AUGUSTA COUNTY [VIRGINIA] ROAD ORDERS

1745-1769

Virginia Genealogical Society
Richmond, Virginia

Published With Permission from the

Virginia Transportation Research Council
(A Cooperative Organization Sponsored Jointly by the Virginia
Department of Transportation and
the University of Virginia)

HERITAGE BOOKS
2008

HERITAGE BOOKS
AN IMPRINT OF HERITAGE BOOKS, INC.

Books, CDs, and more—Worldwide

For our listing of thousands of titles see our website
at
www.HeritageBooks.com

Published 2008 by
HERITAGE BOOKS, INC.
Publishing Division
100 Railroad Avenue #104
Westminster, Maryland 21157

Copyright © 1998, 2003 Virginia Genealogical Society

All rights reserved. No part of this book may be reproduced or transmitted in any form or by any means, electronic or mechanical, including photocopying, recording or by any information storage and retrieval system without written permission from the author, except for the inclusion of brief quotations in a review.

International Standard Book Number: 978-0-7884-3668-0

AUGUSTA COUNTY ROAD ORDERS 1745-1769

by

Nathaniel Mason Pawlett
Faculty Research Historian

Ann Brush Miller
Research Scientist

Kenneth Madison Clark
Research Associate

and

Thomas Llewellyn Samuel, Jr.
Research Assistant

Virginia Transportation Research Council
(A Cooperative Organization Sponsored Jointly by the Virginia
Department of Transportation and
the University of Virginia)

Charlottesville, Virginia

June 1998
Revised July 2003
VTRC 99-R17

HISTORIC ROADS OF VIRGINIA

Louisa County Road Orders, 1742-1748, by Nathaniel Mason Pawlett. 57 pages, indexed, map.

Goochland County Road Orders, 1728-1744, by Nathaniel Mason Pawlett. 120 pages, indexed, map.

Albemarle County Road Orders, 1744-1748, by Nathaniel Mason Pawlett. 57 pages, indexed, map.

The Route of the Three Notch'd Road, by Nathaniel Mason Pawlett and Howard Newlon. 26 pages, illustrated, 2 maps.

An Index to Roads in the Albemarle County Surveyor's Books, 1744-1853, by Nathaniel Mason Pawlett. 10 pages, map.

A Brief History of the Staunton and James River Turnpike, by Douglas Young. 22 pages, illustrated, map.

Albemarle County Road Orders, 1783-1816, by Nathaniel Mason Pawlett. 421 pages, indexed.

A Brief History of Roads in Virginia, 1607-1840, by Nathaniel Mason Pawlett. 41 pages.

A Guide to the Preparation of County Road Histories, by Nathaniel Mason Pawlett. 26 pages, 2 maps.

Early Road Location: Key to Discovering Historic Resources? by Nathaniel Mason Pawlett and K. Edward Lay. 47 pages, illustrated, 3 maps.

Albemarle County Roads, 1725-1816, by Nathaniel Mason Pawlett. 98 pages, illustrated, 8 maps.

"Backsights," A Bibliography, by Nathaniel Mason Pawlett. 29 pages, revised edition, 1986.

Orange County Road Orders, 1734-1749, by Ann Brush Miller. 323 pages, indexed, map.

Spotsylvania County Road Orders, 1722-1734, by Nathaniel Mason Pawlett. 159 pages, indexed.

Brunswick County Road Orders, 1732-1749, by Nathaniel Mason Pawlett. 81 pages, indexed.

Orange County Road Orders, 1750-1800, by Ann Brush Miller. 394 pages, indexed, map.

Lunenburg County Road Orders, 1746-1764, by Nathaniel Mason Pawlett and Tyler Jefferson Boyd. 394 pages, indexed.

Culpeper County Road Orders, 1763-1764, by Ann Brush Miller. 22 pages, indexed, map.

DEDICATION

This volume is dedicated to the memory of
Katherine Gentry Bushman (1919-1997)
Historian and Genealogist

FOREWORD

by

Ann Brush Miller

Augusta County Road Orders 1745-1769 is one of several compilations of early Virginia road orders left unfinished by Nathaniel Mason Pawlett, longtime Faculty Research Historian of the Virginia Transportation Research Council, at his death in 1995. Mr. Pawlett began work on the first volumes of published Virginia road orders in the early 1970s and over the next twenty years produced more than dozen volumes of road order transcriptions and histories of Virginia roads.

A number of individuals worked together to complete this volume. Tyler Jefferson Boyd assisted Mr. Pawlett in the initial work on the transcription of the Augusta County road orders. I, as principal historian, completed this volume with Kenneth Madison Clark and Thomas Llewellyn Samuel, Jr.

We are particularly indebted to the late Katherine Gentry Bushman (Mrs. William Bushman) of Staunton, Virginia, one of the greatest authorities on Shenandoah Valley history, for her long-term interest and encouragement regarding this project, and for her assistance in deciphering some of the vagaries of spelling and handwriting of the early Augusta county clerks. Sadly, Mrs. Bushman did not live to see the publication of this work, which we dedicate to her memory.

This volume is the nineteenth entry in the *Historic Roads of Virginia* series, initiated by the Virginia Transportation Research Council (then the Virginia Highway & Transportation Research Council) in 1973. *Augusta County Road Orders 1745-1769* is also the first volume of published road orders to be concerned wholly with territory west of the Blue Ridge, although portions of the Shenandoah Valley were covered by a previous publication, *Orange County Road Orders 1734-1749*, which included the period the territory was part of Orange County, prior to 1745.

A NOTE ON THE METHODS, EDITING AND DATING SYSTEM

by

Nathaniel Mason Pawlett

The road and bridge orders contained in the order books of an early Virginia county are the primary source of information for the study of its roads. When extracted, indexed, and published by the Virginia Transportation Research Council, they greatly facilitate this. All of the early county court order books are in manuscript, sometimes so damaged and faded as to be almost indecipherable. Usually rendered in the rather ornate script of the time, the phonetic spellings of this period often serve to complicate matters further for the researcher and recorder.

With these road orders available in an indexed and cross-indexed published form, it will be possible to produce chronological chains of road orders illustrating the development of many of the early roads of a vast area from the threshold of settlement through much of the eighteenth century. Immediate corroboration for these chains of road orders will usually be provided by other evidence such as deeds, plats, and the Confederate Engineers maps. Often, in fact, the principal roads will be found to survive in place under their early names.

With regard to the general editorial principles of the project, it has been our perception over the years as the road orders of Louisa, Hanover, Goochland, Albemarle, and other counties have been examined and recorded that road orders themselves are really a variety of "notes," often cryptic, incomplete, or based on assumptions concerning the level of knowledge of the reader. As such, any further abstracting or compression of them would tend to produce "notes" taken from "notes," making them even less comprehensible. The tendency has, therefore, been in the direction of restraint in editing, leaving any conclusions with regard to meaning up to the individual reader or researcher using these publications. In pursuing this course, we have attempted to present the reader with a typescript text that is as near a type facsimile of the manuscript itself as we can come.

Our objective is to produce a text that conveys as near the precise form of the original as we can, reproducing all the peculiarities of the eighteenth-century orthography. While some compromises have had to be made because of the modern keyboard, this was really not that difficult a task. Most of their symbols can be accomodated by modern typography, and most abbreviations are fairly clear as to meaning.

Punctuations may appear misleading at times, with unnecessary commas or commas placed where periods should be located; appropriate terminal punctuation is often missing or else takes the form of a symbol such as a long dash, etc. The original capitalization has been retained insofar as it was possible to determine from the original manuscript whether capitals were intended. No capitals have been inserted in place of those originally omitted. The original spelling and syntax have been retained throughout, even including the obvious errors in various places, such as repetitions of words and simple clerical errors. Ampersands have been retained throughout to include such forms as "&c" for "etc." Superscript letters have also been retained where used in y^e, y^t, s^d. The thorn symbol (y), pronounced as "th," has been retained in the aforesaid "y^e," pronounced "the," and "y^t" (that), along with the tailed p ( ) which the limitations of the modern keyboard have forced us to render as a capital "p" (P). This should be taken to mean either "per" (by), "pre," or "pro" (sometimes "par" as in "Pish" for parish) as the context by the order may demand. For damaged and missing portions of the manuscripts we have used square brackets to denote the [missing], [torn] or [illegible] portions. Because of the large number of ancient forms of spelling, grammar, and syntax, it has been deemed impracticable to insert the form [sic] after each one to indicate a literal rendering. Therefore, the reader must assume that apparent errors are merely the result of our literal transcription of the road orders, barring the introduction of typographical errors, of course. If, in any case, this appears to present insuperable problems, resort should be made to the original records.

As to dating, most historians and genealogists who have worked with early Virginian records will be aware of the English dating system in use down to 1752. Although there was an eleven-day difference from our calendar in the day of the month, the principal difference lay in the fact that the beginning of the year was dated from March 25 rather than January 1, as was the case from 1752 onward to the present. Thus, January, February, and March (to the 25th) were the last three months in a given year, and the new year came in only on March 25.

Early Virginian records usually follow this practice, though in some cases dates during these three months will be shown in the form 1732/3, showing both the English date and that in use on the Continent, where the year began January 1. For researchers using material with dates in the English style, it is important to remember that under this system (for instance) a man might die in January 1734 yet convey property or serve in public office in June 1734, since June came *before* January in a given year under this system.

INTRODUCTION

by

Nathaniel Mason Pawlett

> The roads are under the government of the county courts, subject to be controuled by the general court. They order whenever they think them necessary. The inhabitants of the county are by them laid off into precincts, to each of which they allot a convenient portion of the public roads to be kept in repair. Such bridges as may be built without the assistance of artificers, they are to be built. If the stream be such as to require a bridge of regular workmanship, the court employs workmen to build it, at the expense of the whole county. If it be too great for the county, application is made to the general assembly, who authorize individuals to build it, and to take a fixed toll from all passengers, or give sanction to such other proposition as to them appears reasonable.
>
> ¥ Thomas Jefferson, *Notes on the State of Virginia*, 1781

The establishment and maintenance of public roads were among the most important functions of the county court during the colonial period in Virginia. Each road was opened and maintained by an Overseer of the Highways appointed by the Gentlemen Justices yearly. He was usually assigned all the "Labouring Male Titheables" living on or near the road for this purpose. These individuals then furnished all their own tools, wagons, and teams and were required to labour for six days each year on the roads.

Major projects, such as bridges over rivers, demanding considerable expenditure were executed by commissioners appointed by the court to select the site and to contract with workmen for the construction. Where bridges connected two counties, a commission was appointed by each and they cooperated in executing the work.

At its creation from Orange County in 1745, Augusta County extended from the Blue Ridge to "the utmost limits of Virginia." Although legislated into existence along with Frederick County in 1738, Augusta did not commence operation until 1745 when it was felt it had sufficient population to support a government.

From 1745 to 1770, Augusta was a giant parent county, although early nibbled by the creation in 1754 from it of Hampshire County (now West Virginia). Indeed, what is strange is that it maintained as much of its territory as it did until 1770. Much of this must be attributed to the turmoil of the French and Indian War and its retarding effect on settlement.

The road orders contained in this volume cover the period from 1745, when Augusta's county government became operational, down to the creation of Botetourt from it in 1770. As such, they are the principal extant evidence concerning the early development of roads over a vast area of western Virginia from the Blue Ridge to the furthest reaches of settlement.

THE DEVELOPMENT OF AUGUSTA COUNTY

Note: As originally published in paper format, this volume included maps showing the evolution of the county. These maps are not included in the revised/electronic version due to legibility and file size considerations. Instead, a verbal description is provided.

Prior to 1720, a small portion of the area that later became Augusta County was included within newly-formed Spotsylvania County, which included the present counties of Spotsylvania, Orange, Greene, Culpeper, Madison, and Rappahannock east of the Blue Ridge Mountains, and a portion of the Shenandoah Valley as far west as the Shenandoah River.

In 1734, Orange County was created from Spotsylvania County. A giant county at its formation, Orange included the present-day counties of Orange, Greene, Culpeper, Madison, and Rappahannock east of the Blue Ridge Mountains, as well as the territory west of the mountains extending, at least nominally, to the Mississippi River. A 1738 enabling act provided for the creation of two new counties, Frederick and Augusta, from that that part of Orange west of the Blue Ridge. This was to take effect as soon as there was sufficient settlement in the region: the first court of Frederick County was held in 1743; Augusta County's government became operational in 1745.

Augusta County's original territory included most of western and southwestern Virginia, as well as most of what would become the state of West Virginia, the future state of Kentucky, and the Illinois territory. Major reductions to Augusta's territory included the creations of the counties of Hampshire (1754) and Botetourt (1770), and the loss of the other far western lands of the county (the creation of Yohogania, Monongalia, and Ohio counties from the District of West Augusta in 1776 and the creation of Illinois County in 1778). The subsequent creations of the counties of Rockingham and Rockbridge (both 1778), Pendleton (1788), and Bath (1791) brought Augusta County to its current boundaries

Augusta County, 1745-1769

Book I, 1745-47

10 December 1745 Old Style, p. 3
On the Petition of James Carter and Others, it's Ordered that Mathew Edmondson James Carter and John Finla View a way from Andrew Hamiltons in the Calf pasture thro Jenning's Gap to John Finla's and report their proceedings to next Court--

10 December 1745 O. S., p. 4
Daniel Dennison is hereby Appointed Overseer of the Road in the room of John Pickens and it's Ordered that he cause the high ways to be cleared and the Bridges to be repaired in the said Precinct According to Law--

10 February 1745 O. S., p. 5
On the Petition of Samuel Wallace & Others it's Ordered that a Road be cut from William Kings to this Court House and from thence to Samuel Gays and it's further Ordered that William King Morrice Ofrield and John Trimble or any three of them lay if the Same to the Court House and William Hutchison James Trimble lay of the Residue from the Court House to the s^d Gays and Make report of their proceedings to Next Court--

10 February 1745 O. S., p. 5
John Grymes is Appointed Overseer of the Road laid of and View'd by Edmondson and Others in the Calf Pasture on the Other Side the Ridge and Robert Armstrong is appointed Overseer of the s^d Road on this side the Ridge and ordered that they keep the same in repair According to Law--

11 February 1745 O. S., p. 8
Ordered that William Pierce and Adam Miller View and Mark away from the Top of the Blew Ridge at the head of Swift run to Capt. Downs place formerly Alexander Thomsons and make report of their proceedings to Next Court--

11 February 1745 O. S., p. 8
Ordered that William Smith and Robert Gay be overseers from David Davis Mill to the Top of the Mountain above William Kings and it's Ordered that they clear the same According to Law--

11 February 1745 O. S., p. 8
Daniel Holdman and Samuel Wilkins are hereby Appointed Overseers from Benjamin Allens Mill to the North River and it's further Ordered that they cause the s^d Road to be Clear'd According to Law--

11 February 1745 O. S., p. 8
William McGill and Thomas Stinson are appointed Overseers of the Road from the North River to John Andersons & it's further Ordered that they clear the s^d Road According to Law

11 February 1745 O. S., p. 8
John Anderson and Andrew Lewis are Appointed Overseers from the s^d Andersons to this Court House and it's further Ordered that they Clear the Same According to Law--

10 March 1745 O. S., p. 20
Ordered that the Road blazed by Order of Orange County from the Inhabitants of Roan Oak to the top of the Blew Ridge to the Bounds of Brunswick County & Mark Evans William Kervine John Mcfarron & James M^tGomerie are Appointed Overseers of the s^d Road & it's further Ordered that Capt. Robinson & John Mills lay of to each of the s^d. Overseers their respective Precincts & tithables to work on the s^d Road--

10 March 1745 O. S., p. 20
Thomas Scot is hereby Continued Overseer of the road from the Top of the Ridge to Alexander Thomsons

12 May 1746 O. S., p. 44
Simon Aires is hereby Appointed Overseer of the Road in the room of William Kerwin and it's Ordered that he with the tithables that was the s^d Kerwin Clear & keep the s^d. Road in Repair According to Law

12 May 1746 O. S., p. 45
Robert Armstong is hereby Appointed Overseer of the Road from Jenning's Gap to Daniel M^canairs and from thence to John Finlas Cooper and so to the Court House and it's Ordered that he Clear and keep the Same in Repair According to Law and it's further Ordered that all the Male labouring Tithables within four Miles on Each Side of the s^d. Road Assist in Clearing the Same

12 May 1746 O. S., p. 45
Ordered that a Road be laid of and Marked from the great Lick in the Cow Pasture Adjoyning Col^o. Lewis Land to Andrew Hamiltons in the Calf Pasture and that Andrew Lewis and George Lewis mark and lay of the same and make report of their proceedings to the Next Court--

13 May 1746 O. S., p. 46
The Petⁿ. of William Lusk for turning the Road Round his Plantation is granted him

13 May 1746 O. S., p. 47
Thomas Lockey is hereby Appointed Overseer of the Road in the Room of James Gill from the North river where the s^d. Gill dwelt to the South River and it's Ordered that the s^d Lockey keep the s^d Road in repair According to Law with the Tithables that fomerly worked on the s^d. Road--

18 June 1746 O. S., p. 49
On the Petition of Richard Crunk and Others for a Road it's Ordered that Daniel Richeson Michael Stump and Benjamin Hardin or any two of them View the Road Petitioned for & make report of their proceedings to the Next Court--

18 June 1746 O. S., p. 49
Ordered that Morice Offrield John Trimble & William King mark and lay of the Remainder of the Way from the Top of the North Mountain to the s^d. Kings and from thence to the Court House--

19 June 1746 O. S., p. 51
Henry Spears and Mathias Seltser are hereby Appointed Overseers of the Road that Leads over Thorns Gap to begin at the South River and that they Work on their respective roads till they Meet and then with their Gangs Work on the same to the Extent of the County & Clear the s^d Roads According to Law.

20 June 1746 O. S., p. 67
Capt John Denton and Jonas Denton are hereby Appointed Overseers of the Road from the County line to Stoney Creek and it's Ordered that the Tithables Convenient to them work on the s^d Road and that they Clear and keep the same in repair According to Law.

20 June 1746 O. S., p. 68
Griffith Thomas and John Ruddle Senior are hereby Appointed Overseers of the Road from the s^d. Creek to the Place where the New Road is Opened and it's Ordered that they With the most Convenient Tithables Work & keep the same in repair According to Law.

20 June 1746 O. S., p. 68
Alexander Herrin is Appointed Overseer of the Road from Robert Cravens to Samuel Wilkins and it's Ordered that with the Most Convenient Tithables he keep the s^d Road in repair According to Law.

20 June 1746 O. S., p. 68
Thomas Harrison and Jeremiah Harrison are Appointed Overseers of the Road from Craven's to the Indian Road and it's Ordered that they keep the s^d Road in repair According to Law.
And its further Ordered that Capt Scholl lay of their proper precincts & Tithables.

16 July 1746 O. S., p. 70
Ordered that John Maxwell and William Thompson View and mark a Way from this Court House to the Tinkling spring and report their proccedings to the Next Court--

16 July 1746 O. S., p. 71
Ordered that a Road be cleared from this Court House to the Clerks Office and the Tithables belonging to John Madison Gent William Nut James McCorkle Robert McClenahan and James Armstrong Clear and keep the same in repair According to Law.

20 August 1746 O. S., p. 72

On the Petition of Henry Downs and Others it's Ordered that a Way be Marked from the Road that Leads of the Mountain Near Alexander Thompsons to the lower Meeting House and that William Thompson j^r. Samuel Givens and John Campbell mark and lay of the Same.

20 August 1746 O. S., p. 72
John Trimble William King and Morice Ofield Pursuant to an Order of Court to them directed returned that they have marked and laid of the Most Convenient Way from the top of the North Mountain to William Kings and from thence to the Court House. Ordered that Robert Davis be Overseer of the road from the North Mountain to William Kings (Already marked and laid of by John Trimble and Others) and that the following tithables work on the s^d. Road Viz^t. George Kill Patrick Hugh Young Jam^s. Young Samuel Kinkead James Mills William Mills Robert McClellan William M^{c}feeters Adrew Pickens James Clark Jacob Lockart Henry Crestwell and John Trishell and it's further orderd that wth. the s^d Tithables he Clear and keep the s^d road in repair According to Law.

20 August 1746 O. S., p. 73
Ordered that John Brown be Overseer of the road from William Kings to the Court House as already mark' and laid of by John Trimble and Others and that the following Tithables Work on the s^d. Road Viz^t. Hugh Spears James Phillips John Spears John McKenney James Bell Samuel Wallace Thomas Peary George Vance William McClintock John Bartley James Montgomerie John Davis Patrick Martin and Thomas Killpatrick and it's further Ordered that with the s^d Tithables he Clear and keep the s^d road in repair according to Law.

20 August 1746 O. S., p. 73
Ordered that William Thompson Gent be Overseer of the road from the Court House to the tinkling Spring already Viewed and that the following Tithables Work on the s^d Road Viz^t. John Lynn and his three Sons John Henderson David Stuart John Mitchell John Ramsey James Coile John Hutchison John Preston Joseph McClelhill Andrew Russell William Palmer Alexander Thompson George Caldwell and his two Sons and it's further Ordered that the s^d Thompson with the s^d. Tithables Clear and keep the s^d. Road in repair According to Law.

20 August 1746 O. S., p. 73
a road being Cleared from those Inhabitants of Roan Oak that are part of this County to the top of the Ridge Adjoining to Luningsburgh County it's Ordered that James Montgomerie and George Robinson Gent wait on that Court and request the s^d. Court to Order a road to be Cleared to meet the s^d. Road at the Top of s^d Ridge in Order to have a road out of this County into that and Make report of the s^d. Court's Answer.

20 August 1746 O. S., p. 73
On the Petition of William Buchanan and Others it's Ordered that a Road be Cleared from the s^d Buchanans to this Court House and that John Buchanan Gent Patrick Cook and Alexander Walker mark and lay of the same that also they Appoint Proper Overseers and gangs to work on the same and lay of their respective Precints and make return of their proceedings to the next Court--

20 August 1746 O. S., p. 74
Ordered that John Graham be Overseer of the road Appointed to be Cleared from James Carters Mill to this Court House as farr as the first ford above Bells Land and that all the Tithables from John Millers to the head of the River assist in Clearing and keeping the same in repair According to Law.

20 August 1746 O.S., p. 74
Ordered that Capt. Daniel M^{c}anare be Overseer of the Road appointed to be Cleared from the first ford above Bells land to the Court House and that the following Tithables Work on the same to wit, Samu'l Wallis James Bell Robt. Renix Alexander Crawford James Mills Francis Gardner John Elliot James Dyer John Trimble David Trimble Chas. Clendening Thomas Bard John Hogshead William Hogshead Robt. Gilkason Alexander Gardner Robt. Raltstone John Archer Sampson Archer John Moffet William Anderson Alexander Gibson Samuel Lusk John Spears Robt. Davis James Phillips John McKenny Thomas Gardner Daniel Brealey William Brady Walter Trimble Matthew Edmondston Robert Armstrong John Sixby James Trimble James Miller David Stuart and John Farguson and it's further Ordered that the s^d. M^{c}anare with the s^d Tithables Clear and keep the s^d Road in repair According to Law.

20 August 1746 O.S., p. 74
It's Ordered that James McCune be Overseer of the road in the room of Francis McCune and that with the usual Gang he Clear the Same Immediatly and keep the Same in repair According the Law--

22 August 1746 O.S., p. 86
Robert Patrick is hereby Appointed Overseer of the Road whereof Capt. Gay was Overseer and Ordered that he keep the s^d Road in repair according to Law wth. the Same Gang that work'd under s^d Gay.

19 November 1746 O. S., p. 130
Ordered that a road be Cleared from the North fork of James River to Looneys ford on the south fork of James River as already Laid of by Richard Burton Gent Joseph Lapsley and John Mathews are hereby Appointed Overseers of the s^d Road it's also further Ordered that the Male Tithables of all the Families between the s^d Rivers work on the same John Boyn Jos. Long and John Peter Sallings Families Excepted as also all the male Inhabitants from the South branch Downwards Clear and keep the same in repair According to Law.

19 November 1746 O. S., p. 130
Ordered that a Road be Cleared from the reed Creek the Nighest way to Eagle Bottom and from thence to the Top of the ridge that Parts the Waters of New River and those of the South fork of Roan Oak & it's further Ordered that George Ezekiel W^m and Patrick Colhoon Bryant White Wm Handlon Peter Rentfro and his two sons George the Tinker Jacob Woolman & two Sons John Black Simon Hart Michael Clanie John Stroud Samuel Starknecker and all the Dunkers that are able to Work on the Same and all Other Person in that Precinct are Ordered to Work under James

Colhoon and Charles Hart who are Appointed Overseers & it's further Ordered that wth the s^d Gang they Clear & keep the s^d road in repair According to Law.

19 November 1746 O. S., p. 130
Ordered that a road be cleared from Adam Harmons to the River and North branch of Roan Oak and it's further Ordered that George Draper Israel Larton & son Adam and George Herman Thomas Looney Jacob Harman and three Sons Jacob Castle John Lane Valintine Harman Adrew Moser Humberston Lyon James Skaggs Humphrey Baker John Davis Frederick Hering & two Sons and all Other Persons Setling in the Precincts work on the s^d Road Under the s^d Adam Harman who is hereby appointed Overseer of the s^d Road with the s^d Gang to Clear & keep the s^d Road in repaire according to Law.

19 November 1746 O. S., p. 131
Ordered that a road be Cleared from the Ridge above Tobias Brights that Parts the Waters of New river from the brances of roan Oak to the Lower ford of Catabo Creek and it's further Ordered that William English and two Sons Thomas English and son Jacob Brown George Bright Benjamin Oyle Paul Garrison Elisha Isaac John Donalin Philip Smith Mathew English and the rest of the Tithables as Nominated by George Robinson and James Montgomerie Gent Work on the s^d Road under Tobias Bright who is hereby appointed Overseer of the s^d Road with the s^d Gang to Clear and keep the same in repair according to Law.

19 November 1746 O. S., p. 131
Ordered that a Road be Cleared from the Ridge that Devides the Waters of New river from the waters of the South branch of Roan Oak to end in a road that heads Over the Blew ridge and further Ordered that Col Wm Robinson & his Sons Thos Wilson and his two Sons Wm Bens and his Brother all the Ledfords Samuel Brown Henry Brown Samuel Niely James Burk James Bean Francis Estham Ephraim Voss and servants Fran^s Summerfield John Mason Tasker and Thomas Tosh John and Peter Dill Uriah Evan's Sons Mathusaleth Griffeths and sons John Thomas Peter Kender and all Others that George Robinson and James Montgomerie Gent shall Nominate to Work on the Same under James Cambell and Mark Evans who are hereby Appointed Overseers to Clear and keep the s^d road in repair According to Law.

20 November 1746 O. S., p. 133
Hugh Thompson and Thomas Stinson are hereby appointed Overseers of the road from William Thompsons to the meeting House and it's Ordered that they summon the most Convenient Tithables to Work on the same and keep it in repair according to Law

21 November 1746 O. S., p. 135
Adam Miller and Ludwick Francisco are hereby appointed Overseers of the Road from Alexander Thompsons to Swift run gap and it's further Ordered that all the Male Labouring Tithables from Jacob Cobers to Samuel Scots at the upper end of the Peaked Mountain on both sides the river assist in Clearing & keeping the same in repair according to Law.

22 November 1746 O. S., p. 142

Ordered that Public Notice be given by the Sherif to the respective Overseers of the roads in this County that at every Cross road & where the roads fork they set up Posts of Directions according to Law.

22 November 1746 O. S., p. 142
Ordered that a road be Cleared from the Court House to the Timber Broge as the Same is to be laid of by John Buchanan Gent Alex^r. Walker and Patrick Cook David Suart James Lockart and John Hays are hereby Appointed Overseers of the same and it's further Ordered that all Male Labouring Titheables from the s^d Road to the North mountain and all within three Miles of the s^d Road on the Opposite side work on the same under the s^d Overseers and Clear and keep the same in repair acc^d. to Law.

18 February 1746 O. S., p. 151
The Petition of Sundry of the Inhabitants of Roan Oak for a Road is Granted and Ordered that the Several Persons mentioned in the s^d Petition Clear & keep the same in Repair According to Law.

19 February 1746 O. S., p. 159
The Petition of Adam Dickinson for a Road being read is rejected

18 March 1746 O. S., p. 168
Ordered that a road be Cleared from Lower end of Cowpasture to Carters Mill and that Adam Dickenson with the following Persons lay of and Clear the same to Wit James Scot W^m. Galespy James Simpson Wm Donerly Andrew Muldrough Hugh Coffey John Donerly Alexander McKoy John Mitchell John Moore Ralph Laverty John Cockmill James Hay Wm Hugh James Stuart & James McKoy and it's further Ordered that they keep the Same in repair According to Law.

18 March 1746 O. S., page 168
On the Petition of Sundry the Inhabitants for a road from Calep Jones Mill Down to the County Line Ordered that James McKoy wth the s^d Petitioners clear the same Viz^t. Moses McKoy Henry Harding John Hill Philip Crim Thomas Land Wm Hurst Thomas Burk Wm Harrel Thomas Grubbs Wm Hankins Zachery McKoy [blank in book] Joshua Job James McNeal Adam Cuningham Jacob Kerrell Charles Cox Charles Buck Ephraim Leech and Calep Job & further Ord^d. that they keep the same in repair According to Law.

18 March 1746 O. S., p. 168
On the Petition of Sundry the Inhabitants for a road from the Top of the Ridge to John Terralds and James Beards Ordered that John Bomgardner and Jacob Harmon / after the County Road is Cleared with the Petitiones Clear the Same to Wit Robert Scot Samuel Scot John Stevenson Robert Hook Wm Burk Mathew Thompson Charles Duel Nicholas Noal Jacob Harmon John Lawrence Jacob Pence Henry Dickens Valintine Pence George Scot John Viare Jacob Harmon Senr Mathew Sharp John Harmon Robert Frazier James Beard Mathew Thompson John Rolston Stiffell Francisco Wm Lamb Samuel Lockard and Robert Smith and it's further Ordered that they keep the same in repair According to Law

19 March 1746 O. S., p. 175
Ordered that John Smith and David Davis mark and lay of a Way from this Court House to the top of the Ridge near Rockfish Gap and that they View the Most Convenient Way from thence to the road that Leads to the Falls of James River and Fredericksburg and Make report of their proceedings to Next Court and that they bring in their Charge for the same at laying the County Levy

21 May 1747 O. S., p. 199
On the Petition of Sundry the Inhabitants Ordered that John Dobikin John Smith Jacob Dye Thomas Moore and Wm Brown View and lay of a Way from the Fork of the New road near Jumping run or Colletts to this Court House and Marke report of their Proceedings to Next Court

21 May 1747 O. S., p. 199
[Grand Jury Presentments]

... James Campbell and Mark Evans for not Clearing and Keeping the Road whereof they are Overseers in repair Acc^d to Law on the Information of Col^o John Buchanan

21 May 1747 O. S., p. 200
Ordered that David Stuart and Andrew Russell View and lay of a Road from this Court House to Tinkling Spring, which was formerly laid of by Wm Thompson and report their Proceedings to the next Court

21 May 1747 O. S., p. 200
Ordered that the road formerly Cleared from James Youngs Mill to Wood's Gap be altered as the respective Overseers see Convenient and that this Order be sent to James McCowns John Hays Jo^s. Coulton, Patrick Hays & Charles Campbell and that all the Titheables within three Miles of the South River Work on the s^d Road with the two last Overseers to the s^d Gap besides their former Gang.

21 May 1747 O. S., p. 200
Ordered that John Allison have Licence on his Petition to keep a Ferry from his Landing to Harbert McClures

21 May 1747 O. S., p. 200
Ordered that the Road formerly Cleared from Alexander Thomsoms to the Top of Ridge Leading to Louisa by Order Orange County Court be repaired and that William Thompson j^r. with the Titheables from the South Mountain a Cross by the Peaked Mountain to the North Mountain and from South Mountain by Robert Turks a Cross by John Andersons to the s^d North Mountain Assist in Clearing and keeping the Same in repair According to Law

21 May 1747 O. S., p. 202

Ordered that Henry Downs Gent wait on the Court of Orange and inform them there is a Road Cleared through this County to the Top of the Ridge near Swift run Gap and Desire and Order for another to meet the s^d Road as the Law Directs

17 June 1747 O. S., p. 220
The Petition of Benjamin Borden & Others for a Road is rejected

19 June 1747 O. S., p. 239
On the Petition of John Pickens Gent Ordered that Robert Patterson and James Allen View a Road from the s^d Picken's Mill to the Lower Meeting House & Make report of their Proceedings to ye next Court

19 June 1747 O. S., p. 239
Ordered that Andrew Lewis and Robert Poge View a Road from Pickens Mill to this Court House and Appoint Proper Overseers and Titheables to Work on the s^d Road and Make report of their Preceedings to the next Court

19 August 1747 O. S., p. 248
Ordered that John Pickens and William Bell be Overseers of the Road View'd by Andrew Lewis and Robert Poge from the s^d Pickens Mill to this Court House and that William Lewis James Robertson Thomas Gordon Wm Baskins James Lasley James Wallis Daniel Deniston Daniel Deniston j^r. William Bell j^r. John Poge & George Crawford Clear and keep the Same in repair According to Law.

19 August 1747 O. S., p. 250
The Petition of James McCown and Sundry of the Inhabitants is Continued & Ordered that Patrick Hays Chas Campbell Isaac White & Samuel Steel be Summoned to Attend the Same and that Andrew Pickens Patrick Cook Patrick Martin William M^{c}feeters John Anderson & Wm Anderson View the s^d Road Petitioned for from the Cross Road below Patrick Hay's as Also the Road that Leads by Edward Halls to their meeting at the foot of the Mountain and that they return the Most Convenient and best Way to the Next Court and that they Meet to View the s^d Road the fourth of September Next and that Charles Campbell and Isaac White Pilate them the Way that leads by Halls & William Christian & Thomas Stewart Pilate them the Other Way

20 August 1747 O. S., p. 255
John Smith and others being appointed to View and Lay of a road from Abrah^m Coletts to this Courthouse and they having made their return that the said road is a Convenient road Therefore its ordered that ye sev^l. Persons who petitioned for ye same Clear and keep the said Road in repair according to Law.

20 August 1747 O. S., p. 255
Robert Craven and Saml Wilkins are hereby appointed Overseers of the road from the Courthouse to the Indian road near ye s^d Cravens's in the room of Alex^r Herren Thos Harrisson & Jeremiah Harrisson and its ordered that they keep ye same in repair according to Law.

22 August 1747 O. S., p. 268
Grand jury v. James Campbell
Presentm^t for not keeping the road wherof he is the Overseer in repair
The Deft not appearing and the Sheriff having returned on the sumons Executed Its Considered that the said Deft be fined to our Sorereign Lord the King fifteen Shill^s: Curr^t Money for ye s^d Offence according to Law & the Deft in Mercy &^{c}

22 August 1747 O. S., p. 269
Grand jury v. Mark Evans
Presentment for not keeping the road whereof he is Overseer in repair
The Deft not appearing and the Sheriff having returned the summons Executed on ye Deft. Its Considered by ye Court that for ye s^d Offence he be fined fifteen Shillings Curr^t Money to our Sovereign Lord the King together with ye Costs of this Presentment & ye Deft in Mercy &^{c}

16 September 1747 O. S., p. 288
Ordered that the road from the Cross road below Hays on the North Side the South river to the ridge be Cleared by the subscribers and that Thos Stuart and Wm Christian be Overseers of ye said road and cause ye same to be Cleared according to Law

16 September 1747 O. S., p. 288
The Complaint of Robert Davies ag^t the Overseers of the road from the Tinkling Spring is dismisd --

18 September 1747 O. S., p. 303
Ordered that a road be cleared from the Tinkling Spring Meeting house to Col^o Pattons Bridge and that James Pattons Tithables Edwd Hall Samuel Davids Robert Gibson Wm Thomson & Geo: Caldwells Tithables work on the said Road under James Patton & Wm Thomson Gents who are hereby appointed Overseers of ye s^d Road and are hereby ordered to clear ye s^d Road & keep ye Same when cleared in repair according to Law.

18 September 1747 O. S., p. 303
Ordered that James Lockhard John Buchannan & Benjn Walker lay of and mark a road from the Courthouse to where the Church is to be built and from thence to the Timber Grove and make report of their Proceedings to the next Court

18 November 1747 O. S., p. 319
Ordered that Robert Ramsey & David Mitchell view mark and lay of a way from Timber Grove to the Place where the Church is to be built And that James Lockhart and Wm Ledgerwood lay of and mark a way from thence to ye Courthouse & make return of their proceedings to ye next Court--

19 November 1747 O. S., p. 321
Ordered that Mathias Seltzer be continued Overseer of the road whereof he was Overseer till May Court

20 November 1747 O. S., p. 331-2
[Grand Jury Presentments]

We Present Henry Speer Overseer of a road from the Pass run that leads Over thorns Gapp for not clearing it according to Law by the information of Mathias Seltzer

* * *

We Present Robert Davis & John Brown Overseers of a road from the top of ye Mountain by William kings to ye Courthouse for not clearing the Same according to Law by our own knowledge

We Present the Overseers of the road from Charles Miligans to Luneys Creek to George Robinsons for not clearing the Same according to Law by ye Information of John Braham & Wm Pierce--

18 February 1747 O. S., p. 346
John Brownlee is hereby appointed Overseer of the Indian road in the room of Patrick Campbell & its further ordered that he keep ye said road in repair according to Law--

19 February 1747 O. S., p. 356
Ordered that Thomas Stinson be Overseer of the road from Henry Downs jun^r to ye Meeting house and that he keep the Same in repair with the Same hands that formerly worked on ye said road

17 March 1747 O. S., p. 360
John Pickens Gent is hereby appointed Overseer of the road in the room of Daniel Deniston and its ordered that with those tithables that formerly were under ye s^d Deniston he cause the said road to be kept in repair according to Law--

17 March 1747 O. S., p. 363
Ordered that John Briant be Overseer with Robert Cravens of ye road from the said Cravens to the Indian road & that he keep ye Same in repair according to Law--

Book II, 1747-1751

18 May 1748 O. S., p. 5
Samuel Wallace is hereby appointed Overseer of the road in the room of John Brown Gent & its ordered that he Cause the same to be repaired according to law

18 May 1748 O. S., p. 5
Ordered that Adam Rider & Charles Daley view and Mark a Way from Wm Waldings to meet the road near Thos Moores & make report of their proceedings to ye next Court--

18 May 1748 O. S., p. 6

The Pet^n of Sundry Inhabitants of James River for a road is granted them & its ordered that the several Subscribers clear ye same and that James Montgomery and John McPharron divide the Same into two precints

18 May 1748 O. S., p. 6
Stephen Rentfro is hereby appointed Overseer of the road from Charles Milkins to the first fording on Catabo Creek and its ordered that he cause the Same to be cleared and kept in repair according to Law

18 May 1748 O. S., p. 7
Morris Offrail is hereby appointed Overseer of the road in the room of Robert Davis and its orderd that he keep the said road in repair according to Law

18 May 1748 O. S., p. 7
Joseph Canady & James Walker are hereby appointed Overseers of ye road in the room of Joseph Coulton & its ordered that ye Cause the said road to be kept in repair according to Law

18 May 1748 O. S., p. 8
Ordered that Isaac Taylor and W^m McClung be Overseers of the road from Benj^a Bordens to James ffultons & its ordered that they cause the said road to be cleared and kept in repair according to Law

19 May 1748 O. S., p. 9
Wm Pierce is hereby appointed Overseer of the road in the room of Ludwick Francisco and its ordered that he Cause the said road to be cleared and kept in repair according to Law

19 May 1748 O. S., p. 9
Jacob Coger is hereby appointed Overseer of the road in the room of Adam Miller and its ordered that he Cause the said road to be Cleared and kept in repair according to Law

19 May 1748 O. S., p. 9
Paul Luny is hereby appointed Overseer of ye road in the room of Mattias Seltzer and its ordered that he Cause the said road to be cleared & kept in repair according to Law

19 May 1748 O. S., p. 9
Daniel Stover is hereby appointed Overseer of the road in the room of Henry Spear and its ordered that he Cause the said road to be cleared & kept in repair according to Law

19 May 1748 O. S., p. 9
Daniel Holdman is hereby appointed Overseer of the road in the room of Thos Loakey and its ordered that he Cause the said road to be cleared and kept in repair according to Law

21 May 1748 O. S., p. 27

Ordered that John Harrison with his gang clear out the road that was formerly blazed by Andrew Bird and his former gang--

21 May 1748 O. S., p. 28
ffrancis Donnerly is hereby appointed Overseer of ye road in the room of Robert Gay and its orderd that he keep ye s^d road in repair according to Law

21 May 1748 O. S., p. 30
On the Motion of Benjamin Borden Its ordered that James Thompson clear the road already Petitioned for from Gilbert Campbells ford to ye s^d Bordens & that ye s^d Borden clear ye s^d road from thence to Beverley Mannor Line & its ordered that ye Cause ye s^d Road to be cleared and kept in repair according to Law

21 May 1748 O. S., p. 30
Ordered that David Stuart and Andrew Russell be overseers of the road from the Courthouse to ye tinkling Spring & the are ord^d to keep ye Same in repair

21 May 1748 O. S., p. 30
Ordered that James Edmondson & Alex^r: Thompson Survey and Lay of a road the Most convenientest way from tinkling Spring into the road whereof Wm Christian and Thos Stuart are Overseers.

21 May 1748 O. S., p. 30
James Lofton is hereby appointed Overseer of ye road from Pickins's to the tinkling Spring and its ordered that he keep ye same in repair according to Law

21 May 1748 O. S., p. 34
[Grand Jury Presentment]

We Present Thomas Stevenson for not clearing the road from the Lower Meeting house to Henry Downs Junr. on the Information of Henry Downs

21 May 1748 O. S., p. 43
On the Motion of Patrick Hays Its ordered that he have Liberty to turn the road round his plantation and that he Clear ye same with his own people--

26 May 1748 O. S., p. 44
A Proposition and Grievances of Sundry the Inhabitants of the West side of the blue Ledge for help to make the way over the blue ridge more convenient was presented into Court and orderd to be certifyed to the next Assembly

17 August 1748 O. S., p. 48

John Pickens Gent and David Stevenson are hereby appointed Over Seers of the road Laid of from the said Pickins's Mill to ye Lower meeting house which they are orderd to keep in repair according to Law

17 August 1748 O. S., p. 50
David Edmiston is hereby appointed Overseer of the road from tinkling Spring to Stuart and Christians road and its ordered that James and John Campbell Archibald Stuart Charles Dollis James Hamilton Richard Pilsher David Henderson George Vance Robt McCutchin Saml McCune Robert Moody John ffrazier John Thompson Wm Johnson Alex^r Henderson, Saml Henderson & Saml ffarguson work on ye s^d Road under the said Edmiston their Overseer and its further ordered that he Cause the Said road to be kept in repair with ye s^d Hands according to Law

18 August 1748 O. S., p. 52
Wm Thomson Junr. is herby appointed Overseer of ye road from the lower meeting house to Henry Downs Junr: in the room of Hugh Thompson & its orderd that he keep ye said road in repair according to Law

20 August 1748 O. S., p. 59
A Propositition from Sundrey the Inhabitants for a road to be cleared Over the ridge &^c: received and ordered to be certifyed to the General Assembly for Allowance--

20 August 1748 O. S., p. 63
Ordered that Robert and Wm Christian lay out a road from Black James Armstrong to Wm Longs Mill & from thence to ye Corner of James Alexanders ffence[?] and that ye following Persons work on ye Same to wit James Armstrong Geo: Rutlidges Thos Rutlidge James Caldwell James Armstrong James ffram Wm Robb John Christian James Alex^r John Blair John Wilson Anthony Black Wm Wright & W^m & John Robinson And its further ordered that the s^d tithables work on ye said road & clear the same immediately according to Law under the said Robt & Wm Christian their Overseers--

19 October 1748 O. S., p. 67
Ordered that Saml Brown & Jacob Brown upon Roan Oak Survey lay off and mark a road from the fork of Roan oak to the top of the ridge that divides the Waters of Roan oak and Massisippi and that Col^o John Buchannan appoint two men to mark & Lay off a road from where the former road ends to reed Creek & that the make return to their proceeding to the next Court

19 October 1748 O. S., page 67
Ordered that John ffinla Mathew Edmondson & David Trimble be overseers of the road from Jennings Gapp to this Courthouse in the room of Daniel M^{c}anaire Gent and that the Gang formerly under the Said M^{c}anaire work thereon and its further ordered that they Cause the said road to be kept in repair according to Law

18 May 1749 O. S., p. 114
William Hamilton is Appointed surveyor of the Highway in the room of Captain W^m. Smith in the Calf Pasture who is discharged from that Office

18 May 1749 O. S., p. 114
Ordered that Joseph Cannaday and Joseph Coulton marke and lay of a Road from the Timber Grove to the north mountain meeting House and that James Lockard and Wm Ledgerwood mark and lay of a Road from the s^d. Meeting House to the Court House of this County and make report of their proceeding to the next Court

18 May 1749 O. S., p. 115
John Lynn is Appointed Surveyor of the Highway in the room of John Stevenson who is hereby discharge from that Office

18 May 1749 O. S., p. 115
On the Petition of Sundry the Inhabitants of the South Branch of Potowmack River in this County It is Ordered that John Smith and Mathew Patton mark and Lay of a Way from John Pattons to the Forks of the Dry River and that Henry Smith and Gabriel Pickins mark it from thence to Capt John Smith's and from the s^d Smiths to the Court House of this County and make report of their Proceedings to the next Court--

18 May 1749 O. S., p. 117
Ordered that all Male Labouring work on the Road formerly laid of from Calop Jones Mill to the County line under the Present Overseer of the s^d Road within five miles on Each side the same

18 May 1749 O. S., p. 119
Ordered that William Jackson mark and lay of a way from Jacksons River to Col^o. John Lewis Land in the Cow Pasture and that James Mays be Overseer of the road Already marked from the s^d Lewis Land to Wm Hamiltons in the Calf pasture & It is further Ordered that all male Labouring Titheables above James Hugarts work on the Same

19 May 1749 O. S., p. 126
Ordered that all former Overseers of the Indian Road from Frederick County line to Toms Creek be Continued untill they Clear the s^d Road and Set up Posts of Directions According to Law

19 May 1749 O. S., p. 126

Michael Kaufman is Appointed Overseer of the Road in the room of Paul Long who is hereby discharged from that Office.

19 May 1749 O. S., p. 126
William Frazier is hereby Appointed Overseer of the Road in the room of Wm Pierce who is discharged from that Office

19 May 1749 O. S., p. 126
Henry Long is hereby Appointed Overseer of the road in the room of Jacob Coger who is discharged from that Office & It is Order that all the male Labouring Tithables down the river as low as the s^d Coger's Work on the same

19 May 1749 O. S., p. 126
Ordered that James Montgomerie and Richard Burton or any one of them wait on the Court of Luninburg and Acquaint that the Inhabitants of Augusta County have Cleared a Road to the s^d County Line and desire that they will Clear a Road from the Court House of Luninburg to meet the Road already Cleared by the Inhabitants of Augusta

19 May 1749 O. S., p. 127
Francis McCown is Appointed Overseer of Road in the room of James McCown who is hereby discharged from that Office

19 May 1749 O. S., p. 127
Andrew Pickens is hereby Appointed Overseer of the road in the room of Moric Offrield who is discharged from that Office

19 May 1749 O. S., p. 127
On the Petition Sundry the Inhabitants It is Ordered that Jacob Rogers Robert Scot and James Beard Survey and Mark a way from John Mizers to the Stone Meeting House Adjoining to the Court House Road and make report of their proceedings to the next Court--

20 May 1749 O. S., p. 129
Ordered that James Carr be Overseer of the Road from Long Meadow Bridge to the South River at Israil Christians and that all Male Labouring Titheables from the s^d Carrs to Robert Moodys work under & assist the s^d Carr in repairing the s^d Long Meadow bridge & keeping the s^d Road in Repair According to Law

20 May 1749 O. S., p. 129
Ordered that Robert Patrick be Surveyor of the Highway from the South River at Christians to the Top of the Mountain at Woods Gap and that with the Male Labouring Titheables from Christians Clayman's to Edward Halls on the South River he Clear & keep the Same in repair Acc^d to Law.

22 May 1749 O. S., p. 148

John Maxwell and Robert M^c^Clenahan are Appointed Overseers of the Road in the room of David Stuart And^r^ Russell and Ordered that they keep same in repair acc^d^ to Law.

22 May 1749 O. S., p. 148
Joseph Tees is hereby Appointed Surveyor of the high way from the foot of the Mountain at Woods Gap to James Bells on the South River

22 May 1749 O. S., p. 148
Ordered that all the Male Labouring titheables from Long Meadow Run to the Top of the blew Ridge be added to Robert Patrick's Gang who is Overseer of the s^d^ Road

22 August 1749 O. S., p. 151
On the Petition of Sudry the Inhabitans for a Road from Picken's Mill to the Indian Road near Givens old place Ordered that Samuel Givens and W^m^. Baskins mark and lay of the same that they with Hugh Thompson John Gwins Wm Thompson John Pickens Wm Bell Robert Scot Robert Patterson and James Givens the Subscribers Clear & keep the s^d^ Road in repair Acc^d^ to Law.

22 August 1749 O. S., p. 151
John Anderson is Appointed Overseer of the Highway from this Court House to the Middle River whereof Saml Wilkins was Overseer and Ord^d^. that he Clear & keep the Same in repair Acc^d^ to Law.

22 August 1749 O. S., p. 151
James Allen is Appoint Surveyor of the High way from the Middle River to the Lower Meeting House and Ordered that he Clear & keep the Same in repair Acc^d^ to Law.

22 August 1749 O. S., p. 151
David Stevenson is Appointed Overseer of the High way from the Lower Meeting House to Naked Creek and Ordered that they Clear and keep the Same in repair According to Law.

22 August 1749 O. S., p. 151
Samuel Wilkins is Appointed Surveyor of the Highway from Naked Creek to Robert Craven's bounds and Ordered that he clear and keep the same in repair Acc^d^ to Law.

[Page 162 is followed by page 263]

24 August 1749 O. S., p. 263
William Stevenson and Peter Horse are hereby App^d^. Surveyors of the Highway from John Pattons to the forks of the dry River and It is ordered that with the Adjacent titheables they clear and keep the same in repair according to law

24 August 1749 O. S., p. 263

Henry Smith and Gabriel Pickins are hereby Appointed Surveyors of the High way from the forks of the Dry river to the court House of this County as already laid of by John Smith & others and It is Ordered that with the Adjacent titheables they Clear and keep the same in repair acc^d to law.

26 August 1749 O. S., p. 278
James Beard is hereby appointed Surveyor of the Highway from the New Meeting House to Robert Scots and with the adjacent Titheables It is Ordered that he Clear & keep the same in repair According to Law

26 August 1749 O. S., p. 278
John Craig is hereby appointed Surveyor of the High way from Robert Scots to the Smiths Shop near Jacob Roger's and with the Adjacent Tithea^s It is ordered that he Clear & keep the same in repair According to Law

26 August 1749 O. S., p. 278
Jacob Rogers is hereby appointed Surveyor of the High Way from the Smith Shop near him to John Magorts and with the Adjacent Titheables It is Ordered that he clear & keep the same in repair According to Law

26 August 1749 O. S., p. 278
On the motion of Gabriel Jones on behalf of the Justices of Culpeper County It is Ordered that James McCoy and Richard Harrold mark & Lay off a way from the s^d McKoys to Frederick County Line and make report of their proceedings to the next Court--

29 November 1749 O. S., p. 289
James Brown is hereby appointed Surveyor of the Highway from the Court House of this County opposite to Robert Poages, and It is ordered that he Set up Posts of Directions & Clear and keep the s^d Road in repair According to Law.

29 November 1749 O. S., p. 290
John Anderson Gent is hereby appointed Surveyor of the Highway from Robt. Poages to the River near his own House and It is ordered that he set up Post of Directions and Clear and keep the s^d Road in repair Acc^d to Law

29 November 1749 O. S., p. 292
William Smith in hereby Appointed Surveyor of the Highway in the room of Daniel Deniston and it's Ordered that he Clear & keep the same in repair according to Law.

1 December 1749 O. S., p. 297
John Moore is hereby Appointed Surveyor of the high way in the room of John Hayes & Its Ordered that he Clear & keep the same in repair According to Law.

2 December 1749 O. S., p. 311

Ordered that James Moodey William Nutt Robert Ramsey and Hugh Fulton mark a road the Most Convenient Way from the Court House to Moores Mill and make report of their proceedings to the Next Court

27 February 1749 O. S., p. 312
James Lockart Gent and William Ledgerwood having returned that they have laid of a way from the North Mountain Meeting House to the Court House of this County It is Ordered that they with the adjacent Titheables Clear the same from the s^d Meeting House as Low as John Campbells field and that they keep the same in repair According to Law

27 February 1749 O. S., p. 312
Ordered that John Henderson and John Lynn be overseers of the Road Laid of by James Lockart and William Ledgerwood from John Campbells field to the Court House of this County and that they with the adjacent Titheables Clear & keep the same in repair According to Law

27 February 1749 O. S., p. 313
Andrew Hayes and John Moore are hereby Appointed Surveyors of the Highway from the North Mountain Meeting House to the s^d. John Moores and It is Ordered that with the Adjacent Titheables they Clear and keep the same in repair According to Law

22 May 1750 O. S., p. 356
William Armstrong Daniel Evans and John Robinson are hereby appointed Surveyors of the high way in the room of James Campbell & it is Ordered that the Set up Sign Posts with directions & Clear & keep the Same in repair According to Law

22 May 1750 O. S., p. 358
On the Motion of John Pickens it is Ordered that John Anderson and Thomas Gordon review the Road formerly laid of by William Baskins and Samuel Givens & make report of their proceedings to the next Court

22 May 1750 O. S., p. 359
Thomas Moore and Riley Moore are hereby Appointed Surveyors of the High Way in the room of Daniel Holdman and it is Ordered that they set up posts of Directions and Clear & keep the same in repair According to Law.

22 May 1750 O. S., p. 359
Daniel Davison is Appointed Surveyor of the High Way from John Harrisons to the Meeting House road and it is Ord^d. that he Set up Posts of Directions & Clear & keep the Same in repair According to Law

22 May 1750 O. S., p. 359

Nicholas Long is hereby Appointed Overseer of the Highway in the room of Michael Kaufman decd and it is Ordered that he Set up Posts of directions & Clear and keep the Same in repair According to Law

22 May 1750 O. S., p. 363
Ordered that Robert Graham be Surveyor of the highway in the room of William Hamilton and that he Set up Posts of Directions and Clear & keep the Same in repair Acc^d. to Law

23 May 1750 O. S., p. 363
William McCutcheon is hereby Appointed Surveyor of the High Way from the North Mountain Meeting House as high as Bordens line and it is Ordered that he Set up Posts of Directions and Clear and keep the Same in repair According to Law

23 May 1750 O. S., p. 364
Ordered that a road be Cleared from John Hays Mill to Providence Meeting House from thence to the County Road and that And^r. Hays Set up Posts of Direction and with the adjacent titheables Clear & keep the Same in repair According to Law

23 May 1750 O. S., p. 369
The Petition of David Hayes and Others for a Road is rejected

23 May 1750 O. S., p. 370
On the Petition of Sundry the South West Inhabitants of this County It is Ordered that John Vance and Alexander Sayers mark and lay of a Road from Ezekiel Colhouns to Wood's River and that John Stroud and James Conley mark and lay of a road from thence to the top of the Dividing Ridge beween Wood's River & the South fork of Roan Oak and that John M^{c}farland and Joseph Crocket be Surveyors of the s^d Road from Cohouns to Wood's River and William Crisp and William Pellam be Surveyors of the Road from Wood's River to the top of the af^d. Ridge and that with the adjacent titheables and Henry Ballon Mordicai Earley, John Mcfarland, Jacob Goldman, John Downing, John Goldman, Charly Sinclar, Nathaniel Wiltshire, William Sayers, Jacob Goldman, William Hamilton, Humberston Lyon, Frederick Carlock, Robert Norris James Miller, James Cave Samuel Montgomerie Steven Lyon, John Conley, Andrew Linam, James Willbey Samuel Stonlick, James Mairs Robert M^{c}farlin, James Harris, John Vance, John Stride, Robert Miller, Alexander Sayers, John Miller, Jacob Castle, Robert Alcorn John Forman and William Miller they Clear and keep the same in repair According to Law

23 May 1750 O. S., p. 371
Erwin Patterson Gent is hereby desired to Wait on the Court of Luninburg and Acquaint them that the Inhabitants of this County have Cleared a Road from the forks of Roan Oak to their County Line, Thereupon pray that a Road may be Cleared from Lunenburg Court House to meet the same

23 May 1750 O. S., p. 371

Ordered that Andrew Cowan James Mitchell Samuel Downey and James Fulton be Surveyors of the High Way from the Court House of this County to Moores Mill and that they Set up Posts of Directions & Clear & keep the same in repair According to Law

24 May 1750 O. S., p. 372
William Williams is hereby Appointed Surveyor of the highway in the room of John Lynn Gent and it is Ordered that he Set up Post of directions and Clear and keep the Same in repair According to Law

24 May 1750 O. S., p. 372
Ordered that the Road marked from the North Mountain Meeting House to this Court House by James Lockart Gent and Wm Ledgerwood be Cleared thro James Millers field the way the said Road was first laid of

24 May 1750 O. S., p. 373
On the Petition of Sundry the Inhabitants for a Road from the County line to John Staly Mill It is ordered that Joseph How, Set up posts of directions and with the titheables persons within one Mile of the s^d Road and John Elswick, Andrew Viney, John Dunbarr, William M^cbride, Francis M^cbride, Robert Denton, James Thomas, James Scot, James Hamiltons William Miller and Valentine Sevier, the Subscribers he Clear & keep the Same in repar According to Law

25 May 1750 O. S., p. 381
A Road being Cleared over the blew Ridge of Mountains at the place known by the Name of Wood's Old pass to the line of Albemarle It is Ordered that the Clerk of this Court Acquaint the Court of Albemarle thereof desiring them to Clear a Road from Albemarle Court House to meet the Same

25 May 1750 O. S., p. 381
Richard Burton Robert Renix John Poage and Peter Wallace are hereby appointed Surveyors of the highway from Looneys Ferry to the North branch of James River and that John Mathews and Richard Woods Gent. lay of their respective gangs and precincts and it is further Ordered that they set up posts of directions and Clear and keep the Same in repair According to Law

25 May 1750 O. S., p. 381
Benjamin Borden gent John Thompson Isaac Taylor & William McClung are hereby appointed Surveyors of the high way from the North River till it intercepts with the County Road and it is Ordered that John Lyle Gent & John Stevenson lay of their respective gangs and precincts & that they Set up posts of directions and Clear & keep the Same in repair According to Law.

25 May 1750 O. S., p. 381

James Bell James Alexander and John M{c}Clure are hereby appointed Surveyors of the High way from the Piney Run to Israel Christians & it is Ordered that Thomas Steuart and Robert Cuningham gent lay of their respective gangs and precincts

25 May 1750 O. S., p. 382
Ordered that William Finley and Robert Patrick lay of and be Overseers of a road from Israel Christians to meet the road Cleared over the blew Ridge of Mountains by Thomas Steuart and that they Set up Posts of Directions and with the Titheables within fifteen Miles of the s^d. Road they Clear & keep the Same in repair According to Law

25 May 1750 O. S., p. 382
Mathew Edmondson is hereby appointed Surveyor of the High way from Daniel M^{c}anares thro^g. Jenning's gap to the Waters of the Cowpasture and that John Graham Settle the bounds between the s^d waters & that the s^d Edmondson with the Adjatient titheables Clear & keep the same in repair According to Law

25 May 1750 O. S., p. 382
James Hall is hereby appointed Surveyor of the highway from the Waters of the Cowpasture to Lewis great bottom and that with the Adjacent titheables he Clear & keep the same in repair According to Law. & its is further Ordered that W^m. Jackson mark and lay of a Way from Jacksons River to meet the Same

25 May 1750 O. S., p. 382
Wm Thompson and Joseph McClelhill are hereby appointed Surveyors of the high Way in the room of Robert McClenahan and John Maxwill and Ordered that with the Adjacent Tith^s. they Set up posts of directions & Clear and keep the Same in repair According to Law

25 May 1750 O. S., p. 382
Peter Thorn and Lambert Pooper are hereby Appointed to lay of and be Surveyors of a Road from Coburns Mill to the County Line and that James Rutledge gent lay of the titheables to Clear the Same

25 May 1750 O. S., p. 382
Edward Erwin is Appointed Surveyor of the high Way in the room of William Thompson on the Middle River and it is Ordered that John Stevenson lay of his precincts & nominate the Titheables to work on the Same and it is further Ordered that he Set up posts of directions and Clear and keep the same in repair According to Law

25 May 1750 O. S., p. 382
John Craig is hereby Appointed Surveyor of the Indian Road in the room of Robert Cravens and it is Ordered that with the Adjacent titheables he Set up posts of Directions and Clear and keep the Same in repair According to Law

25 May 1750 O. S., p. 383

Daniel Love is hereby Appointed Surveyor of the highway from the North River as low as Craven's and it is Ordered that he Set up posts of Directions and with the Adjacent Titheables Clear & keep the Same in repair According to Law

28 August 1750 O. S., p. 415
On the Petition of Sundry the Inhabitants of the Calf Pasture for a Road from Wm Gays to Robert McCutcheons & from thence to Robert Campbells It is Ordered that Robert McCutcheon with Wm Elliot Thomas Fulton, John Meek, John Gay, William Gay, Thomas Meek, John Gay, John Fulton & James Sevenson Clear & keep the same in repair According to Law.

28 August 1750 O. S., p. 418
William Beard is hereby Appointed Surveyor of the High Way in the Room of James Galespy / it being that part of the Indian Road whereof Wm Thompson was formerly Overseer / and it is ordered that he Set up Posts of Directions and Clear and keep the same in repair According to Law

1 September 1750 O. S., p. 459
David Logan is hereby Appointed Surveyor of the Highway / in the room of John Craig / whereof Robert Craven was formerly Overseer and it is Ordered that he Set up posts of Directions & with the Usual Gang Clear and keep the Same in repair According to Law

27 November 1750 O. S., p. 485
On the Petition of Sundry the Inhabitants of the Cow pasture for a road from Patrick Davis's to the Road that Leads from Col^o John Lewis' Land to Beverley's Bigg Meadows It is Ordered that James Mays Adam Dickenson & David Davis lay of the Same & make report of their proceedings to the next Court

28 November 1750 O. S., p. 495
[Grand Jury Presentments]

We Present the Overseers of the Road Over Swift run Gap on the Blue Ridge for not keeping the Same in Repair on the Information of Henry Downs

*　*　*

We also present the Overseers of the Road from Henry Downs j^r to the Stone Meeting House for being not Sufficient
We Present the Overseers of the Road from George Scots at the Middle River to John Harrisons not being Sufficient

28 November 1750 O. S., p. 500
John Mitchell is hereby Appointed Surveyor of the Highway in the room of John Buchanan and it is ordered that with the Usual Gang he Clear & keep the same in repair According to Law.

27 February 1750 O. S., p. 523

Joseph Langdon is hereby Appointed Surveyor of the Highway in the room of Jonas Denton and its Ordered that with the Titheables that Usually work'd under the s^d Denton / he Set up Posts of Directions and Clear & keep the Same in repair According to Law

27 February 1750 O. S., p. 523
John Philips is hereby Appointed Surveyor of the Highway in the room of Daniel Deniston and it's Ordered that with the Titheables that Usually work'd Under the s^d. Denton he Set up Posts of Directions and Clear and keep the Same in repair According to Law

27 February 1750 O. S., p. 523
James Mays and John Dickenson are hereby Appointed Surveyors of the High Way from Patrick Davis' to the Road that Leads to Beverleys bigg Meadow, and It is ordered that Adam Dickenson Gent lay of their respective Gangs and precincts and that with the Same they Set up Posts of Directions and Clear and keep the Same in repair According to Law

2 March 1750 O. S., p. 558
The King agst. The Overseers of the Road Over Swift run Pass
On Pres^t of the Grand jury for not keeping the High Way in repair According to Law

The Sherif having returned on the Summons Not found". on the Motion of the Attorney of our L^d the King an Alias Summons is Awarded agst. them returnable here the Next Court

2 March 1750 O. S., p. 559
The King agst. The Overseers of the Road from Down's to the Stone Meeting House
On Pres^t of the Grand Jury
The Sherif having returned on the Summons not found, on the Motion of the Attorney of our Lord the King an Alias Summons is Awarded agst. them returnable here the next Court

2 March 1750 O. S., p. 559
The King agst. The Overseers of the Road from Scots to the Middle River
On Presentm^t of the Grand Jury
The Sherif having returned on the Summons "Not found" on the Motion of the Attorney of our Lord the King an Alias Summons is Awarded agst. them returnable here the next Court.

28 May 1751 O. S., p. 566
Robert Scot is hereby appointed Surveyor of the Highway in the Room of James Beard and It is ordered that he set up Posts of Directions and with the usual Gang that worked on the s^d Road Under the s^d Beard he Clear and keep the same in repair According to Law.

28 May 1751 O. S., p. 566
On the Petition of Robert Campbell & Others It is Ordered that John McCreary Wm Lockart and James Wilson lay of a Road from between Captain Wilsons and John McCrearys to the South Side of James Lockarts Field thence to the South Side James Wilsons Field and from thence the Nearest and best Way by Capt Christians to the Road that Leads from Pattons Mill to the

Tinkling Spring and It is further Ordered that James Lockart John Wilson James Wilson, and James Moody be Overseers and with the Titheable persons within four Miles on Each Side of the s^d Road they Clear and keep the same in repair According to Law. & that the s^d Lockart & Wilson lay of their Respective Gangs & precincts

28 May 1751 O. S., p. 568
David Kerr is hereby Appointed Surveyor of the highway in the Room of Andrew Hays and its' Ordered that he Set up Posts of Directions and with the Gang that Usually worked on the s^d Road Under the s^d Hays he Clear and keep the Same in repair According to Law.

28 May 1751 O. S., p. 568
William Wortlow is hereby Appointed Surveyor of the highway in the room of John Moore and it's Ordered that he Set up Posts of Directions & with the Gang that Usually worked on the s^d Road Under the s^d Moore he Clear & keep the Same in repair According to Law.

28 May 1751 O. S., p. 568
George Caldwell is hereby appointed Surveyor of the highway in the Room of Wm Thompson and it's Ordered that he set up Posts of Directions and with the Gang that Usually Worked on the s^d Road Under the s^d Thompson he Clear & keep the same in repair According to Law

28 May 1751 O. S., p. 568
[Grand Jury Presentments]

We present John Robinson Overseer of the Road in his precincts for not Clearing the s^d Road According to Law. We also present Isaac Taylor for Stoping the s^d Road Erwin Patterson Informer

28 May 1751 O. S., p. 569
Ordered that a Road be Cleared from or Near James McCowns to Pattons Mill place on Christians Creek, and that James Buchanan John Shields and James Mitchell be Overseers and that the s^d Buchanan & Shields lay of their respective precincts and Appoint their Gangs, and it's further Ordered that with the s^d Gangs they Set up Posts of Directions and Clear & keep the s^d Road in Repair According to Law.

28 May 1751 O. S., p. 569
Ordered that a Road from Pattons Mill / formerly belonging to Andrew McCord / to the Tinkling Spring be kept in repair & that John Christian & Robert Coningham Gent with Usual Gang Appointed by Orange Court Clear & keep the same in repair Acc^d. to Law.

28 May 1751 O. S., p. 570
William Hutcheson is hereby Appointed Surveyor of the Highway in the room of James Lesley & it is Ordered that with the Titheables that usually worked on the s^d Road under the s^d Lestley he / set up Posts of Directions & Clear & keep the Same in repair According to Law.

8 May 1751 O. S., p. 570
Ordered that a Road be Cleared from Timber Ridge to New Providence and that John Lyle and Andrew Hill [?] be Surveyors and Appoint their Gangs & lay of their Precincts & it's further Ordered that they set up Posts of Directions and wth their respective Gangs Clear & keep the s^d Road in repair According to Law.

28 May 1751 O. S., p. 570
Ordered that a Road be Cleared from the Court House of this County by John Buchanans Mill to the Indian Road that leads by Fultons and that James Lockart Gent lay of the Titheables and appoint Overseers to Clear the Same and its further Ordered that the s^d Overseers wth. the Gang app^d by the s^d Lockart / Set up posts of Directions / and Clear & keep the same in repair According to Law

28 May 1751 O. S., p. 570
Samuel Monsey is hereby Appointed Surveyor of the highway in the room of John Bryant and it's Ordered that with the adjacent Titheables / he Set up posts of Directions / & Clear and keep the Same in repair According to Law.

28 May 1751 O. S., p. 570
Ordered that a Road be Cleared from Crockets to Kings Gap and that Thomas Weems & William Hamilton be Surveyors, and Set up Posts of Directions, amd with the Adjacent Titheables Clear & keep the Same in repair According to Law.

28 May 1751 O. S., p. 571
Ordered that a Road be Cleared from Calep Jobs to James McKoys Crossing the River at a Place Called the brush bottom Ford and so Along the River by Henry Spears Plantation and that the s^d Spears with Mason Combs, John Sollers, Richard Shirly William Hurst, William Overall, Thomas Hues, Zachariah McKoy Terrance Carroll, Wm Dickinson, Steven Philips, Alexander Gunnoe, James McNeal, John Hankins, Benj^a. Grider, Ephraim Leath, Charles Williamson, Josiah Parent William Parent Thomas Parent Edmond Bollen, Wm Parent, Adam Coningham & Francis Grubbs / Set up posts of Directions and / Clear & keep the s^d Road in repair According to Law.

28 May 1751 O. S., p. 572
Robert McMahon is hereby Appointed Surveyor of the Highway in the Room of Wm Beard and it is Ordered that he Set up Posts of Directions & with the Tithables that usually worked on the s^d Road under the s^d. Beard he Clear & keep the Same in repair According to Law.

29 May 1751 O. S., p. 574
Ordered that John Davis John Erwin and Thomas Turk mark a way from John Davis's Mill to Wood's New Cleared Gap and that John King with Andrew Erwin John McGill, William McGill, Robert Fowler Hugh Campbell John Erwin, Edward Erwin, Robert Carscaden Edward Erwin, Francis Erwin, William Frame, Benjamin Erwin Charles Campbell Robert Campbell Wm Brown, Michael Dickey Robert Brown Henry Smith Hugh Diver, Charles Diver, David McCammis John

Davis, Daniel Smith James Anderson, John Frances, Wm Alexander Robert Gamble, Andrew Combs James Patterson Francis Brown and Gabriel Pickens Set up posts of Directions & Clear & keep the Same in repair According to Law.

29 May 1751 O. S., p. 574
Ordered that James Lockart Gent and John Henderson be Surveyors of the highway from John Campbells field to this Court House & that they Set up Post of Directions and with the Adjacent Titheables Clear & keep the Same in repair According to Law.

29 May 1751 O. S., p. 574
Alexander Painter and John Staley are hereby Appointed Surveyors of the Highway from Cape Caphon till it meets with the road near Thomas Moores, and it's Ord^d. that with the Adjacent titheables they Clear & keep the Same in repair According to Law.

29 May 1751 O. S., p. 576
John Magoit is hereby Appointed Surveyor of the Highway in the room of Henry Long & it is Ordered that he set up Post of Directions & with the Titheables that usued to work on the s^d Road under the s^d. Long Clear & keep the same in repair According to Law.

29 May 1751 O. S., p. 576
George Lewis is hereby Appointed Surveyor of the highway in the room of James Hall, and it is Ordered that he Set up Posts of Directions & with the Titheables that usued to work on the s^d Road under the s^d Hall Clear & keep the Same in repair According to Law.

29 May 1751 O. S., p. 577
Paul Lung is hereby Appointed Surveyor of the highway in the room of Nicholas Lung and it is Ordered that he Set up Posts of Directions and with the Titheable Persons that worked on the s^d Road under the s^d Niho^s. Lung Clear & keep the same in repair According to Law.

29 May 1751 O. S., p. 577
Samuel O'Dell is hereby Appointed Surveyor of the highway in the room of Daniel Stover and it is Ordered that he set up Posts of Directions & with the Titheables Persons that Usually worked on the s^d Road under the s^d Stover he Clear & keep the same in repair According to Law.

29 May 1751 O. S., p. 577
William Carroll is hereby Appointed Surveyor of the highway in the room of Riley Moore, and it is Ordered that he Set up posts of Directions and with the Titheable Persons that Usually Worked on the s^d Road Under the s^d Moore he Clear and keep the same in repair According to Law.

29 May 1751 O. S., p. 577
Francis Hughs is hereby is hereby Appointed Surveyor of the highway in the room of Thomas Moore and it is Ordered that he Set up Posts of Directions and with the Titheable Persons that

Usually Worked on the s^d Road under the s^d Moore he Clear & keep the same in repair According to Law.

29 May 1751 O. S., p. 577
Mathew Lyle is hereby Appointed Surveyor of the highway in the room of Benjamin Borden Gent and it is Ordered that he Set up Posts of Directions and with the Titheable Persons that Usually worked on the s^d Road under the s^d Borden he Clear & keep the same in repair According to Law.

29 May 1751 O. S., p. 577
William Moore is hereby Appointed Surveyor of the highway in the room of W^m. McClung and it is Ordered that he Set up Posts of Directions and with the Titheable persons that Usually worked on the s^d Road Under the s^d McClung he Clear & keep the Same in repair According to Law.

29 May 1751 O. S., p. 577
David Drydon is hereby Appointed Surveyor of the highway in the room of James Thompson and it is Ordered that he Set up Posts of Directions and with the Titheable persons that Usually worked on the s^d Road Under the s^d Thompson he Clear & keep the Same in repair According to Law.

29 May 1751 O. S., p. 577
Joseph Lapsley is hereby Appointed Surveyor of the highway in the room of Peter Wallace and it is Ordered that he Set up Posts of Directions and with the Titheable persons that Usually worked on the s^d Road Under the s^d Wallace he Clear & keep the same in repair According to Law.

29 May 1751 O. S., p. 578
John Mason is hereby Appointed Surveyor of the Highway in the room of William Armstrong, and it is Ordered that he Set up Posts of Directions, & with the usual titheables that worked on the s^d Road under the s^d Armstrong he Clear & keep the same in repair According to Law.

29 May 1751 O. S., p. 578
Thomas Tosh is hereby Appointed Surveyor of the highway in the room of Daniel Evans and it is Ordered that he set up posts of Directions and with the Titheable persons that usually worked on the s^d Road Under the s^d Evans he Clear & keep the Same in repair According to Law.

29 May 1751 O. S., p. 578
The Petition of John Paxton to turn the Road by his Door is granted and it is Ordered that with his own hands he Clear & keep the same in repair According to Law.

29 May 1751 O. S., p. 580
On the Petition of Sundry the Inhabitants of the Cow Pasture, Ordered that Wallace Estill with Robert Carlile, John Carlile, Loftus Pullen Rich^d. Bodkin, Samuel Farguson, Mathew Harper, Thomas Wright Michael Harper Hance Harper, John Miller, William Price, James Anglen, Ja^s. Hall, Philip Phegan, John Shaw Herculus Wilson, William Carlile & John Carlile lay of and

Clear a Road from his Mill to the Road on the head of the Calf Pasture, and that he Set up Post of Directions & keep the s^d Road in repair According to Law.

29 May 1751 O. S., p. 581
Samuel Tincher is hereby Appointed Overseer of the Road in the room of Andrew Hamilton and it is Ordered that With the Titheable persons that usually worked on the s^d Road under the s^d Hamilton he / Set up Posts of Directions & / Clear & keep the same in repair According to Law.

29 May 1751 O. S., p. 581
On The Petition of Sundry the Inhabitants of the South branch. It is Ordered that John Patton, Roger Dyer, Daniel Richardson & Duke Collins with the Adjacent Titheables Clear a Road from Pattons Mill the Nearest & best way to Coburns Mill & that they Set up posts of Directions & keep the s^d Road in repair According to Law.

29 May 1751 O. S., p. 582
Joseph Canaday and James Walker are hereby Appointed Surveyors of the Highway in the room of Capt Joseph Coulton and it is Ordered that they Set up Posts of Directions and with the Gangs that shall be appointed them by Benjamin Borden & Alexander Miller they Clear and keep the s^d. Road in Repair According to Law.

29 May 1751 O. S., p. 582
Ordered that a Road be Cleared from Hays's fulling Mill to Timber Ridge Meeting House and that Benjamin Borden Gent lay on their Gangs Overseers & Precincts.

29 May 1751 O. S., p. 583
Henry Downs jun^r. is hereby Appointed Surveyor of the highway from his house to the Stone Meeting House & Its is Ordered that he Set up Posts of Directions & with the Adjacent Titheables Clear & keep the Same in repair According to Law.

29 May 1751 O. S., p. 583
Jacob Anderson and John Huston are hereby Appointed Surveyors of the highway from the North River to Robert Dunlops and it is Ordered that Benjamin Borden and John Lyle Gent lay of their Gangs and precincts.

29 May 1751 O. S., p. 583
On the Motion of Thomas Steuart, John Lyle, Andrew Hays Charles Campbell John Trimble Cooper John Tate, John Anderson, & Joseph Lapsley or any five of them are hereby Ordered to View the Road Cleared by the s^d Steuart Over the blew Ridge of Mountains and that they meet at the s^d Mountains on the first day of August next, and return their proceedings to the next Court, and it is further Ordered that in Case the s^d Road be found Sufficient that all Subscription papers relating thereto be delivered to the s^d Steuart

29 May 1751 O. S., p. 583
Joseph Robinson and John Marshall are hereby Appointed to lay of and be Surveyors of a Road from James Davis' to the Landing Road and it is Ordered that they set up posts of directions and wth. the Adjacent titheables Clear & keep the Same in repair According to Law.

29 May 1751 O. S., p. 583
James Davis is hereby Appointed Surveyor of the highway from the Cherry tree bottom ford to Millikins, and it is Ordered that he Set up Posts of Directions and with the Adjacent titheables Clear & keep the Same in repair According to Law.

29 May 1751 O. S., p. 583
Steven Rentfro is hereby Appointed Surveyor of the highway from Millikins to the first ford on Catapo and it is Ordered that he Set up posts of Directions and with the Adjacent Titheables Clear & keep the same in repair According to Law.

29 May 1751 O. S., p. 583
Ordered that a Road be Cleared from David Moores Mill the Nearest & best way to Robert Poages Mill Place in the forks of James River, and that Archabald Alexander Michael Finney, John Hargrove, John Maxwell & John Peter Salling be Overseers of the Same & it's further Ordered that John Lyle Benjamin Borden Richard Woods & John Mathews lay of their Respective Gangs & Precincts.

31 May 1751 O. S., p. 598
James Downing is hereby Appointed Surveyor of the high way in the room of David Logan and it is Ordered that he Set up Posts of Directions with the titheables that Usual worked on the s^d Road Under the s^d Logan he Clear & keep the same in repair Acc^d to Law.

31 May 1751 O. S., p. 598
Jacob Nicholas is hereby Appointed Surveyor of the highway in the room of John Craige and it is Ordered that he Set up Posts of Directions & with the titheables that Usually worked on the s^d Road Under the s^d Craig he Clear & keep the same in repair According to Law

31 May 1751 O. S., p. 598
Henry Sellore is hereby Appointed Surveyor of the highway in the room of Jacob Rogers and it is Ordered that he Set up Posts of Directions and with the titheables that Usually worked on the s^d Road Under the s^d Craig he Clear & keep the same in repair According to Law.

1 June 1751 O. S., p. 605
Ordered that Henry Smith and Daniel Harrison mark and lay of a way from the South branch Road to Swift run Gap and make a Report of their Proceedings to the next Court

Book III, 1751-1753

27 August 1751 O. S., p. 177

Patrick Frazier is hereby Appointed Surveyor of the highway in the room of Robert McMahon and It is Ordered that with the Titheable persons that usually worked on the s^d Road Under the s^d McMahon he Clear and keep the same in Repair According to Law.

27 August 1751 O. S., p. 179
On the Petition of Sundry the Inhabitants of this County for a Road from John Andersons to the Court House of this County It is Ordered that John Poage and James Allen being first sworn before a Justice of the Peace for this County do View the Most Conveniant way & make report of their proceedings to the next Court

27 August 1751 O. S., p. 179
On the Complaint of William Russell Gent against William Hurst for not keeping the Road whereof he is Overseer in repair According to Law It is Ordered that he be Summoned to Appear at the next Court to answer the s^d Complaint and that William Harrald be Appointed Surveyor of the s^d Road in his Stead and it is further Ordered that James M^ckoy with the Titheable persons on the West Side the South River to Frederick County Line together with those on Goodys Run and on the South Side the River to the afores^d line of Frederick assist the s^d Harrald in Clearing and keeping the s^d Road in repair According to Law.

27 August 1751 O. S., p. 187
Daniel Harrison and Henry Smith having According to an Order of this Court laid of away from the South branch to Swift run Pass. It is Ordered that Robert Craven and James Balley be Surveyors of the Same and that the said Harrison lay of their Precincts & appoint the Titheable persons that shall Clear the Same.

29 August 1751 O. S., p. 189
On the Motion of Thomas Stewart It is Ordered that Alexander Wright John Christian, John Pickens, John Tate, John Anderson & William Hamilton, be Summoned to appear at the road Cleared over the blew Ridge of Mountains by the said Stewart, on the first Monday in Novr. next and that with John Lyle and Andrew Hays or any four of them they View the same & report their proceedings to the next Court--

29 August 1751 O. S., p. 189
Andrew Hays having made Oath that Robert Patrick and William Finlay Overseers of the highway from Israel Christians to the Mountain had not Cleared and kept the said Road in repair According to Law It is Ordered that they be find Each fifteen Shillings Current Money According to Law & that they pay Cost--

29 August 1751 O. S., p. 189
Ordered that Thomas Stewart and James Allen with Robert Finly and Robert Patrick be Surveyors of the Road from Israel Christians to the Mountain and that with the titheable persons Appointed by former Order they Clear and keep the Same in repair According to Law.

29 August 1751 O. S., p. 189
Ordered that James Bell and James Alexander be Summoned to Appear at the next Court for not Clearing the road whereof they are Overseers According to Law.

26 November 1751 O. S., p. 200
Ordered that John Davis and Samuel O'Dell being first Sworn before a Justice of the Peace for this County do lay of and mark the Most Conveniant Way from Thorns Gap to Henry Nethertons and Make report of their proceedings to the next Court

28 November 1751 O. S., p. 208
Ordered that Adam Dickenson David Davis Peter Wright and Joseph Carpenter lay of and be Surveyors of a Road from Wrights Mill to the Cow Pasture near Hugarts or Knoxes and that with the Adjacent Titheables and such as may hereafter Subscribe they Clear and keep the s^d Road in repair According to Law.

28 November 1751 O. S., p. 209
The Petition of Sundry the Lower Inhabitants of the Cow Pasture for a Road from thence to Burdens Tract is granted and it is Ordered that James Scot John Scot, William Memury, James Simpson, James Frame, Robert Montgomerie, James Montgomerie Hugh McDonall and William Galispy the Subscribers to the s^d Petition Clear & keep the same in repair According to Law

3 December 1751 O. S., p. 233
[Grand Jury Presentments]

The King v The Overseers of the High-way that Leads over Swit run gap
On a Presentm^t of the Grand jury
The Sheriff having returned that s^d Overseers was not found in this Bailiwic this Prest^n is dismissed

The King v The Overseers of the Highway from Down's to the Stone Meeting-house
On a Presentm^t of the Grand jury
The Sheriff having returned that the s^d Overseers was not found in this Bailiwic this Suit is dismissed

The King v The Surveyors of the Highway from Scots to the Middle River
On a Present^t. of the Grand jury
The Sheriff having returned that the s^d Overseers was not found in his Bailiwic this Suit is dismissed

* * *

The King v John Robinson

On a Pres^t. of the Grand Jury for not keeping the Road whereof he was Overseer in repair According to Law
The s^d John being returned not to be found on the Motion of his Matys Attorney an Alias Summons is awarded against him returnable to the next Court

The King v Isaac Taylor
On a Presentment of the Grand jury for Stoping the Highway
The defendant being Summon'd Appeared and his Excuse being heard It is Ordered that the Presentment be discontinued

3 December 1751 O. S., p. 239
The Order of Court for Summoning Wm Hurst on the Comp^{ls}. of Wm Russell Gent for not keeping the Road whereof he is Overseer in Repair According to Law is dismissed Neither party Appearing

3 December 1751 O. S., p. 240
The Order of Court for Summoning James Bell and James Alexander for not keeping the road whereof they are Overseers in Repair According to Law is dismissed

19 February 1751 O. S., p. 241
A Petition of Sundry the Inhabitants praying a Sum of Money be by the Public Allowed them for the Clearing of Thorns Gap Over the Blew Ridge of Mountains and Other things therein Mentioned being read was Ordered to be Certified to the next Assembly

20 May 1752 O. S., p. 245
On the Motion of Rubin Harrison It is Ordered that he have leave to turn the main Road near his House round his Plantation he with his own hands Clearing the Same According to Law

20 May 1752 O. S., p. 245
Zebulon Harrison is hereby Appointed Surveyor of the highway in the room of John Philips and it is Ordered that with the Titheable Persons that usually worked on the s^d Road Under the s^d Philips he Clear and keep the Same in repair According to Law

20 May 1752 O. S., p. 247
On the Petition of Hans Magort Overseer of the Highway from Shanando River to the Top of the Blew Ridge It is Ordered that James Urrey, Steven Hans Burger, John Fought William Burk, Samuel Thornhill, John F[illegible]rnice Little Patrick Jacob Miller & Son Adam Miller & Son Charles Cross Henry Lung Jacob Coger and George Warrell be Added to his former Gang & that with the Same he Clear & keep the s^d Road in repair According to Law

20 May 1752 O. S., p. 247
Thomas Armstrong is hereby appointed Surveyor of the highway in the room of Mathew Edmondson and it is Ordered that with the Titheable persons that Usually worked on the s^d road under the s^d Edmondson be clear and keep the same in repair According to Law.

20 May 1752 O. S., p. 247
Ordered that John Finla be Surveyor of the highway from the Middle River to the Court House of this County and that with the adjacent Titheables he Clear and keep the same in repair Acccording to Law.

20 May 1752 O. S., p. 247
Ordered that David Carr be Overseer of the highway in the room of William Worklaw and that with the titheable persons that Usually worked on the s^d Road under the s^d Worklaw he Clear and keep the Same in repair According to Law

20 May 1752 O. S., p. 247
Ordered that Andrew Erwin Thomas Stevenson and Patrick Crawford be Overseers of the Road in the room of John King and that with the Titheable Persons that Usually worked on the s^d. road under the s^d King they Clear and keep the same in repair According to Law.

20 May 1752 O. S., p. 247
James Bartley is hereby appointed Surveyor of the highway in the room of Daniel Love and It is Ordered that with the Usual Titheables that worked on the s^d Road Under the s^d Love he Clear and keep the Same in repair According to Law.

20 May 1752 O. S., p. 247
On the Petition of Sundry the Inhabitants of Linvells Creek It is Ordered that Jonathan Duglass William Smith, John Miller, James Claypole, Willm. Claypole, Robert Williams & Rees Thomas Clear a Road from Brockes Creek to Francis Hughes & from thence to the Main Road that leads to Fredericksburg and that they keep the Same in repair According to Law

20 May 1752 O. S., p. 248
On the Petition of Sundry the Inhabitants of the Calf Pasture It is Ordered that William Smith be Overseer and with the following Persons Viz^t. William Elliot, Robert McCutcheon, William Smith, William Ramsey John Mocke, Robert Foyle, Wm Guy, James Stevenson Robt. Gay, John Guy Samuel Looney, Samuel Guy, John Hanley John Smith and John McGinney he Clear a Road from William Guys to Robert McCutcheons Mill and from thence to Robert Campbells and that with the above mentioned Titheables he keep the Same in repair According to Law.

20 May 1752 O. S., p. 248
On the Motion of Sundry the Inhabitants It is Ordered that a Road be Cleared from Jenning's to Swift run Gap and that Sampson Archer and John Young mark the s^d Road from the begining to the North River & that John Hare and Hugh Campbell mark it from thence to Swift run Gap, and that Wm Hogshead be Overseer of the s^d Road from the begining to the Long Glade, John Francis

to the s^d North River and that Patrick Frazier to the Main Road that Leads to the s^d Swift run Gap and that with the Adjacent titheables they Clear and keep the Same in repair According to Law

20 May 1752 O. S., p. 249
John Beard and Jacob Gum are hereby appointed Surveyors of the highway in the room of Francis Hughs, and it is Ordered that with the Titheable persons that worked on the s^d Road under the s^d Hughs they Clear and keep the same in repair According to Law

20 May 1752 O. S., p. 249
Abraham Collet and William White are hereby appointed Surveyors of the highway in the room of William Carroll and It is Ordered that with the titheable persons that work'd on the s^d Road under the s^d Carroll they Clear & keep the Same in repair According to Law

20 May 1752 O. S., p. 249
Ordered that Nap Grigory lay of and mark a way from the Widow Jacksons to Wms [Williams] Creek and make report of his proceedings to the next Court

20 May 1752 O. S., p. 250
Ordered that Samuel McClure be Overseer of the highway from the Tinkling Spring to Blacks run and that Robert Craig be Overseer from the s^d. run to the Middle River and that with the adjacent Titheables they Clear and keep the Same in repair According to Law

21 May 1752 O. S., p. 251
Thomas Paxton Senr. and John Paul are hereby Appointed Surveyors of the highway in the room of Archibald Alexander and It is Ordered that with the Titheable persons that worked on the s^d Road under the s^d Alexander the Clear and keep the Same in repair According to Law

21 May 1752 O. S., p. 251
Ordered that Benjamin Borden Gent lay of a Road from his House to Providence Meeting House and that John Patton be Surveyor of the Same and with Such Titheable Persons as Shall be Appointed by the s^d Borden and Archabald Alexander he Clear and keep the Same in repair According to Law.

21 May 1752 O. S., p. 251
Ordered that Benjamin Borden and Archabald Alexander Gent^n. Appoint the Titheable Persons to work under the Several Overseers of the Roads from the North River to Beverley Manner line

21 May 1752 O. S., p. 251
Ordered that Joseph Coulton be Summoned to Appear at the next Court to Shew Cause if any he can, why he hath not Cleared the road whereof he is Overseer According to Law.

21 May 1752 O. S., p. 251
On the Motion of John Madison Ordered that a Road be Cleared from Robert Poages to Pickens Mill from thence to the forks of the River near the said Madisons from thence to Swift run gap and that he Appoint Surveyors and Titheable Persons to Clear and keep the same in repair According to Law

21 May 1752 O. S., p. 251
Ordered that John Mathews and Richard Woods Gent Appoint the Several Gangs under the Overseers of the roads in the forks of James River

21 May 1752 O. S., p. 251
Ordered that John Hare be Appointed Overseer of the Road from the North River to naked Creek near David Stevensons from thence to the Stone Meeting House and that with the Adjacent Titheables he Clear and keep the Same in repair According to Law

21 May 1752 O. S., p. 252
James Cadwell is hereby Appointed Overseer of the Road from Nutts Mill Creek near his Meadow to this Court House and It is Ordered that with the adjacent Titheables he Clear and keep the Same in repair According to Law

21 May 1752 O. S., p. 253
John Finla and Archabald Stewart are hereby Appointed Surveyors of the highway from Finla's Spring to the Meeting House and it is Ordered that with the Adjacent titheables they Clear and keep the Same in repair According to Law

21 May 1752 O. S., p. 254
Ordered that Abraham Smith be Overseer of the Road in the room of Henry Smith and Gabriel Pickens from the Little fork of the Dry run to the North River and that Silas Hart Gent Appoint the Titheable persons with which they are Ordered to Clear and keep the same in repair According to Law

21 May 1752 O. S., p. 254
Ordered that Henry Smith and William Anderson mark a Road from the North River near Silas Harts Gent to this Court-house and that John Anderson be Surveyor of the Same from the s^d Harts to the Middle River and John Trimble from thence to the Court House of this County and that with the Convenient Titheables they Clear & keep the Same in repair According to Law

17 June 1752 O. S., p. 260
Ordered that James Galespy and Joseph Tees be Surveyors of the highway in the room of John Finla and Robert Patrick and that with the Titheable Persons within Six Miles of the s^d Road they Clear and keep the Same in repair According to Law

17 June 1752 O. S., p. 260
Wm Gerrott is hereby Appointed Surveyor of the highway in the room of Tobias Bright and it is Ordered that with the Titheable persons that Usually worked on the s^d Road under the s^d Tobias he clear and keep the Same in repair According to Law

17 June 1752 O. S., p. 260
Ordered that Samuel Fincher and Thomas Gilham be Overseers and with the Adjacent Titheables Clear and keep the road from Jenning's Gap to Charles Walkers in repair According to Law

17 June 1752 O. S., p. 260
James Knox is hereby Appointed Overseer of the highway in the room of George Lewis and it is Ordered that with the Titheable persons that Usually worked on the s^d Road under the s^d Lewis he Clear and keep the Same in repair According to Law

17 June 1752 O. S., p. 260
Ordered that Adam Dickenson and Joseph Carpenter being first Sworn before a Justice of the Peace for this County to View away from Peter Wrights to the s^d Dickensons and that the s^d Dickenson & Carpenter be Overseers and with the Titheable Persons from Thomas Thompsons to Patrick Davises and the Convienent Titheables on Jacksons River they Clear and keep the Same in repair According to Law

17 June 1752 O. S., p. 264
Samuel Lockart is hereby Appointed Surveyor of the highway in the room of Patrick Frazier and it is Ordered that with the Titheable persons that worked on the s^d road under the s^d Frazier he Clear and keep the Same in repair According to Law

17 June 1752 O. S., p. 264
Isaac Taylor jun^r. is hereby Appointed Surveyor of the highway in the room of John Robinson and it is Ordered that with the Titheable Persons that Usually worked on the s^c Road under the s^d Robinson he clear & keep the Same in repair According to Law

18 June 1752 O. S., p. 265
Ordered that Peter Scholl Gent Appoint the Titheable Person to work on the Road whereof Zebulon Harrison is Overseer and is further Ordered that with the Same he Clear and keep the Said Road in Repair According to Law

19 June 1752 O. S., p. 279
John Robinson being Summoned to Answer the Presentment of the Grand Jury against him for not keeping the road whereof he is Overseer in repair According to Law Appeared & his Excuse being heard It is Ordered by the Court that the s^d. Presentment be dismised

20 August 1752 O. S., p. 315
Ordered that James Campbell and James Nealy and William Robinson divide and lay of the Precincts for the Several Overseers of the Road from Reed Creek to Warwick & that Wm Robinson be Surveyor of the upper part of the s^d. Road

20 August 1752 O. S., p. 316
Ordered that a Road be Cleared from Youngs Mill to Alexander Richeys Smiths Shop from thence to Buchanans Mill and that Patrick Martin and Alexander Richey be Overseers and with Adam Thompson George Ray Robert Young James Peary John Campbell, John Buchanan James Moody Andrew Cowan, James Callison, John Jameson, Walter Smiley James McCorkle Robert McCorkle Nathan Gilliland and William McNabb they Clear & keep the same in repair According to Law

20 August 1752 O. S., p. 317
Ordered that a Road be Cleared from Wm Clighorns by the Adjacent Titheables to the Waters of Purgatory

22 August 1752 O. S., p. 328
Ordered that a Road be Cleared from Edward Halls to William Longs Mill and that Thomas Stewart be Surveyor and with his Own Titheables, Isaac White, John McClure, Edward Hall James Patton, John Black James & Gabriel Alexander & James Bell he Clear & keep the same in repair According to Law

22 August 1752 O. S., p. 328
Ordered that a Road be Cleared from Wm Longs Mill to Charles Campbells & that the s^d Campbell with his own Tithables, William Long, Joseph Loves, John Wilsons, Wm Wrights Anthony Blacks James Robinsons and Patrick Cambells - Clear and keep the same in repair According to Law

22 August 1752 O. S., p. 328
Ordered that a Road be Cleared from Charles Campbells to the Cross Roads above James Fultons and the s^d Campbell & Fulton be Surveyors and with the titheable persons through which the s^d Road Shall Pass and within One Mile & a half thereof they Clear & keep the Same in repair According to Law.

24 August 1752 O. S., p. 339
On the Motion of Thomas Stewart It is Ordered that Robert Poage Alexander Wright, John Tate, Charles Campbell, William Henderson, John Trimble and William Anderson or any four of them View the Road Cleared by the s^d Stewart Over the blew Ridge on the first Friday in September next and report their proceedings to the next Court

15 November 1752 New Style, p. 361
On the Petition of Sundry the Inhabitants It is Ordered that Samuel Givens and Robt. Patrick being first sworn before a Justice of the Peace for this County View and mark the Most

Convenient way from James Givin's Mill to the Road that leads over Wood's new Gap at the foot of the Mountain and that Robert Patrick, William Hinds, John Homes, Joseph Bell, William Bell, Wm Finla, Arch^d. Stewart, Richard Pilson, Wm Johnston, Robert Wilson John Hind George Skilleron, Hugh Ross, And^r. Baskin, John Gwins, Samuel Henderson, John Ramsey, Alexander Henderson Samuel Henderson, Nathaniel Woodroof David Logan and George Duglass Clear and keep the Same in repair According to Law

15 November 1752 New Style, p. 361
On the Petition of Sundred the Inhabitants of the South branch for a Road from their Waggon Road up the South fork to Peter Reeds Mill It is Ordered that James Simpson & Michael Stump being first Sworn before a Justice of the Peace for this County do View and Mark the Same & that they be Surveyors and with Jeremiah Osborn, George Osburn, Manis Alkin H[illegible] Carlock John Westfall Jacob Westfall, Michael Stump Henry Harris Henry Shipler Philip Moore & Wm Westfall they Clear & keep the Same in repair According to Law

15 November 1752 New Style, p. 363
On the Petition of Rachel Vance Seting forth that by Order of this Court a road is marked thro' her Land Greatly to her Prejudice & Praying relief thereon It is Ordered that James Lockart Gent View & turn the s^d Road as he shall think proper

15 November 1752 New Style, p. 364
John Ward is hereby Appointed Surveyor of the highway in the room of Chas. Campbell and It is Ordered that with the titheable Persons that worked on the s^d Road Under the s^d Campbell he keep the Same in repair According to Law

16 November 1752 New Style, p. 369
[Grand Jury Presentments]

We present William Gerrall Overseer of the Road from the Lower ford of Catapo to Tobias Brights for not keeping the s^d Road in repair according to Law on the Information of James McAfee

***

We do present the Overseer of the Road from the North River to Naked Creek for not keeping the s^d Road in repair According to Law on the Information of Peter Scholl Gent & David Logan

***

We do present Robert Dunlop for Clousing up the highway & not finding Sufficient Ground to turn the Same on the Information of James Edmondson and Samuel Buchanan

We do present the Overseers of the Road from James Cowans to the Indian Road for not keeping the said Road in repair According to Law by two of our Number

21 November 1752 New Style, p. 410
On the Petition of Samuel Wallace Surveyor of the highway from the Top of the North mountain to the Court House It is Ordered that the following Persons be added to his Gang Viz^t. Maurice O'frield, Jno Trimble, William M^{c}feeters, Wm Martain, Jame Young, Jacob Lockart, James Vance, Patrick Martin, W^m McClintock Robert Young, Thomas Piery, John Campbell, James Peary, Robert Davis James Philips John Spear, John M^{c}murry, Alexander McMurry David Stuart, Hugh Young, John Jameson, Robert McClellon & John Brown

21 March 1753 New Style, p. 414
On the Petition of John Buchanan, James Clark, Jacob Lockart Thomas Kirkpatrick, John Berry, John Bartley, Wm Martin Josias Richards, William M^{c}feeters, John Jameson, James Young, Hugh Young, Robert Young, William McClintock, Wm Ledgerwood, John Trimble, Maurice O'frield Samuel Wallace, Robert Davis, Robt. McClenon, James Moody, James Philips, William Akry, Cornelius Donaho, George Peary, Adam Thompson, Thomas Peary John Campbell, James Peary, William McNab, Robert Scot Thomas Reid Abraham Me[_]sha[?], Francis Dunn, Major Scot John Bigham, John Black Samuel Downing, Alexander M^{c}feeters, Andrew Cowan, James McCorkle, John Vance Ja^s. Gilmore and Patrick Martin It is Ordered that Adam Thompson and Alexander Richey be Overseers of a Road layed of by former Order of this Court from James Youngs Mill to the s^d Buchanans Mill and that with the Petitioners and their Male Labouring Titheables they Clear and keep the Same in repair According to Law

21 March 1753 New Style, p. 414
On the Petition of James Gorrell[Gorrett?], Thomas Ingles, John Ingles, Wm Ingles Tobais Bright, George Pearis, William Pepper Adam Loony Elijah Isaac Erick Bright, Thos Hill, Benjamin Ogle, Jacob Brown & John Robinson It is Ordered that they be Exempted from Working on the Road that leads down Catapo Creek farther than from the dividing Waters of New River to the Dividing ridge of Catapo

21 March 1753 New Style, p. 415
On the Petition of Robert Dunlop the Complaint Exhibited against him by John Edmondson for turning the Highway is con^t. untill the next court

21 March 1753 New Style, p. 415
On the Petition of Robert Young and others for a Road from Joseph Longs Mill to James Youngs Mill thence to the Great Road on James Morrisons Plantation It is Ordered that the said Joseph Long and James Young be Overseers and with Robert Young, Joseph Long, Samuel Gibson, Soloman Whitley, John Collier, William Hall, Gilbert Crawford, George Gibson John Ruckman, Thomas Barton William Wadington William Brown, James Moore, John Hannah, James Huston, William Todd James Bats James Todd, James Young Patrick Young John Carr & James Campbell the Subscribers they clear and keep the same in repair According to Law

22 March 1753 New Style, p. 419
On the Petition of William Russell Gent It is Ordered that a Road be Cleared from the Road that leads from Chesters ford to Frederick County line to the Top of the blew ridge of Mountains to meet a Road Cleared by Order of Culpeper Court and that Henry Harden be Surveyor of the Same and with all the Male Labouring Titheables below Flint run on the East Side Shanando River and James McCoys on the West side of the s^d River together with the Titheables below the s^d McCoys to the line of Frederick he Clear and keep the Same in repair According to Law

22 March 1753 New Style, p. 419
Ordered that James Lockart, John Brown and John Trimble being first Sworn before a Justice of the Peace of this County do View and lay of a Road the nearest and best way from this Court House to Browns Meeting House and from thence to the Glebe and report their proceedings to the next Court

23 March 1753 New Style, p. 429
On the motion of George Wilson It is Ordered that he together with Mathew Harper, Loftus Pullen, and Hugh Hicklen or any three of them being first Sworn before a Justice of the Peace of this County View a road already marked from Wallace Estells to the Calf Pasture road as also the Ground thereabouts and see whether a more convenient place can be had and report their proceedings to the next Court

23 March 1753 New Style, p. 430
Ordered that Daniel Harrison Robert Fowler John McGill and David Nelson or any three of them being first sworn before a Justice of the peace of this County do View and Mark a way from the Calf Pasture to Swift run pass and report their proceedings to the next Court

23 March 1753 New Style, p. 430
Joseph Waite is hereby Appointed Surveyor of the highway in the room of James Berkley and It is Ordered that with the titheable persons that Usually work'd on th said road under the s^d. Berkley he Clear and keep the Same in repair According to Law

16 May 1753 N. S., p. 437
[Grand Jury Presentments]

...against the Surveyors of the highway from the Court House to James Moodys for not keeping the same in repair According to Law, Against the Surveyors of the highway from Samuel Brafords Meadow to the Indian Road for not keeping the same in repair According to Law, against the Surveyors of the highway from the Court House to Givins's Mill for not keeping the same in repair According to Law. against Surveyors of the highway from the Stone Meeting House to Robert Poages for not keeping the Same in repair According to Law, against the Surveyor of the highway from the Stone Meeting house to John Davis's Mill for not keeping the Same in repair According to Law...

16 May 1753 N. S., p. 440
Alexander McClure is hereby Appointed Surveyor of the highway from Bordens to the North Branch of James River and It is Ordered that with the titheables that Usually work'd on the s^d Road he Clear and keep the Same in repair According to Law

16 May 1753 N. S., p. 440
Ordered that John Henderson be Surveyor of the highway from John Campbells to the Court House and that with William Ledgerwood John Bigham, George Campbell, William McNabb, James Peary John Campbell, Thomas Peary, Robert Young & Sons John Black and Sons David Stewart Samuel Sprowl, James Miller, James Miller, Abraham Miller Alexander Wright & his Titheables James Brown Samuel Wilson and John Cuningham he Clear and keep the same in repair According to Law

16 May 1753 N. S., p. 440
James Philips is hereby Appointed Surveyor of the highway in the room of John Finla and It is Ordered that with the titheables that Usually work'd on the s^d Road under the s^d Finla he Clear and keep the same in repair According to Law

16 May 1753 N. S., p. 440
William Lockart and William Ledgerwood are hereby Appointed Surveyors of the highway in the room of James Lockart from the north Mountain Meeting House to John Campbells Field and it is Ordered that with the titheable persons that Usually work'd on the said Road under the s^d Lockart they Clear and keep the same in repair According to Law

16 May 1753 N. S., p. 440
Volentine Pence is hereby Appointed Surveyor of the highway from Robert Shanklands to Stoney Run in the Room of Jacob Nicholas and It is Ordered that with the titheables that Usually work'd on the said Road under the s^d Nicholas he Clear and keep the same in repair According to Law

16 May 1753 N. S., p. 440
Nicholas Null is hereby Appointed Surveyor of the highway from Stoney Run to Hance Magots in the room of Henry Seller and It is Ordered that with the titheables that Usually work'd on the said road under the s^d Seller he Clear and keep the Same in repair According to Law

16 May 1753 N. S., p. 440
Robert Huston is hereby Appointed Surveyor of the highway from Isaac Taylors to the Widow Bordens in the room of Daniel Lyle and It is Ordered that with the titheable persons that Worked on the said Road under the said Lyle he Clear and keep the same in repair According to Law

16 May 1753 N. S., p. 442
On the Petition of Peter Rufner It is Ordered that a Road be Cleared from William Bethells Road to the said Rufners Mill and from thence to Philips Lungs Road and that John Davis and Nicholas

Lung be Overseers and with the titheable persons within three Miles on Each Side the Said Road they Clear and keep the Same in repair According to Law

16 May 1753 N. S., p. 442
John Walker is hereby Appointed Surveyor of the highway from Hay's Mill to Providence Meeting House in the room of Andrew Hays and it is Ordered that with the titheables that usually work'd on the said Road under the s^d Hays he Clear and keep the Same in repair According to Law

16 May 1753 N. S., p. 442
Patrick Hays and John Huston are hereby Appointed Surveyors of the road that goes by Kenadays to Patrick Hay's and it is Ordered that with the titheable persons that Usually work'd on the s^d Road they Clear and keep the same in repair According to Law

16 May 1753 N. S., p. 442
John McCutcheon is hereby Appointed Surveyor of the highway from Kenadays Mill to the Court House and it is Ordered that with the titheable persons that usually work'd on the said road under W^m McCutcheon the late Overseer he Clear and keep the Same in repair According to Law

17 May 1753 N. S., p. 444
William Draper is hereby Appointed Surveyor of the Masanuting Road in the room of William White and it is Ordered that with the titheable persons that usually worked on the said Road under the said White he Clear and keep the same in repair According to Law

17 May 1753 N. S., p. 445
James Reaburn is hereby Appointed Overseer of the Road from Jenning's gap to the long Glade in the room of William Hogshead and it is Ordered that with the titheable persons that usually work'd on the s^d Road under the said Hogshead he Clear and keep the Same in repair According to Law

17 May 1753 N. S., p. 446
John McCown is hereby app^d Overseer of the Road in the room of James Davis and It is Ordered that with the titheable persons that usually work'd on the said Road under the s^d Davis he Clear and keep the same in repair According to Law

17 May 1753 N. S., p. 448
Upon the Complaint of Lofty Pullen upon Oath that George Wilson refused to Obey the Order of this Court for Viewing a Road It is Ordered that he be Summoned to appear at the next Court to Shew Cause for the s^d Contempt

17 May 1753 N. S., p. 449
Ludwic Francisco is hereby Appointed Overseer of a road from Robert Cravens's to the Mark'd road that Leads to Swift run Pass and it is Ordered that with the adjacent titheables he Clear and keep the same in repair According to Law

17 May 1753 N. S., p. 449
Daniel Love is hereby Appointed Overseer of the Road from the North River to Robert Craven's from thence by Volentine Seviers and it is Ordered that with the Adjacent titheables he Clear and keep the Same in repair According to Law

17 May 1753 N. S., p. 451
On the Petition of John Risk and Thomas Teat It is Ordered that a road be Cleared from the said Risks Mill to the s^d Teats Shop and that the said John Risk & Samuel McCutcheon with the Adjacent titheables Clear and keep the Same in repair According to Law

18 May 1753 N. S., p. 453
On the Petition of Sundry the Inhabitants for a Road from William Wilsons Mill to Wallace Estells Mill It is Ordered that Stephen Wilson and Hugh Hicklen be Overseers and with John Miller, William Wilson John Wilson, Samuel Gay, Robert Gay Robert Carlile, John Carlile John Hicklen Loftus Pullen and Thomas Hicklen they Clear and keep the Same in repair According to Law

19 May 1753 N. S., p. 457
Israel Christian is hereby Appointed Surveyor of the highway in the room of Joseph McClelhill from the Court House to Christians Creek and it's Ordered that with the Titheable persons that Worked on the s^d Road Under the s^d McClelhill he Clear and keep the Same in repair According to Law

19 May 1753 N. S., p. 457
On the Petition of Sundry the Inhabitants It is Ordered that a Road be Cleared from Browns Bridge to the Glebe Land and that Robert Campbell and John Trimble be Surveyors and with James Lusk Robert Robeson, Samuel McCutcheon William Hunter, James Hunter, Robert Campbells Man, Mathew Wilson William Wilson, John Wilson ju^r. John McCreary, James McCreary, Thos Kilpatrick & Son, James Peiry James Clark, John Clark, James Clark j^r Jacob Lockart, James Lockart, John Bartley Josias Richards, Wm Martin, George Berry, William M^{c}feeters, John M^{c}feeters W^m M^{c}feeters j^r. John Jameson Patrick Martin Joseph Martin William Ward, Maurice Offriel, Robert Philips Robert Davis Thomas Reed, Robert Scot John Vance William Akry, Andrew Foster, James Bell, Wm Bell, Andrew Steel & his Man, Alexander McKenny John McKenny, John Spear, Patrick McCroskey Abraham Shaw, John McClenhan, Robert McClenhan, Robert Young John McCutcheon John Young, Samuel McCutcheon Samuel Young Hugh Young, & his Man, William McClintock, Thomas Peiry John Campbell James McCutcheon George Peiry and Duncan McFarland they Clear and keep the Same in repair According to Law

19 May 1753 N. S., p. 458
Thomas Beard is hereby Appointed Surveyor of the highway in the room of David Carr and it is Ordered that with the Titheables that Work'd on the s^d Road Under the said Carr he Clear and keep the Same in repair According to Law.

21 May 1753 N. S., p. 480
Israel Christian is hereby Appointed Surveyor of the highway from the Court House to Christians Creek and it is Ordered that with the adjacent Titheables he turn the s^d road & make Such Alterations as he shall think proper

21 May 1753 N. S., p. 480
John Cuningham is hereby Appointed Surveyor of the highway in the room of James Brown & It is Ordered that with the titheable persons that work'd on the s^d road under the s^d Brown he Clear and keep the same in repair According to Law

21 May 1753 N. S., p. 480
Ordered that William Preston and John Trimble being first Sworn before a Justice of this County do View and lay of the Most Convenient way from this Court House to William Andersons & that the Surveyor thereof Samuel Wilson Clear the same according to their direction

22 May 1753 N. S., p. 497
The King v Wm Gorrett
On Pres^t of the Grand jury for not keeping the road whereof his Overseer in repair
Alias Summons

22 May 1753 N. S., p. 497
The King v. John Hare
On the Pres^t of the Grand jury agst for not keeping the road whereof he is Overseer in repair
Alias Summons

22 May 1753 N. S., p. 497
The King v. Robert Dunlop
On a Present. of the G^d. Jury for stoping the highway
Alias Summons

22 May 1753 N. S., p. 497
The King v. Chas Campbell & Ja^s Fulton
On Pre^s. Grand Jury for not keep the road Whereof they are Overseers in repair
Alias Summons

22 May 1753 N. S., p. 499
On the Motion of James Patton Gent It is Ordered that the old Road turn'd by John Paxton to his House be by him Opened and that the Same be kept in repair According to Law by the Overseers,

and that no person be Oblidged to work on that part of the Road that leads by the s^d Paxtons House

22 May 1753 N. S., p. 499
Ordered that John Lewis Robert McClenachan & Saml Wilson or any two being first Sworn before a Justice of this County do View & lay of the Most Convenient way from this Court House to Christys Creek & that Israel Christian be Surveyor & with the Adjacent Titheables Clear the same According to their direction

Book IV, 1753-1755

15 August 1753 N. S., p. 4
On the Petition of Ephraim Love and Others It is Ordered that the s^d Love and Jeremiah Harrison being first Sworn before a Justice of the Peace for this County View and Mark the Most Convenient Way from the s^d Ephraim Loves to the Main Road that leads from the South Branch Over Swift run pass and report their proceedings to the next Court

15 August 1753 N. S., p. 6
Mathew Harper and Loftus Pullen being appointed to View a Way Mark'd from Wallace Estills to the Calf Pasture Road as also the Ground thereabouts to See whether a more Convenient way can be had, reported to the Court that the way already laid of is the Most Convenient It is therefore Ordered that the said Road as laid of be Continued

15 August 1753 N. S., p. 7
On the Petition of William Smith and others Seting forth that they are Oblidged to keep in repair three Roads that are not above half a mile Distant & praying the s^d Roads be reduced into One It is therefore Ordered that William Christian, John Mitchell, John Buchanan and Joseph Kenaday or any two of them being first sworn before a Justice of this County View the s^d Roads & report their proceedings thereon to the next Court

15 August 1753 N. S., p. 7
Ordered that the following persons with their Titheables Viz^t. Robert Young, Thomas King John Campbell, James Peiry, John Bigham, William Ledgerwood Samuel McCorkle James Caldwell, Andrew & Thomas Scot, Alexander Wright James Miller David Stewart John Black Nathan Gilliland, John Henderson, Robert McClenahan Robert Breckenridge John Cuningham and Major Scot work on the road whereof John Henderson is Overseer

16 August 1753 N. S., p. 9
Ordered that William Leeper be Surveyor of the highway on New River in the room of Adam Harmon and that with the titheable persons that work'd on the s^d Road under the s^d Harman he Clear & keep the same in repair according to Law

16 August 1753 N. S., p. 9
Ordered that John Stales and Alexander Painter be Overseers and with the Adjacent Titheables Clear and keep in repair a Road from the North Mountain Gap called Brocks Gap near Thomas Neist to the mouth of the Lost River leading to North Shenandore

16 August 1753 N. S., p. 10
Ordered that Patrick Hays and John Huston be surveyors and Clear with the Adjacent Titheables the Road from the forks at the Widow Fultons to Joseph Kenadays Mill

16 August 1753 N. S., p. 11
James Carlile is hereby appointed Surveyor of the highway in the room of Wallace Estell and It is Ordered that with the titheables that usually work'd on the s^d Road under the s^d Estill he Clear & keep the same in repair According to Law

16 August 1753 N. S., p. 11
Ordered that John Crouch and John Cuningham be Surveyors of the highway in the room of Peter Thorn & Lambert Pooper and that with the Titheables that usually work'd under the s^d Thorn & Pooper the Clear and keep the same in repair According to Law

17 August 1753 N. S., p. 15
James Urrey is hereby Appointed Surveyor of the highway in the Room of Hance Magot & It is Ordered that with the titheable persons that work'd on the s^d Road under the said Magot he Clear & keep the same in repair According to Law.

17 August 1753 N. S., p. 16
William McCurry is hereby Appointed Surveyor of the highway in the room of William Robinson from a ford near Esther Robinsons to a mark'd tree near hands Meadow and It is Ordered that with the titheable persons that work'd on the said Road under the s^d Robinson he Clear and keep the same in repair according to Law

17 August 1753 N. S., p. 16
John Stevenson is hereby Appointed Surveyor of the highway from John Wilson by Dooleys, Barnet Manns, John Loves & from thence to James Waits and It is Ordered that with the Convenient titheables he Clear & keep the Same in repair According to Law

17 August 1753 N. S., p. 17
It is Ordered that Jeremiah Early Hance Magot and Francis Kirkley or any two of them being first sworn before a Justice of the Peace for this County View and Mark the Most Convenient Way over the Mountain at Swift run pass and report their proceedings to next Court

17 August 1753 N. S., p. 17
It is Ordered that Robert McClenachan, Alexander Wright, John Hunter, Thomas Stewart, Samuel Steel and Isaac White or any three of them being first sworn before a Justice of this County View Armers and Rock-fish gaps and mark the Most Convenient Way and report their proceedings to the next Court

17 August 1753 N. S., p. 19

John Hare being summoned upon a Presentment of the Grand jury against him for not keeping the road whereof he is Overseer in repair According to Law appeared and his Excuse being heard It is Ordered this presentment agst him be dismis'd.

17 August 1753 N. S., p. 19
Charles Campbell and James Fulton being Summoned upon a Presentment of the Grand Jury against them for not keeping the road whereof they were Overseers in repair According to Law, the said Campbell appeared and his Excuse being heard It is Ordered that this presentment agst him be dismis'd, and this presentment agst. the s^d Fulton is abated by his Death.

17 August 1753 N. S., p. 19
Robert Dalton being summoned upon a presentment of the Grand jury against him for Stoping the highway Appeared and his Excuse being heard It is Ordered that this presentment against him be dismised

17 August 1753 N. S., p. 20
Elijah McClenachan and James Cowan being summoned upon a Presentment of the Grand jury against them for not keeping the road whereof they are Overseers in repair According to Law [blank in book]

17 August 1753 N. S., p. 20
The Sherif having returned upon the Summons for Summoning Samuel Givens for not keeping the Road whereof he is Overseer in repair According to Law that he was not found within his Bailiwic on the Motion of his Matys Attorney an Alias Summons is awarded against him returnable here the next Court

17 August 1753 N. S., p. 20
John Anderson being summoned upon a presentment of the Grand jury against him for not keeping the road whereof he is Overseer in repair According to Law Appeared and his Excuse being heard It is Ordered that this presentment against him be dismised

17 August 1753 N. S., p. 20
The Sherif having returned upon the summons for summoning John King, Andrew Erwin and Michael Dickey for not keeping the road whereof they are Overseers in repair According to Law, not found on the motion of his Matys Attorney an Alias Summons is Awarded against them returnable here the next Court

18 August 1753 N. S., p. 63
Ordered that James Campbell William Carvin, William Byran and Wm Graham or any three of them being first sworn before a Justice of this County mark the Most Convenient Way for a road from Charles Millicans to William Bryans and report their proceedings to the next Court

21 November 1753 N. S., p. 65
[Grand Jury Presentments]

We present the Overseers of the Road from James Roseboroughs to Josephs Kenadays for not Clearing the s^d Road According to Law on the Information of James Lockart
We present the Overseers of the Road from the Court House to Robert Poages for not Clearing the s^d Road According to Law of our own knowledge
We present the Overseers of the Road from James Cowans to where it comes into the Indian Road of our own knowledge

21 November 1753 N. S., p. 65
William Harrald is hereby Appointed Overseer of the Highway in the Room of Henry Harden and It is Ordered that with the Gang that Usually work'd on the said Road under the s^d Harden he Clear & keep the same in repair According to Law

21 November 1753 N. S., p. 65
Ordered that James Timble and John Paxton being first Sworn before a Justice of this County View two Roads that lead through the Land of Joseph Walker and report to the next Court the most Convenient

21 November 1753 N. S., p. 66
Alexander Brownlee is hereby Appointed Surveyor of the highway in the room of John Ward & It is Ordered that with the Gang that Usually work'd on the said Road under the s^d Ward he Clear and keep the Same in repair According to Law

21 November 1753 N. S., p. 66
Edward Shankland and Robert Hooks are hereby Appointed Overseers of the highway in the room of Patrick Frazier and It is Ordered that with the Gang that usually work'd under the s^d Frazier they Clear and keep the said Road in Repair according to Law

21 November 1753 N. S., p. 67
James Robinson is hereby appointed Overseer of the highway in the room of John Bean and It is Ordered that with the titheables that Usually work'd on the s^d Road under the s^d Bean he Clear and keep the Same in repair According to Law

22 November 1753 N. S., p. 70
Ordered that John Stevenson on his Petition have leave to Cut a Road from the Bent of Buffeloe to Michael Dougherty at his own Expence

22 November 1753 N. S., p. 70
On the Motion of Elijah [torn: McC?]lenachan who was presented and find for not keeping a Road whereof [torn] was Overseer in repair According to Law It appearing to the Court the [torn: sa?]me was done by mistake It is Ordered that the s^d fine be remitted

22 November 1753 N. S., p. 71
James Neilly and Henry Brown are hereby Appointed Overseers of the highway in the room of Isaac Taylor and It is ordered that with the Titheable persons that Usually work'd on the Road under the s^d. Taylor the Clear and keep the Same in repair According to Law

23 November 1753 N. S., p. 73
On the Petition of James Trimble It is Ordered that John Paxton be Overseer of a Road from James Edmondsons Mill to the fork Meeting House and that with James Trimble Michael Finney John Berriford William Holdman John Hardin Hugh Means Joseph Lapsley Peter Wallace Samuel McClure Abram Brown John Moore Robert Moore Stephen Arnold Samuel Paxton and James Edmondson he Clear and keep the Same in repair According to Law

23 November 1753 N. S., p. 74
Ordered that George Breckenridge be Overseer of a Road Mark'd by Charles Campbell from his House to Alexander Brownlees and from thence to the Lower End of James Fultons Meadow leaving the s^d Meadow on the Right hand and so on to the forks of the Road above the s^d Fultons House & that with the titheable persons within four Miles on Each Side of the s^d Road he Clear and keep the Same in repair According to Law

23 November 1753 N. S., p. 74
Robert McClanahan is hereby Appointed Overseer of the highway in the room of James Caldwell and It is Ordered that with the titheable persons that work'd on the s^d Road under the s^d Caldwell he Clear & keep the same in repair According to Law

23 November 1753 N. S., p. 74
Ordered that John Carlile be Surveyor of the highway in the room of Wallace Estell and that with the titheable persons that work'd on the s^d Road under the s^d Estell he Clear and keep the same in repair According to Law

23 November 1753 N. S., p. 75
Ordered that a Road be Cleared from the North fork of James River near John Mathews to Renix's Road and that the s^d Mathews be Overseer and with Henry Brown, John Smiley, James Trimble, John Berriford, James Edmondson William Edmondson Michael Finney, William Holdman, Steven Arnold Hugh Means John Hargus, William Scot, Edward Bishop, Alexander McCorkall, Patrick McCorkall, Henry Fuller, Joseph Poin[?], Edward Belay James Baley John Peter Salling James Simpson James Wolson Alexander Beggs John Mathews Joshua Mathews John Maxwell, James Frazier, John Hutcheson Senr John Hutchison j^r. George Salling Richard Belon, William Boil John Sproul John Smith, Samuel McClure John Smiley, John McCuley,

Richard Mathews Sampson Mathews Daniel Sancion Samuel Paxton, William Paxton John Oleston Samuel Oleston & Samuel Walker & their respective Male Labouring titheables he Clear & keep the same in repair according to Law

24 November 1753 N. S., p. 76
It is Ordered that a Road be Cleared the nearest and best way from Samuel Stalnakers on Holdstons River to James Davis's and that the s^d Samuel Stalnaker be Overseer of the Same and with James Davis, and his Sons, Frederick Carlock, David Carlock, George Carlock Conrod Carlock Frederick Stern, Jacob Stalnaker Adam Stalnaker Jacob & Henry Goldman Isaiah Hamilton, Hamilton Shoemaker Timothy Coe, Humphrey Baker, and Son, George Stalnaker Adam Andrews Mathias Sareh, Michael Hook Martin Counce, and Jacob Mires he Clear & keep the Same in repair According to Law

24 November 1753 N. S., p. 76
It is Ordered that a Road be Cleared the nearest and best way from the End of William Carravans Road on his Plantation to William Bryans on Roan Oak and that the said Bryan be Overseer of the same and with James Campbell Joseph Love William Bryan j^r. John Bryan James Bane, Henry Brown j^r James Neilly, Henry Brown Senior, Alexander Ingram, Edward Patterson, Jacob Patton John Wood Erwin Patterson Andrew Cox, Jesper Terry, William Terry, John Woods, Edward Moon Peter Craven, Aron Hart, Miles Hart, Wm Graham Neal McNeal Malcome Campbell Wm Armstrong Tasker Tosh Thomas Tosh Daniel Evans, Uriah Acres, Thomas Acres, John McAdoe, William Akers & the Titheables with them bounds he Clear and keep the s^d Road in repair According to Law.

24 November 1753 N. S., p. 76
It is Ordered that a Road be Cleared the nearest and best way from Charles Millicans to William Carravans & Over a Run near his House and that the s^d Caravin be Overseer and with William Ralston & his Sons Charles Millican James McDonald, Joseph McDonald Edward McDonald Joseph Robinson, David Robinson, James Galliad Arch^d. Graham David Miller Hugh Mills, Richard Kerr, William Miller William Graham, David McCormick, Joshua McCormick Tobias Smith, Steven Rentfro, and all the Titheables with the s^d Bounds he Clear and keep the same in repair According to Law

26 November 1753 N. S., p. 78
Ordered that John Poage Samuel McClure and Robert Renix be Surveyors of the Indian Road from the North fork to the Main Branch of James River and that James Patton and John Mathews Gent lay of their respective Gangs and precincts

27 November 1753 N. S., p. 106
Israel Christian is hereby appointed surveyor of the highway from the Court House to Christians Creek and It is Ordered that with the Titheable persons mentioned a list by him produc'd he Clear & keep the same in repair according to Law

20 March 1754 N. S., p. 108

On the Petition of Sundry the Inhabitants It is Ordered that Jam^s. Patton David Stewart and Robert McClenachan Gent or any two of them agree with workmen to Erect a bridge at the Place commonly called & known by the name of Browns Bridge and that the workmen Undertaking the Same bring in their Charge at Laying the next County Levy

21 March 1754 N. S., p. 114
John Paxton and James Trimble who were appointed to View a way Tho' Joseph Walkers Plantation (on his Petition) return that the way the Road now goes the Most Convenient It is Therefore Ordered that the s^d Pet^n. be rejected

21 March 1754 N. S., p. 116
Ordered that James Patton Robert McClenachan and David Stewart Gent or any two of them agree with workmen to make a causeway over the marsh between this Court House and the tinkling Spring and that the Workmen bring in their Charge at laying the County Levy

22 March 1754 N. S., p. 121
On the Petition of Sundry the Inhabitants It is Ordered that a Road be Cleared from the Glebe of this Parish to John Risks Mill and that John McCleary be Surveyor and with William M^{c}feeters, John M^{c}feeters, William Martin, Alexander Crawford, John Perry John Kirkpatrick, John Timble John Jones Samuel Wallace, James Clark John Wilson William Wilson Thomas Kirkpatrick and John Risk he Clear & keep the same in repair According to Law

23 March 1754 N. S., p. 126
It is Ordered that a Road be Cleared from Campbells School House to Renix's Road and that Samuel Walker be Overseer and with William Bradshaw, John Maxwell, James Frazier John McColley John Peter Salley George Salley Henry Fuller, Joseph Ryon John Hutchings John Hutchings j^r. John Sproul, Mathew Vance Richard Burton William Burt John Smith Joseph Smith John Allison William Byers Richard Mathews Sampson Mathews Samuel Walker Thomas Shaw Stephen Arnold Jonathan John Peteet William Noble and Samuel Allison he Clear and keep the Same in repair According to Law

23 March 1754 N. S., p. 126
It is Ordered that a Road be Cleared from the North river to Campbells School House and that John Mathews j^r. be Overseer and with Alexander McCorkle, John Smiley James Bealey Samuel Paxton James Trimble, James Edmondson John Berriford Edmond Crump William Holdman John Harges William Scot Edward Bishop Michael Finney Hugh Manes Patrick McCorkle Alexander Smiley, Michael Johnston, John Noble, John Stevenson, William Paxton, Alexander Baggs Joshua Mathews James Simpson and James Wilson[?] he Clear and keep the Same in repair According to Law

23 March 1754 N. S., p. 127
Ordered that a Road be Cleared from Charles Millicans to the End of Carwins Road and from thence to the Widow Sloans and that John McGown and Hugh Caruthers with the gangs already appointed them Clear and keep the same in repair According to Law

23 March 1754 N. S., p. 128
Ordered that Mathew Patton and Henry Holdston lay of a Road from the mouth of John Creek thro the Mountains to the Waggon Road by James McAfees And that Jacob Patton and Henry Holdston by Surveyors thereof and with the titheable persons on the said Creek and the Waters thereof they Clear and keep the Same in repair According to Law

23 March 1754 N. S., p. 128
Ordered that Henry Holdston Senior and Plunkard Seilar mark a way from the mouth of Johns Creek to John M^{c}farrons the nearest and best way over the Mountains and that John Lowry and Henry Holdston be Surveyors and with the Titheable persons on Craigs Creek and the Waters thereof they Clear and keep the Same in repair According to Law

23 March 1754 N. S., p. 128
Richard Hull is appointed Overseer of the highway from the New river near Garret Zinns to the Waters of Roan Oak in the room of William Pellam and that with the titheables that usually work'd on the said Road under the s^d Pellam he Clear & keep the Same in repair According to Law

25 March 1754 N. S., p. 142
Ordered that a Road be Cleared from Bingamans Ferry to the Waters of Roan Oak near Tobias Brights as also from the Widow Drapers to Jacob Browns and that William Leopard be Overseer and James Patton Gent appoint the Titheables to work thereon

25 March 1754 N. S., p. 142
Ordered that a Road be Cleared from Bingamans Ferry to Robinsons Land above John Bingamans j^r. and that John Bingaman Senior & Henry Cook be Surveyors and that James Patton Gent appoint the Titheables to work thereon

25 March 1754 N. S., p. 142
Ordered that a Road be Cleared from the End of Bingamans Road on Robinsons Land to James Millers on Reed Creek and that James Miller be Surveyor and that John Buchanan Gent Appoint the titheables to Work thereon

25 March 1754 N. S., p. 142
Ordered that a Road be Cleared from Alexander Sayers Mill to James Davisons on Holdstons river and that James Davis and James McCall be Overseers and that John Buchanan Gent appoint the Titheables to work thereon

25 March 1754 N. S., p. 142

Ordered that a Road be Cleared from Jacob Browns on Roan Oak to Isaac Taylors and John Robinson Senior and Jacob Brown be overseers and with the titheable persons on Roan Oak between the s^d Robinsons and Browns they Clear and keep the Same in repair According to Law

25 March 1754 N. S., p. 147
Ordered that a Road be Cleared from Frederick Hartsaws Mill On Craigs Creek up the said Creek and a Cross a mountain to James M^{c}afees and that Henry Holdston junior be Surveyor and with the Titheables on Craigs Creek he Clear and keep the Same in repair According to Law

25 March 1754 N. S., p. 147
Ordered that a Road be Cleared from Frederick Hartsaws Mill on Craigs Creek to the Catapo and that Jo^n. Lowry be Surveyor of the Same and with the Titheables on the s^d Creek he Clear and keep the Same in repair According to Law

25 March 1754 N. S., p. 147
On the Motion of Israel Christian It is Ordered that the Main Road be turnd that leads through his Lott Number six in the Town of Staunton

27 March 1754 N. S., p. 184
Upon the presentment of the Grand jury agst John Cuningham for not keeping the Road whereof he was Overseer in repair According to Law The s^d Cuningham Appeared and his Excuse being heard It is Ordered that this presentment against him be dismis'd

27 March 1754 N. S., p. 184
Upon the presentment of the Grand jury agst. Elijah McClenachan and James Cowan for not keeping the Road whereof they were Overseers in repair According to Law The s^d McClenachan appeared & his Excuse being heard It is Ordered that this presentment agst him be dis^d. & that an alias Summons Issue agst the s^d Cowan returnable here the next Court

27 March 1754 N. S., p. 185
The order for summoning George Wilson on the Complaint of Loftus Pullin for refusing to obey an order of this Court in Viewing and laying off a Road is dis'^{d} neither party appearing

27 March 1754 N. S., p. 185
John Madison having Inform'd the Court that the Road that Leads from Henry Down's through this Plantation formerly Wm Thompsons to the Stone Meeting House is of little Use and that the Same is prejudicial to him It is Therefore Ordered that the s^d Road be discontinued

15 May 1754 N. S., p. 189-90
[Grand Jury Presentments]

We present the overseers of the Road from the South River at Ramseys Over the Mountain for not keeping the Same in repair According to Law,

* * *

We present the Over seers of the road from James Cowans Meadow to Patrick Campbells run by Information of Jacob Gray and Richard Woods

15 May 1754 N. S., p. 191
James Greenlee is hereby Appointed Surveyor of the highway in the room of Mathew Lyle and It is Ordered that with the titheable persons that work'd on the said Road under the s^d Lyle he Clear and keep the Same in repair According to Law.

15 May 1754 N. S., p. 191
John Thompson is hereby appointed overseer of the highway in the room of George Caldwell and It is Ordered that with the titheable persons that work'd on the s^d road under the s^d Caldwell he Clear & keep the Same in repair According to Law

15 May 1754 N. S., p. 191
John Ramsey is hereby appointed overseer of the highway from the South River to the foot of the Old Gap in the room of James Galespy and It is Ordered that with the titheable persons that work'd on the s^d Road under the s^d Galespy he keep the same in repair according to Law

15 May 1754 N. S., p. 192
Baptist McNab is hereby Appointed Surveyor of the highway in the room of Alexander McClure and It is Ordered that with the titheables that usually work'd on the s^d road under the s^d. McClure he Clear and keep the Same in repair According to Law

15 May 1754 N. S., p. 192
William Mathews is hereby Appointed Overseer of the highway in the room of James Reaburn and It is Ordered that with the Titheable persons that work'd on the s^d Road under the s^d Reaburn he Clear & keep the Same in Repair According to Law

15 May 1754 N. S., p. 192
William Finla is hereby appointed Overseer of the highway in the room of Archibald Stewart and It is Ordered that with the titheable persons that Work'd on the s^d Road under the s^d Stewart he keep the same in repair According to Law

15 May 1754 N. S., p. 193
Robert Poage is hereby appointed overseer of the highway in the room of John Cuningham and It is Ordered that with the Titheable persons that Usually work'd on the said Road under the s^d Cuninigham he keep the Same in repair According to Law

15 May 1754 N. S., p. 193
Robert Breckenridge is hereby Appointed Overseer of the highway in the room of Elijah McClenachan and It is Ordered that with the Titheable persons that usually work'd on the s^d road under the s^d McClenachan he keep the Same in repair According to Law

15 May 1754 N. S., p. 193

John Underwood is hereby appointed overseer of the highway in the room of John Paul and It is Ordered that with the Titheable persons that usually worked on the said Road under the s^d Paul he Clear & keep the same in repair Acc^d to Law

15 May 1754 N. S., p. 193
Robert Gibson is hereby Appointed overseer of the highway in the room of James Patton Gent and It is Ordered that with the titheable persons that worked on the s^d Road under the s^d Patton he keep the same in repair Acc^d to Law

15 May 1754 N. S., p. 194
Robert Patterson is hereby Appointed Overseer of the highway from Picken's Grist Mill to the Stone Meeting House and It is Ordered that with the Titheables that usually work'd on the said Road under John Pickens the former Overseer he keep the Same in repair According to Law

15 May 1754 N. S., p. 194
Ordered that a Road be Cleared from the Widow Sloans Plantation to the End of Caravans New Road and that John McGown be Surveyor & with the titheable persons as Shall be Appointed him by James Patton Gent he Clear & keep the Same in repair According to Law

16 May 1754 N. S., p. 194
Robert Armstrong is hereby appointed Surveyor of the highway in the room of John Poage and It is Ordered that with the titheable persons that Work'd on the s^d Road under the s^d Poage he Clear & keep the Same in repair According to Law

16 May 1754 N. S., p. 195
James Campbell and Robert Bratton are hereby appointed Overseers of the highway from Samuel Jackson[?] to the Second ford on Jenings's Branch and It is ordered that with the Adjacent Titheables they Clear and keep the same in repair According to Law

16 May 1754 N. S., p. 195
Nicholas Cuin is hereby Appointed Surveyor of the highway in the room of John Slater and It is Ordered that with the titheable persons that work'd on the s^d Road Under the said Slater he Clear & keep the same in repair According to Law

16 May 1754 N. S., p. 196
James Baggs is hereby Appointed Surveyor of the highway in the room of Alexander Pointer and It is Ordered that with the titheable persons that work'd on the said Road Under the said Pointer he keep the Same in repair According to Law

16 May 1754 N. S., p. 196
Joseph Kenaday is hereby appointed overseer in the room of Patrick Hays of the highway and It is Ordered that with the Such Titheable persons as Shall be appointed him by the s^d Hays he keep the same in repair According to Law

16 May 1754 N. S., p. 198
Ordered that John Anderson j^r. and John Francis being first Sworn before a Justice of the Peace of this County do View & mark the Nearest and best Way from Silas Harts to the Court House of this County & make report thereof to the next Court

16 May 1754 N. S., p. 198
Charles Campbell is hereby Appointed Surveyor of the highway from Longs Glade to the North River in the room of John Francis and It is Ordered that with the Titheable persons that work't on the s^d Road under the s^d Francis he Clear & keep the Same in repair According to Law

16 May 1754 N. S., p. 200
Ordered that Edward McDonald be Surveyor of the highway in the room of Stephen Rentfro and It is Ordered that with the Titheable persons that work'd on the said Road under the said Rentfro he keep the Same in repair according to Law.

18 May 1754 N. S., p. 244
Ralph Laverty is hereby Appointed Surveyor of the highway in the room of John Dickenson and It is Ordered that with the titheable persons that work'd on the s^d Road under the s^d Dickenson he keep the Same in repair According to Law

20 May 1754 N. S., p. 252
On the Petition of James Cowan Seting forth that he as Surveyor of the highway was presented by the Grand jury and find notwithstanding the s^d Road was in good repair and the Same Appearing by Witness It is Ordered that he be of the Said fine Acquitted

21 May 1754 N. S., p. 252
Alexander Wright is hereby appointed Surveyor of the highway in the room of Israel Christian and It is Ordered that with the titheable persons that work'd on the s^d Road under the s^d Christian he Clear & keep the Same in repair According to Law

21 August 1754 N. S., p. 255
Henry Gay is hereby appointed Surveyor of the highway in the room of James Knox and It is Ordered that with the titheable persons that Usually work on the s^d Road under the s^d Knox he Clear & keep the Same in repair According to Law.

21 August 1754 N. S., p. 255
On the Petition of Sundry the Inhabitants of the Cow and Calf Pastures for a Road from Andrew Hamiltons to the turn of the Waters by Charles Walkers It is Ordered that William Wilson John

McCleary and Robert Bratton or any two of them being first Sworn before a Justice of this County do View the Road Petitioned for and report their proceedings to the next Court--

21 August 1754 N. S., p. 256
Jacob Anderson is hereby appointed Surveyor of the highway in the room of John Hays dec^d and It is Ordered that with the titheables that usually work'd on the s^d Road under the s^d Hays he Clear and keep the Same in repair According to Law.

21 August 1754 N. S., p. 257
Ordered that a Road be Cleared from Jeremiah Earleys to the Top of the Ridge at Swift Run and that Gabriel Jones Thomas Lewis and John Madison appoint the Gangs and Overseers provided they be Such as Occupy the s^d Road

21 August 1754 N. S., p. 257
Ordered that Gabriel Jones Thomas Lewis Francis Tyler and John Madison or any one of them apply to the Court of Orange County and desire they will Order a Road to be Cleared to meet a Road Clear'd by the Inhabitants of this County to the Top of the Mountain at Swift Run Pass.

21 August 1754 N. S., p. 257
Ordered that Robert McClenachan, Alexander Wright, Thomas Stewart and Samuel Steel or any three of them being first Sworn before a Justice of the Peace for this County do View the Mountains from Wood's Gap to the head of Rockfish and report the Most Convenient way over the s^d Mountains to the next Court--

21 August 1754 N. S., p. 259
Ordered that William Hines be Surveyor of the highway in the Room of Samuel Givens and It is Ordered that with the titheable persons that work't under the s^d Givens he Clear the s^d Road as laid of by the s^d Givens According to Law

21 August 1754 N. S., p. 259
Samuel Givens who was presented by the Grand jury for not keeping the Road whereof he is Overseer in repair according to Law being Summoned and failing to appear It is Ordered that for the s^d Offence he make his fine with our Lord the King by the paiment of fifteen Shillings & Cost & may be taken &^c

23 August 1754 N. S., p. 271
James Robinson is hereby Appointed Surveyor of the highway in the room of William Bell and It is Ordered that with the titheables persons that work't on the s^d road under the s^d Bell he Clear and keep the same in repair According to Law

24 August 1754 N. S., p. 290
Ordered that Thomas Tosh John Mason Jacob Harmon j^r. William Hall j^r. & John Buchanan or any three of them View and lay of a Road from Ephraim Voss to the New River and report their proceedings to the next Court

27 August 1754 N. S., p. 316
The Summons against John King on a Presentment of the Grand jury for not keeping the Road whereof he is Overseer in repair According to Law not being Ex^d. It is Ordered that an alias Summons Issue against him returnable here the next Court

27 August 1754 N. S., p. 316
The Sherif having returned on the Summons against David Carr on the Presentment of the Grand jury against him for not keeping the Road whereof he was Overseer in repair According to Law Not Ex^d. It is Ordered that the s^d Presentment be dis^d.

27 August 1754 N. S., p. 316
The Summons against Robert Patrick and William Finla on the Presentm^t. of the Grand jury against them for not keeping the road whereof they were Overseers in repair According to Law not being Executed It is Ordered that an alias Sum^s Issue against them returnable here the next Court

27 August 1754 N. S., p. 316
The Summons against Alexander Brownlee on the presentment of the Grand Jury against him for not keeping the Road whereof he was Overseer in repair According to Law not being Executed It is Ordered than an alias Summons Issue against him returnable here the next Court

20 November 1754 N. S., p. 320
On the presentment of the Grand jury against John King and Andrew Erwin for not keeping the road whereof they were Overseers in repair According to Law the s^d King Appeared & his Excuse being heard It is Ordered that the s^d presentment agst. him be dismised and the Other Def Andrew Erwin not being Summoned It is further Ordered that an Alias Summons Issue against him returnable here the next Court

20 November 1754 N. S., p. 322
[County Levy]

To Robert Breckenridge for the Use of John Brown to be p^d him When a Bridge by him Undertaken is finish'd   6840

20 November 1754 N. S., p. 323
Upon the presentment of the Grand Jury against Robert Patrick & William Finlay for not keeping the Road whereof they were Overseers in repair According to Law their Excuse being heard It is Ordered by the Court that the s^d presentment against them be dismisd they paying Clerks and Sherifs fees.

20 November 1754 N. S., p. 323
Upon the presentment of the Grand jury against Alexander Brownlee for not keeping the Road whereof he was Overseer in repair according to Law his Excuse being heard It is Ordered by the Court that the s^d. Presentment against him be dismisd he paying Clerks & Sherifs fees

21 November 1754 N. S., p. 325
Daniel Deniston is hereby Appointed Surveyor of the higway in the room of James Robinson and It is Ordered that with the titheables that work'd on the s^d. Road under the s^d Robinson he Clear and keep the Same in repair According to Law

21 November 1754 N. S., p. 326
John McCroskey j^r is Appointed Surveyor of the highway from Alex^r. Millers to Robert Dunlops and It is Ordered that with the titheables persons that Shall be Appointed him by Andrew Hays he Clear and keep the Same in repair According to Law

21 November 1754 N. S., p. 326
Ordered that Jacob Anderson with Such titheable persons as Shall be app^d. him by Andrew Hays Clear and keep the Road whereof he is Overseer in repair According to Law

21 November 1754 N. S., p. 328
John Wilson is hereby Appointed Surveyor of the highway from Risks Mill to Samuel Wallaces and It is Ordered that with the titheables as shall be Appointed him by James Lockart he Clear and keep the Same in repair According to Law

22 November 1754 N. S., p. 330
James McDowell is hereby Appointed Surveyor of the Highway from Providence meeting House to Timber Ridge and It is Ordered that with the usual titheables that work'd on the s^d Road he Clear and keep the same in repair According to Law

19 March 1755 N. S., p. 376
Alexander Stewart is hereby Appointed Overseer of the highway in the room of John McClure and It is Ordered that with the titheable persons that Usually work'd on the said Road under the said McClure he Clear and keep the same in repair According to Law

19 March 1755 N. S., p. 376
Ordered that the Road from Samuel Wallaces to James Youngs be discontinued

19 March 1755 N. S., p. 378
William Wilson and John McCleary having by Order of this Court Viewed & laid of a Road from Andrew Hamiltons to the turn of the Calf Pasture Waters by Charles Walkers It is Ordered that Andrew Hamilton be Surveyor thereof and that with James Campbell James Carlile, John Carlile, John Kingkade, Jacob Clements, Thomas Gilham, Robert Gay, Thomas Fulton, Robert Lockridge, and William Hodge he Clear and keep the Same in repair According to Law.
[Note: Pages 379 to 382 are missing]

20 March 1755 N. S., p. 383
Ordered that Robert Looney j^r. be Surveyor of the higway from James River to to the forks below Charles Millicans and that with Such titheable persons as Shall be Appointed him by Major John Smith he Clear and keep the same in repair According to Law

20 March 1755 N. S., p. 383
Ordered that John Lowry and John Potts being first Sworn before a Justice of the Peace for this County do mark and lay of a way from Henry Holdstons to the tavern Spring beyond James Montgomeries and that the s^d Lowry and Plunkard Scilar[Seilar?] be Surveyors of the same and with the titheable persons on Johns Creek and on Craigs Creek as low as Hans Morris's he Clear and keep the Same in repair According to Law

20 March 1755 N. S., p. 384
On the presentment of the Grand jury against Andrew Erwin for not keeping the Road whereof he was Surveyor in repair According to Law the s^d Erwin being Summoned Appeared and his Excuse being heard It is Ordered that he be discharged on paying Clerks and Sherifs fees--

20 March 1755 N. S., p. 384
Ordered that William Bell j^r. Appoint the Several Precincts to Patrick Crawford Andrew Erwin and Thomas Stevenson Overseers of the highway from Davis's Mill to John Ramseys on the South River--

24 March 1755 N. S., p. 411
Ordered that Archibald Alexander John Lyle and John McKay or any two of them being first sworn before a Justice of the Peace for this County do View & Mark the nearest and best way from Isaac Taylors to Tarrs Shop and report their proceedings to the next Court

22 May 1755 N. S., p. 423
Samuel Black is hereby Appointed Surveyor of the highway in the room of John Henderson and It is Ordered that with the titheable persons that Usually work'd on the s^d Road under the said Henderson he keep the same in repair According to Law

22 May 1755 N. S., p. 423
Moses McClure is hereby Appointed Surveyor of the highway in the room of Baptist M^{c}nabb and It is Ordered that with the titheable persons that Usually work'd on the s^d Road under the s^d M^{c}nabb he keep the Same in repair According to Law.

22 May 1755 N. S., p. 423
Richard Bodkin is hereby Appointed Surveyor of the highway in the room of John Carlile And It is Ordered that with the titheables that Usually work'd on the s^d Road Under the s^d Carlile he keep the Same in repair According to Law

22 May 1755 N. S., p. 423
John Ledford is hereby appointed Surveyor of the highway in the room of Henry Brown And It is Ordered that with the titheables that Usually work'd on the s^d Road Under the s^d Brown he keep the Same in repair According to Law

22 May 1755 N. S., p. 423
William Ledford is hereby appointed Surveyor of the highway in the room of W^m M^{c}murry and It is Ordered that with the titheables that usually workd on the s^d Road Under the s^d M^{c}murry he Clear and keep the same in repair According to Law

22 May 1755 N. S., p. 423
John Thompson is hereby Appointed Surveyor of the highway in the room of James Kerr and It is Ordered that with the titheables that usually work'd on the said Road under the s^d Kerr he Clear and keep the Same in repair According to Law

22 May 1755 N. S., p. 423
James McGill is hereby Appointed Surveyor of the highway in the room of Andrew Erwin and It is Ordered that with the titheables that Usually work'd on the s^d Road under the s^d Erwin he keep the Same in repair According to Law

22 May 1755 N. S., p. 424
Sampson Archer is hereby Appointed Surveyor of the Highway from Jening's Gap to the Waters of the long Glade and It is Ordered that with the Adjacent titheables he Clear & keep the Same in repair According to Law

22 May 1755 N. S., p. 424
John Timble is hereby appointed Surveyor of the Highway from the Middle River to the Court House in the room of James Philips and It is Ordered that with the titheables that Usually Work'd on the s^d Road Under the said Philips he Clear and keep the Same in repair According to Law

22 May 1755 N. S., p. 424
Charles Campbell is hereby appointed Surveyor of the Highway in the room of John Francis and It is Ordered that with the titheables that Usually work'd on the s^d Road under the s^d Francis he Clear & keep the Same in repair According to Law

22 May 1755 N. S., p. 424
James Simpson is hereby Appointed Surveyor of the high way in the room of Robert Armstong and It is Ordered that with the Titheables that Usually work'd on the s^d Road Under the s^d Armstrong he Clear & keep the same in repair According to Law

22 May 1755 N. S., p. 424
Archibald Alexander and Others being appointed to View a Road from Isaac Taylors to Tarrs Shop made return that the New Road is the Nearest & best Way It is Therefore Ordered that

Robert Huston and Moses McClure be Surveyors thereof and that with the Adjacent titheables they Clear & keep the Same in repair According to Law

22 May 1755 N. S., p. 426
Ordered that John Anderson Senr David Hogshead and John Davis being first Sworn before a Justice of the Peace for this County View the Several Roads that have been already Petitioned for from this Court House to Silas Harts and report the Most Convenient to the next Court

22 May 1755 N. S., p. 427
On the Motion of John Stevenson It is Ordered that David Bell be Summoned to Appear at the next Court to Answer his Complaint ag^st him for Stoping the High Way near his Plantation--

22 May 1755 N. S., p. 427
James Galespy is hereby Appointed Surveyor of the highway in the room of Patrick Crawford and It is Ordered that with titheable persons that Usually work'd on the s^d Road Under the said Crawford he keep the Same in repair According to Law

22 May 1755 N. S., p. 427
Andrew Vought is hereby Appointed Surveyor of the highway in the room of Samuel Lockart And It is Ordered that with the titheable persons that Usually work'd on the s^d Road under the s^d Vought he keep the Same in repair According to Law

22 May 1755 N. S., p. 427
Ordered that William Ledgerwood and James Mitchell being first Sworn before a Justice of the Peace for this County View two Roads from Charles Campbells to the forks of the Road above Fultons and report the Most Convenient to the next Court--

22 May 1755 N. S., p. 427
William Graham is hereby appointed Surveyor if the highway from Carvins to Millicans in the room of William Carvin and It is Ordered that with Such Titheable's as Shall be Appointed him by John Mills and David Miller he keep the Same in repair According to Law

22 May 1755 N. S., p. 427
Henry Reaburn is hereby Appointed Surveyor of the highway from James Beards ford to Chamberlaines run and Alexander Walker from the s^d Run to the Stone Meeting House and It is Ordered that with the Most Convenient Titheables they Clear and keep the Same in repair according to Law

22 May 1755 N. S., p. 428
Ordered that the Several persons Mentioned in a list produced by William Henderson work on the road whereof he is Overseer

22 May 1755 N. S., p. 428
James Waits is hereby Appointed Surveyor of the highway in the room of Robt. Craven and It is Ordered that with the Titheable persons that formerly work'd on the s^d Road under the s^d Craven he keep the Same in repair According to Law

23 May 1755 N. S., p. 435
On the Petition of Sundry of the Inhabitants Seting forth that there might be a More Convenient Road from Thomas Moores to the Court House of this County than the one Already Used It is Ordered that Robert Patterson Wm Brown and John King being first Sworn before a Justice of this County View the Present Road as also the one Petitiond for & report the Most Convenient to the next Court

23 May 1755 N. S., p. 439
Patrick Sharkey is hereby Appointed Surveyor of the highway from David Cloyds to John M^{c}farrons in the room of John Marshall and It is ordered that with the Titheable Persons that Work'd on the s^d Road Under the s^d Marshall he Clear & keep the Same in repair According to Law

23 May 1755 N. S., p. 439
David Cloyd is hereby appointed Surveyor of the highway from his Plantation to the Roan Oak Road and It is Ordered that with the Most Convenient Male Titheables he Clear and keep the Same in repair According to Law.

23 May 1755 N. S., p. 439
Jacob Patton is hereby appointed Surveyor of the highway from James Campbells to the Catapo Road and It is Ordered that with the most Convenient Titheables he Clear & keep the Same in repair According to Law.

23 May 1755 N. S., p. 439
Richard Reed is hereby appointed Surveyor of the highway from the Catapo Road to Warwick Gap And It is Ordered that with the Most Convenient Male Titheables he Clear and keep the same in repair According to Law.

23 May 1755 N. S., p. 439
John Ledford is hereby appointed Surveyor of the highway from James Campbells to the head of Roan Oak Waters and It is Ordered that with the most Convenient Titheables he Clear and keep the same in repair According to Law.

23 May 1755 N. S., p. 439
Ordered that Robert Montgomerie and Thomas Ramsey being first Sworn before a Justice of the Peace for this County do Mark the Most Convenient Way from the Tavern Spring in the Gap to Robert Looneys Mill and that Wm Preston Gent Appoint the Surveyor & Titheables to Clear the Same.

20 November 1755 N. S., p. 499
James McGill was Appointed Surveyor of the highway in the room of Andrew Erwin having Complained that the s^d Erwin had not put the s^d Road whereof he is Overseer in good repair It is Therefore Ordered that the s^d Erwin Continue Overseer of the Same untill he shall have Clear'd it according to Law.

20 November 1755 N. S., p. 499
Ordered that Baptist M^cnabb remain Overseer of the Road whereof he was formerly Surveyor the present Overseer Moses McClure not being Convenient to the s^d Road.

21 November 1755 N. S., p. 504
Ordered that John Paxton Joseph Lapsley & Joseph Long being first Sworn before a Justice of the Peace for this County View the Ground and lay of a Road from William Halls to the Mountain Road and make report to the next Court

Book V, 1755-1757

25 November 1755 N. S., p. 3
James Caldwell is hereby appointed Surveyor of the highway from Nutt's Mill Creek to this Court House in the room of Robert McClenachan and It is Ordered that with the Titheable persons that Usually work'd on the s^d Road Under the s^d McClenachan he Clear and keep the Same in repair According to Law

17 March 1756 N. S., p. 33
On the Petition of David Moore praying a road may be laid of from the Indian Road to his Mill It is Ordered that Nath Evans and Thomas Wilson being first Sworn before a Justice of the Peace for this County View the s^d Road & make report to the next Court.

19 May 1756 N. S., p. 111
George Rankins is appointed Surveyor of the high Way in the room of Saml Givens And It is Ordered that with the Titheables that Worked Under the s^d Givens he keep the same in repair Acc^d to Law

19 May 1756 N. S., p. 111
Evan Evans is Appointed Surveyor of the highway in the room of Andrew Fought And It is Ordered that with the Titheables that work'd on the s^d Road under the s^d Fought he keep the Same in repair Acc^d to Law

19 May 1756 N. S., p. 111
John Campbell is Appointed Surveyor of the high Way in the room of Charles Campbell And It is Ord^d. that W^h. the Tith^s. that Usually Work'd Under the s^d. Campbell he keep the Same in repair Acc^d to Law

19 May 1756 N. S., p. 111

Thomas Wilson is Appointed Surveyor of the highway in the room of John Underwood and It is Ordered that with the Tith^s. that usually work'd Under the s^d. Jno. he keep the Same in repair Acc^d. to Law.

19 May 1756 N. S., p. 111
John Buchanan is App^d. Surveyor of the highway in the room of Rob Breckenridge And It is Ord^o. that with the Tith^s that Usually work'd under the s^d Rob. he keep the Same in repair Acc^d to Law

19 May 1756 N. S., p. 111
Felix Gilbert is appointed Surveyor of the highway in the room of Ja^s. Knox And It is Ordered that with the Tith^s that usually Work'd under the s^d James he keep the same in repair Acc^d to Law.

19 May 1756 N. S., p. 111
Walter Davis & George Caldwell are appointed Surveyors of the highway in the room of Wm Henderson & It is Ordered that with the Tith^s that usually work'd under the s^d W^m they keep the Same in repair According to Law.

20 May 1756 N. S., p. 119
John Anderson and David Hogshead having been appointed to View two Several Roads from this Court House to Silas Harts made their report, that the Lower Road is the Most Convenient, It is therefore Ord^d. that John Young & John Francis be Overseers of the Same and that with the Convenient Titheables they keep the Same in repair Acc^d to Law

21 May 1756 N. S., p. 124
Moses McClure is Appointed Surveyor of the highway in the room of Thomas Paxton and It is Ordered that with the Titheable Persons that Usually work'd under the s^d Paxton he keep the Same in repair According to Law.

21 May 1756 N. S., p. 124
William Dyer and Michael Props are appointed Surveyors of the highway in the room of Peter Haws & Wm Stevenson and It is Or^d. that with the titheable Persons that Usually work'd under the s^d Haws & Stevenson they keep same in repair According to Law

21 May 1756 N. S., p. 124
William Stevenson is appointed Surveyor of the highway in the room of Abraham Smith and It is Ordered that with the Titheables that usually work'd under the s^d. Smith he keep the Same in repair According to Law

21 May 1756 N. S., p. 124
Robert Huston is appointed Surveyor of the highway in the room of Baptist McNab and It is Order that with the Titheables that Usually work'd under the s^d M^{c}nab he keep the Same in repair According to Law

21 May 1756 N. S., p. 125

Ordered that Silas Hart & Rob McClenachan appoint Surveyors & and titheable Persons to Work on two Roads from this Court House to the s^d Harts

21 May 1756 N. S., p. 126
William Hall & Low Todd are hereby appointed Surveyors of the highway in the room of Robert Young and It is Ordered that with the Titheables that formerly work'd on the s^d Road under the s^d. Young they keep the Same in repair According to Law.

22 May 1756 N. S., p. 134
Samuel Black is hereby appointed Surveyor of the highway in the room of James Black and It is Ordered that with the Titheables that usually work'd under the s^d James he keep the Same in repair according to Law.

18 November 1756 N. S., p. 246
On the Petition of Robert Shankland Seting forth that the Road that Leads from James Beards tho^r. his Land to the North River is Verry Inconvenient and Praying to have the Same turned It is Ordered that Henry Downs being first Sworn View the Same together with the Way Proposed by the Petitioner and make report to the next Court

15 June 1757 N. S., p. 366
John Bigham is Appointed Surveyor of the highway in the room of John Henderson and It is Ordered that with the Tithables that Usually worked Under the said Henderson he keep the same in repair According to Law

15 June 1757 N. S., p. 366
John Hinds is Appointed Surveyor of the Highway in the room of George Rankins and It is Ordered that he with the Titheables that Usally worked under the said Rankins he keep the same in repair According to Law

15 June 1757 N. S., p. 369
Mathew Thompson is Appointed Surveyor of the highway in the room of Evan Evans and It is Ordered that with the Tithables that Usally worked under the s^d Evans he keep the same in repair According to Law

15 June 1757 N. S., p. 369
Ludwick Waggoner and Pasley Hover are Appointed Surveyors of the highway from John Pattons old place to the little fork of Dry River and It is Ordered that with the Tithables that Usally worked on the Road they keep the same in repair According to Law

17 June 1757 N. S., p. 375
On the Petition of Sundry the Inhabitants of the South branch for a Road from the South fork of Potowmack to the Main Road Near Abraham Smiths It is Ordered that William Dyer and Mathew Patton being first Sworn Veiw the Road from Already Cleared together with the one Petitioned for and report to the next Court

18 August 1757 N. S., p. 440
William Finla is Appointed Surveyor of the highway in the room of Alexander Stewart and It is Ordered that with the Tithables that Usually worked under the said Stewart he keep the same in repair According to Law

Book VI, 1757-1761

19 August 1757 N. S., p. 17
Ordered that James Galespie be Surveyor of the highway from Ramsay's to the foot of the South Mountain and that with the Several Tithables in a List delivered in Court he keep the same in Repair According to Law

19 November 1757 N. S., p. 72
Ordered that the Several Persons that Work on the highway from Ramsays to the South Mountain be Exempted from the Working on Other Roads

20 March 1758, p. 125
Henry Miller is Appointed Surveyor of the highway in the room of James Orry and It is Ordered that with the Tithables person that Usally worked under the said James Orry he keep the same in repair According to Law

20 March 1758, p. 141
The Complaint of John Stevenson against David Bell For Stoping up the Highway is dismised

17 May 1758, p. 145
John McCroskey is hereby Appointed Surveyor of the highway from Alexander Millers to Beverly Manor line and It is Ordered that with the Tithables that shall be Appointed by Andrew Hays he keep the same in repair According to Law

17 May 1758, p. 145
Charles Hays is hereby Appointed Surveyor of the highway from Adrew Hays Mill to Captain Kenadys and that with such Tithables person as formerly worked on the said Road Under John Walker he Clear and keep the same in repair According to Law

17 May 1758, p. 145
Alexander McClure is hereby Appointed Surveyor of the hghwaye from the North River to William Lusk and that with the adjacent Tithable person he keep the same in repair According to Law

17 May 1758, p. 147
Ordered that the Several Persons Mentioned in a List Given in by Henry Reaburn work on the Road whereof he is Overseer

17 May 1758, p. 147
Jacob Anderson is hereby appointed Surveyor of the highway from the North River to Alexander Millers and that with the adjatient Tithable person he keep the same in repair According to Law

17 May 1758, p. 147
James Fulton is hereby Appointed Surveyor of the highway from James Cowans line to David Moores and that with the Convenient Tithable person he keep the same in repair According to Law

18 May 1758, p. 158
Alexander Blair and Alexander Craig are appointed Surveyors of the highway in the room of John Young and John Anderson and It is ordered that they with the Tithable person that Ussally worked under the s^d John Young and John Anderson they keep the same in repair According to Law

17 August 1758, p. 181
Isaac Anderson is hereby Appointed Surveyor of the highway from Hays Mill to Alexander Millers in the room of Andrew Hays and that with such Tithable persons as formerly worked on the said Road under Andrew Hays he Clear and keep the same in repair According to Law

15 November 1758, p. 211
Ordered that Alexander Miller Joseph Coulton and Archibald Alexander they being first sworn before a Justice of this County do Veiw and Mark a way from Hays Mill to Timber Ridge Meeting House and report to the next Court

21 March 1759, p. 236
On the Petition of Sundry the Inhabitants of this County It is Ordered that Andrew Soduskie Martin Wiltsil and Uriah Humble or any Two of them of them being first Sworn Veiw the nearest and Most Convenient Way from Jacob Haldermans to Hampshire County Line and make report thereof to the next Court

22 March 1759, p. 241
On the Motion of Patrick Campbell leave to turn the road round his plantation is granted him

22 March 1759, p. 244
John Miller Junior is Appointed Surveyor of the highway in the room of Nicholas Cain and It is Ordered that with the Tithable persons that Usally worked under the said Cain he keep the same in repair according to Law

16 May 1759, p. 258
Andrew Steel is appointed Surveyor of the highway in the room of William Berry and It is Ordered that with the Tithable person that Usally worked under the said Berry he keep the same in repair According to Law

16 May 1759, p. 259
John Wortlaw is hereby Appointed Surveyer of the highway from the Wilderness Bridge to Beverly Manor line and It is Ordered that with the Adjacent Tithables he Clear and keep the same in repair According to Law

16 May 1759, p. 259
Samuel Buchanan is hereby Appointed Survey of the highway from Hays to Kenadays Mill and It is Ordered that with the Adjacent Tithables he Clear and keep the same in repair According to Law

16 May 1759, p. 259
Archibald Armstrong and William Elliot are Appointed Surveyors of the highway in the room of Thomas Weems and It is Ordered that With the Tithable person that Usally worked under the said Weems they Clear and keep the same in repair According to Law

16 May 1759, p. 259
Alexander Brownlee and Samuel Steel are hereby Appointed Surveyors of the highway from from Cowans Line to David Mores and It is ordered that with the adjacent Tithables they Clear and keep the same in repair According to Law

16 May 1759, p. 259
James Bell is hereby Appointed Surveyor of the Highway from the Pine Run to Adam Maurys and It is Ordered that with the adjacent Tithables he Clear and keep the same in repair According to Law

16 May 1759, p. 259
Patrick Hays is hereby appointed Surveyor of the highway from Beverly Manor line to the Indian Road and It is ordered that with the adjacent Tithables he Clear and keep the same in repair According to Law

16 May 1759, p. 260
James Beard is hereby Appointed Surveyor of the Highway from John Stevenson to Andrew Leepers, and It is Ordered that with the Adjacent Tithables he Clear and keep the same in repair According to Law

Henry Parkey is hereby Appointed Surveyor of the Highway in the room of Robert Hook and It is Ordered that with the Tithable person that Usally worked under the said Hook he Clear and keep the same in repair According to Law

16 May 1759, p. 260
George Poage is hereby appointed Surveyor of the room of Alexander Walker and It is Ordered that with the Tithable person that Usually worked Under the said Walker he Clear and keep the same in repair According to Law

16 May 1759, p. 261
Patrick Hays and John Montgomerie are hereby Appointed Surveyor of the Highway from Joseph Kenady to the Landing Road and It is ordered that with the Adjacent Tithables they Clear and keep the same in repair according to Law

16 May 1759, p. 264
Thomas Sheilds and James Mitchell are hereby Appointed Surveyors of the highway from Joseph Mays to James Balls and It is Ordered they devide the Tithables and Precints and Clear & keep the same in repair According to Law

16 May 1759, p. 264
Robert Young and John Allison are hereby Appointed Surveyor of the highway from the Widow Longs to James Thompson and It is Ordered that with the Adjacent Tithables they Clear and keep the same in repair According to Law

16 May 1759, p. 264
Henry Long is appointed Surveyor of the highway from Fraziers to Hance Magorts and John Early from thence to the top of the Ridge at Swift Run pass and that Francis Kirkley j^r devide the Tithables that Ussally worked on the said Road and that they Clear and keep the same in repair According to Law

17 May 1759, p. 264
John Stuart is appointed Surveyor of the highway in the room of John Bigam and It is Ordered that with the Tithable persons that Ussally worked under the said Bigam he Clear and keep the same in repair According to Law

15 August 1759, p. 288
On the Petition of sundry Inhabitants It is Ordered that a Road formerly Cleared from John Archers to John Ramsey's be again repaired and that William Anderson Archibald Hamilton and James Anderson be Surveyors of the Road and that they devide their Precents and with the Convenient Tithables they keep the same in repair According to Law

17 August 1759, p. 292
Nathaniel Evans is Appointed Surveyor of the highway from Evans Run to Beverly Manor line in the room of David Moore and It is Ordered that with the Tithable person that Usally worked under the said Moore he Clear and keep the same in repair according to Law

22 November 1759, p. 319
Ordered that John Mitchell and James Mitchell they being first sworn Veiw a Road from the North Mountain Meeting House to John Tates Mill and make report thereof to the next Court

26 November 1759, p. 339
Ordered that the Sherif Imploy Workmen to repair the Bridge near John Browns and that they bring their Charge at the Laying the next County Levy

20 May 1760, p. 348
Thomas Mitchell is herby Appointed Surveyor of the Highway from James Cowans to Bordens line in the room of Alexander Brownlee and It is Ordered that with the Adjacent Tithables that Usally worked under Brownlee he Clear and keep the same in repair According to Law

20 May 1760, p. 348
William Brown is hereby Appointed Surveyor of the Highway from the South branch to Staunton Between Mossey Creek and Middle River in the room of Alexander Blair and It is Ordered that with the Adjacent Tithables he Clear and keep the same in repair According to Law

20 May 1760, p. 348
William Hunter is hereby Appointed Surveyor of the highway in the room of Samuel Downing and It is Ordered that with the Adjacent Tithables he Clear and keep in repair According to Law

20 May 1760, p. 349
William Patterson is hereby Appointed Surveyor of the Highway [in the?] room of William Finley and It is ordered that with the Tithable persons that Usally worked under the said Finley he Clear and keep the same in repair According to Law

20 May 1760, p. 350
Andrew Cowan is hereby Appointed Surveyor of the highway in the room of James Moody and It is Ordered that he with the Tithable persons that Usally Worked Under the said Moody he Clear and keep the same in repair According to Law

20 May 1760, p. 350
James Hunter is hereby Appointed Surveyor of the Highway in the room of John Risk and It is Ordered that he with the Tithable persons that Usally worked under the said Risk he Clear and keep the same in repair According to Law

20 May 1760, p. 350
Robert Patterson is hereby Appointed Surveyor of the Highway in the room of Alexander Craige and It is Ordered that with the Titheable persons that usally worked under the said Craige he Clear and keep in repair according to Law

20 May 1760, p. 350
Robert Allison is hereby Appointed Surveyor of the Highway in the room of Alexander McClure and It is Ordered that with the Tithable persons that Usually worked under the said McClure he Clear and keep the same in repair According to Law

20 May 1760, p. 351
John Fulton is hereby Appointed Surveyor of the highway in the room of Patrick Hays and It is ordered that with the Tithable persons that Usally Worked under the said Patrick Hays he Clear and keep the same in repair According to Law

20 May 1760, p. 351
John Stewart is hereby Appointed Surveyor of the highway in the room of Samuel Buchanan and It is Ordered that with the Tithable persons that Usally worked Under the said Samuel Buchanan he Clear and keep the same in repair according to Law

20 May 1760, p. 351
John Handley is hereby appointed Surveyor of the Highway in the room of Andrew Steel and It is Ordered that with the Tithable persons that Usally worked Under the said Andrew Steel he Clear and keep the same in repair According to Law

20 May 1760, p. 351
Thomas Turk is hereby Appointed Surveyor of the Highway in the room of William Hind and It is Ordered that with the Tithable persons that Usally worked under the said William Hind he Clear and keep the same in repair According to Law

20 May 1760, p. 351
John Ramsey is hereby Appointed Surveyor of the highway in the room of James Galespy and It is Ordered that with the Tithable person that Usally worked under the said James Galespy he Clear and keep the same in repair According to Law

20 May 1760, p. 351
Robert Moody is hereby Appointed Surveyor of the Highway in the room of John Thompson and It is Ordered that with the Tithable persons that Usally worked Under the said John Thompson he Clear and keep the same in repair According to Law

20 May 1760, p. 351
Thomas Baggs is hereby Appointed Surveyor of the Highway from Brocks Gap to Hampshire County Line and It is ordered that with the Adjacent Tithables he Clear and keep the same in repair according to Law.

20 May 1760, p. 352
Ordered that John Buchanan John Poage Audley Paul and Richard Mathews or any three of them do Veiw a road from Simpsons Place on Buffaloe Creek by the Plantation of John Poage to the road Commonly Called Mathews's joining said Road at Chittams place and with Mathews's road to the Great Spring ware it is to join the old road and make report thereof to the next Court

20 May 1760, p. 352
William Craven and Edward Shankland is hereby Appointed Surveyors of the highway from Brocks Gap to said Shanklands and It is Ordered that with the adjacent Tithables he Clear and keep the same in repair According to Law

20 May 1760, p. 352
William Logan is hereby Appointed Surveyor of the Highway from the Tinckling Spring to the Great Spring belonging to John Finley in the room of John Finley and It is Ordered that with the Tithable persons that Ussally Worked Under the said John Finley he Clear and keep the same in repair according to Law

20 May 1760, p. 352
Joseph Gamble is hereby Appointed Surveyor of the Highway in the room of John Stewart and It is Ordered that with the Tithable person that Usally worked Under the said John Stewart he Clear and keep the same in repair According to Law

20 May 1760, p. 352
Ordered that the Sherif of this County Imploy Workmen to repair the Bridge below this Court House on Lewis Creek as also a Bridge on the Upper part of the same in the Town of Stanton and bring in his Charge at the Laying of the next County Levy

20 May 1760, p. 352
On the Petition of Sundry the Inhabitants for to have road Cleared from Basson Hovers on the South fork of the South Branch of Potomak by the Bryery Branch to Silas Harts is granted and It is Ordered that Henry Pickle be Surveyor thereof & that with the Persons Mentioned in the s[d] Petition he Clear and keep the same in repair According to Law

21 May 1760, p. 353
David M[c]Croskey is hereby Appointed Surveyor of the Highway from Andrew Hays to Robert Kilpatricks and that the Old road Williams Bohanons place be discontinued & It is ordered that with the Adjacent Titheables he Clear and keep the same in repair According to Law

21 May 1760, p. 354

John Davis is hereby appointed Surveyor of the Highway from James Bairds to the Lick by Robert Scotts and It is Ordered that with the Adjacent Tithables he Clear and keep the same in repair According to Law

21 May 1760, p. 354
Valintine Pence is hereby Appointed Surveyor of the Highway from Cub run to Robert Scotts and It is Ordered that with the Adjacent Tithables he Clear and keep the same in repair According to Law

21 May 1760, p. 355
William Campbell is hereby Appointed Surveyor of the Highway from John Tates to the North Mountain Meeting House and It is Ordered that with the Adjacent Tithables he Clear and keep the same in repair According to Law

21 May 1760, p. 355
James McCleary is hereby Appointed Surveyor of the Highway from Parson Jones to Rusks Mill in the room of John Wilson and It is Ordered that with the Adjacent Tithable he Clear and keep the same in repair According to Law

21 May 1760, p. 355
Thomas Stewart and John Black is hereby Appointed Surveyor of the Highway from the tinkling Spring Meeting House to James Balls in the room of Walter Davis and George Caldwell and It is ordered that with the Tithable person that Usally worked under the said Walter Davis and George Caldwell they Clear and keep the same in repair according to Law

21 May 1760, p. 358
Silas Hart Gent is hereby Appointed Surveyor of the Highway in the room of William Stevenson deceased and It is Ordered that with the Tithable persons that Usally Worked Under the said Stevenson he Clear and keep the Same in repair According to Law

22 May 1760, p. 363
Ordered that Robert Brackenridge and Felix Gilberts veiw the Bridge repaired by John Brown and make their report to the next Court

22 May 1760, p. 363
Patrick Young is Appointed Surveyor of the Highway in the room of John Allison and It is Ordered that with the Tithable persons that Usally Worked under the said John Allison he Clear and keep the same in repair According to Law

19 August 1760, p. 390
Daniel Lyle is hereby Appointed Surveyor of the highway from John Bowyers to William Lusks in the room of Robert Houston and It is Ordered that With the Tithable persons that Usally worked Under the said Huston he Clear and keep the Same in repair According to Law.

19 August 1760, p. 390
John Paxton and Abraham Brown are hereby Appointed Surveyors of the highway from the North River to James Simpsons place and It is Ordered that with the Adjacent Tithables they Clear and keep the same in repair According to Law

19 August 1760, p. 391
On the Petition of Mathew Robertson & others for leave to turn the Road from the Stone Meeting House to King Mill thro the fenced Ground of William Hamilton It is Ordered that John Anderson John Pattison and David Bell do Veiw the Same and report the Conveniences or Inconveniences Attending such Alteration to the next Court

19 August 1760, p. 391
On the Petition of Joseph Walker for leave to turn the road between Halls Mill and the Main County Road round his Fence It is Ordered that Richard Woods John Allison and Daniel Lyle do veiw the same and report the Conveniences or inconveniences Attending such Alteration to the next Court

20 August 1760, p. 394
On the Petition of William Ramsay and Others ordered that a Road be Cleared from George Taylors feild to said Ramsays Mill and from thence to the Waggon ford of the North river and that Nathaniel McClure be Surveyor thereof and that with such Tithable persons as are willing to work on the same he Clear and keep the same in repair According to Law

20 August 1760, p. 395
William Logan Overseer of the Road from John Finlas great Spring to the Tinkling Spring Meeting House returned a List of Tithables which are Convenient to work on the said road It is Ordered by the Court that the said Tithables are to work Accordingly

20 August 1760, p. 395
Ordered John Dickenson and James Lockridge Gent do devide the Tithables to work on the road between John Willsons Gap and the Panther Gap and return the Lists respectively into Court

22 August 1760, p. 406
John Buchanan and John Maxwell Gent are hereby Appointed Surveyors of the Highway from the Broad Spring in the forks of James River to the Ferry and It is Ordered that with the Convenient Tithables they Clear and keep the same in repair According to Law

23 August 1760, p. 421
Felix Gilbert and Robert Breckenridge Gent being Appointed to Veiw a Bridge Built by John Brown Near his House made report that the same was done on a good and Workmanlike Manner

23 August 1760, p. 422
Johnston Hill is Appointed Surveyor of the highway in the room of William Stevenson and It is Ordered that with the Tithable persons that Usally worked Under the said Stevenson he Clear and keep the same in repair According to Law

23 August 1760, p. 422
Alexander Herron and Daniel Love are hereby Appointed Surveyors of the Highway from the Dry River Gap to the Road that leads over Swift run Gap and It is Ordered that Daniel Smith Gent devide their Precents and that they with the Tithables persons as Shall be Appointed them by the said Smith they Clear and keep the same in repair According to Law

21 November 1760, p. 439
Ordered that John Dunkle and Nicholas Havenor they being first Sworn Veiw a Way from Michael Props to the County Line and make report thereof to the next Court

21 November 1760, p. 439
Ordered that John Dunkle and Nicholas Havener they being first sworn Veiw the Ground from Michael Props to Daniel Harrison's and make report whether or no a waggon Road Can be had to the next Court

24 November 1760, p. 458
Ordered that Robert Christian William Henderson John Tate Thomas Stuart and Felix Gilbert they being first sworn Veiw the most Convenient way from the Widow Tee's to the top of the Ridge at Kingkades Gap and make report thereof to the next Court

24 November 1760, p. 459
Ordered that James Alexander and William Hinds they being first sworn Veiw the Most Convenient way from Samuel Davis to the Mountain at Woods Gap and make report thereof to the next Court

24 November 1760, p. 459
Ordered that James Trimble and Archibald Alexander they being first sworn Veiw the Road from Paxtons ford at the North River to the foot of the Poplar Hill tho Browns Land and make report thereof to the next Court

24 November 1760, p. 459
Israel Christian Gent having Informed the Court that the Road now goes by the Reason of Steepness of the Heill thro a Valuable Lott of his to his great Prejudice It is Therefore Ordered

that CoL° Preston John Poage and Felix Gilbert Gent veiw the Same and make report thereof to the next Court

24 November 1760, p. 459-60
[Grand Jury Presentments]

The King against Robert McClenachan
On a Presentment of the Grand jury for not keeping the road whereof he is Overseer in repair
Continued by Consent

* * *

The King against The Overseers of the Road from Kenadys to Walkers
On Presentment of the Grand jury for not keeping the Highway in repair According to Law
The Sherif having returned that the said Overseers was not found in his Bailiwick this Suit is dismised.

* * *

The King against The Overseers of the Road from the Court House to Christians Creek
On Presentment of the Grand jury for not keeping the Highway in repair According to Law
The Sherif having returned that the said Overseers was not found in his bailiwick this Suit is dismised from

* * *

The King against The Overseers of the Road from Saml Youngs to Browns
On Presentment of the Grand jury for not keeping the Highwway in repair According to Law
The Sherif having returned that the said Overseers was not found in his Bailiwick this Suit is dismised

17 February 1761, p. 463
The Petition of William Hall Habert McClure to have the road turned round Joseph Walkers Plantation reveiwed is rejected

17 February 1761, p. 463
On the Petition of Randall Lockart for Leave to turn the road that Leads thro' his Plantation It is Ordered that John Anderson George Anderson and John Hutcheson they being first sworn Veiw the Ground and Make report to the next Court

17 February 1761, p. 462 II
James Hamilton and Samuel McClure are hereby appointed Surveyors of the Highway from the tinkling Spring to Blacks Draft and It is Ordered that with the Persons Mentioned in a List they Clear and keep the same in repair According to Law

17 February 1761, p. 462 II
On the Petition of Sundry the Inhabitants James Allen is hereby Appointed Surveyor of the Highway from Kings Mill to the Stone Meeting House and It is Ordered that with the said Petitioners he Clear and keep the same in repair According to Law

18 February 1761, p. 463 II
Ordered that James Trimble and Archibald Alexander they being first sworn Veiw the Road from the North River ford to Buffallow Creek ford and make report thereof to the next Court

18 February 1761, p. 463 II
Ordered that the Road by John Paxtons House to Buffalow Creek be kept Open and in repair According to Law

18 February 1761, p. 472
Ordered that Abraham Smith John Hopkins and John McCoy Lay of the most Convenient Road from this Court House to Brocks Gap and It is Ordered that Abraham Love John Malcome and Robert Gray be Surveyors of the said Road and that with the Tithables as shall be Appointed them by Silas Hart and Daniel Smith Gent they Clear and keep the same in repair According to Law

18 February 1761, p. 472
Ordered that a Road be Cut from the old Road that leads thro' the Dry River Gap of the Mountain and that Gabriel Pickens be Surveyor of that Part the South side of the Mountain and Mark Swatley from their to Sivers's Mill Mathew Patton from their to Charles Wilsons and Charles Wilson from their to the County Line and It is Ordered that with the Adjacent Tithables they Clear and keep the same in repair According to Law

20 February 1761, p. 476
Samuel Davidson is hereby Appointed Surveyor of the highway from Samuel Davidsons to Woods Gap & It is Ordered that with the Adjacent Tithables he Clear and keep the same in repair Acccording to Law

20 February 1761, p. 476
Felix Gilbert Gent is hereby Appointed Surveyor of the highway from the Court House to Christian Creek and It is Ordered that with the Usal Tithables together with those in the town of Staunton he Clear and keep the same in repair According to Law

23 February 1761, p. 493
Ordered that William Preston and John Trimble be Overseers from this Court House to the Middle river and that the said Preston with the Tithables in Staunton Clear the said Road to the head of the Race paths and the s^d Trimble with the Tithable persons that Usally worked Under him from thence to the Middle river and that they Clear and keep the same in repair According to Law.
Book VII, 1761-1763

19 May 1761, p. 1
David Drydon is hereby Appointed Surveyor of the highway from the North branch of James River to William Lusk and It is ordered that with the Adjacent Tithables he Clear and keep the same in repair According to Law

19 May 1761, p. 1
Moses Hall is Appointed Surveyor of the highway in the room of William Brown and It is Ordered that with the Tithable persons that Usally worked Under the said Brown he Clear and keep the same in repair According to Law

19 May 1761, p. 1
Alexander Kyle is Appointed Surveyor of the highway in the room of John Hare and It is Ordered that with the Tithable person that Usally worked under the said Hare he Clear and keep the same in repair According to Law

19 May 1761, p. 2
Robert Brown is Appointed Surveyor of the highway in the room of William McGill and It is Ordered that with the Tithable persons that Usally worked Under the said McGill he Clear and keep the same in repair According to Law

19 May 1761, p. 2
William McCrorie is Appointed Surveyor of the highway in the room of Thomas Wilson and It is Ordered that with the Tithable persons that Usally worked under the said Wilson he Clear and keep the same in repair According to Law

19 May 1761, p. 2
Robert Belshire is Appointed Surveyor of the highway in the room of James Beard and It is Ordered that he with the Tithable persons that Usally Worked Under the said Beard he Clear and keep the same in repair According to Law

19 May 1761, p. 5
Thomas Stevenson j^r is Appointed Surveyor of the Highway in the room of David Stevenson and It is ordered that with the Tithable persons that Usally worked Under the said David Stevenson he Clear and keep the same in repair According to Law

19 May 1761, p. 5
John Stevenson is hereby Appointed Surveyor of the Highway from Waters feild to the Stone Meeting House and It is Ordered that With the Adjacent Tithables he Clear and keep the same in repair According to Law

19 May 1761, p. 5
Mathew Robertson is hereby Appointed Surveyor of the Highway in the room of Thomas Stevenson and It is Ordered that with the Adjacent Tithable persons that Usally worked Under the said Stevenson he Clear and keep the same in repair According to Law

19 May 1761, p. 5
Alexander Thompson is hereby Appointed Surveyor of the Highway from Christians Creek to the Tinkling Spring and It is Ordered that he with the Tithables Mentioned in a List by him delivered in Court he Clear and keep the Same in repair According to Law

19 May 1761, p. 5
James Gamble is Appointed Surveyor of the Highway in the room of Robert Patterson and It is Ordered that with the Tithable persons that Usally Worked under the said Patterson he Clear and keep the same in repair According to Law

19 May 1761, p. 5
David Doak is hereby Appointed Surveyor of the Highway from Tates Mill to Alexander Kellys and It is Ordered that with the Adjacent Tithables he Clear and keep the same in repair According to Law

19 May 1761, p. 6
Ordered that Richard Woods Gent he being first Sworn Veiw the Nearest and best way from Paul Whitleys to the Main Road between the North River and the Poplar Hills and make report thereof to the next Court

19 May 1761, p. 7
Patrick Crawford is Appointed Surveyor of the Highway in the room of John Hinds and It is Ordered that with the Tithable persons that Usally worked Under the said Hinds he Clear and keep the same in repair According to Law

19 May 1761, p. 7
Upon the return of Archibald Alexander and James Trimble who were Appointed to Veiw the Nearest and best way from the North River to Buffalo ford It is Ordered that the Petition for turning the same be rejected

20 May 1761, p. 10
John Campbell is Appointed Surveyor of the Highway in the room of William Patterson and It is Ordered that with the Tithable persons that Usally worked Under the said Patterson he Clear and keep the same in repair According to Law

20 May 1761, p. 10
Ordered that Andrew Hays and Jacob Anderson they being first sworn veiw a road from Andrew Hays Mill on back Creek to Timber ridge Meeting House and that they report the Conveniences or Inconveniences of the same to the next Court

21 May 1761, p. 16
John Thomas and Abraham Bird are hereby Appointed Surveyors of the Highway from John Grattons to the County Line on the south side of the North Mountain and that Daniel Smith Gent lay of their precents and Appoint the Tithables to work on the same they Clear and keep the same in repair According to Law

21 May 1761, p. 16
Michael Finney is hereby Appointed Surveyor of the Highway of the Lower Road from the North river Upwards and that Richard Woods and James Trimble devide their Bounds from the North River to Looneys for the Several Overseers and Appoint the Tithables for each Overseer on both roads

21 May 1761, p. 17
Thomas Boyd is Appointed Surveyor of the Highway in the room of Nathaniel Evans and It is Ordered that with tithable persons that Usally worked Under the said Evans he Clear and keep the same in repair According to Law

21 May 1761, p. 18
Ordered that the Surveyor Thomas Armstrong with his gang work on the road from Jenings Gap to the turn of the Waters near the head of the Calf pasture

21 May 1761, p. 18
Michael Hogshead is Appointed Surveyor of the Highway in the room of Sampson Archer and It is Ordered that with the Tithable persons that Usally worked Under the said Archer he Clear and keep the same in repair According to Law

21 May 1761, p. 18
William Christian is hereby Surveyor of the Highway from Longs Saw Mill to Andrew Scots and It is Ordered that with the Adjacent Tithables he Clear & keep the same in repair According to Law

22 May 1761, p. 31
Ordered that the Overseer with the Usal Tithables turn the road petitioned for by Randal Lockart According to the report of the Veiwers

23 May 1761, p. 48
Thomas Fulton is hereby Appointed Surveyor of the highway in the room of Joseph Gamble and It is Ordered that with the Tithable person that Usally worked Under the said Gamble he Clear and keep the same in repair According to Law

23 May 1761, p. 49
John Williams is Appointed Surveyor of the highway in the room of James Anderson and It is Ordered that with the Tithable persons that Usally worked Under the said Anderson he Clear and keep the same in repair According to Law

18 August 1761, p. 54
John Mathews is hereby Appointed Surveyor of the highway from the North River to Joining the Road near Sharps and It is Ordered that with the Tithables Mentioned in a List by him delivered in Court he Clear and keep the same in repair According to Law

18 August 1761, p. 54
On the Petition of Sundry the Inhabitants for to have a road Cleared from Andrew Leepers to the Mountain Opposite to John Madisons is granted and It is Ordered that Robert Craig and Thomas Fimster be Surveyors and that Samuel Henderson Appoint the Tithables to work on the same and that they Clear and keep the same in repair According to Law

19 August 1761, p. 56
Ordered that Alexander Walker and James Gay they being first sworn veiw the Road from Alexander Walkers to the Painter Gap and make report thereof to the next Court

19 August 1761, p. 56
Ordered that Henry Smith and John Malcome they being first sworn Veiw the Ground from M^r. Harts to the Meeting House on Cooks Creek and make report thereof to the next Court

19 August 1761, p. 58
Ordered that the Road from Abraham Smiths to this Court House be discontinued and that Moses Hall the Surveyor thereof be Exempted from Working thereon

19 August 1761, p. 60
William Preston and Felix Gilbert Gent. being Appointed to Veiw and report the Damage done Israel Christian Gent by reason of the Main road going tho' one of his Lots are of Opinion that he Sustains damage thereby to Five pounds ten Shillings It is Therefore Ordered that the Sherif pay him out of the Money in his hands Five pounds ten Shillings and that the road be Continued

19 August 1761, p. 60
Thomas Harrison is hereby Appointed Surveyor of the Highway from Robert Cravens to the fork of the Road below John Harrisons and It is Ordered that with the Adjacent Tithables he Clear and keep the same in repair According to Law

19 August 1761, p. 61
Ordered that Silas Hart and Daniel Smith Gent Appoint such Tithables as are to Work on the Pensylvania and Brocks Gap Roads

20 August 1761, p. 62
Archibald Alexander Felix Gilbert Andrew Hays John Tate and John Buchanan are hereby Appointed Surveyors of the Highway from Archibald Stuarts to the top of the Mountain near Rockfish Gap and It is Ordered that with the Tithables as the Roads runs from Woods Gap to Jenings Gap and so between the North and South Mountain to the North River they Clear and keep the same in repair According to Law

22 August 1761, p. 75
George Lewis is hereby Appointed Surveyor of the highway from his Own House to Charles Walkers and It is Ordered that with the Adjacent Tithables he Clear and keep the same in repair According to Law

22 August 1761, p. 75
Robert Bratton is hereby Appointed Surveyor of the Highway from Charles Walkers to Robert Gays and It is Ordered that with the Adjacent Tithables he Clear and keep the same in repair According to Law

24 August 1761, p. 100
William Crow and John Stuart are hereby Appointed Surveyors of the Highway from this Court House to William Christians and It is Ordered that with the Adjacent Tithables they Clear and keep the same in repair According to Law

24 August 1761, p. 101
William Armstrong is hereby Appointed Surveyor of the Highway from William Christians to the Saw Mill and It is Ordered that with the Adjacent Tithables he Clear and keep the same in repair According to Law

24 August 1761, p. 102
The King against Robert McClenachan
On a Presentment of the Grand jury for not keeping the road whereof he is Overseer in repair
The Attorney of our Lord the King saith that he will not further prosecute of and Upon the Premises It is therefore Ordered that this Presentment be discontinued

24 August 1761, p. 103
The King against Joseph Gamble
On a Presentment of the Grand jury for not keeping the road whereof he is Overseer in repair
Continued

24 August 1761, p. 103
The King against Daniel Love
On a Presentment of the Grand jury for not keeping the road whereof he is Overseer in repair
The Sumons against the said Defendant being returned not executed on the Motion of his Majestys Attornoy an Alias Sumons is Awarded against him returnable here the next Court

24 August 1761, p. 103
The King against Henry Parkey and Edward Shanklin
On a Presentment of the Grand jury for not keeping the road whereof they are Overseers in repair
The Sumons against the said Defendants being returned not Executed on the Motion of his Majestys Attorney an Alias Sumons is Awarded against them returnable here the next Court

24 August 1761, p. 103
The King against James Lockart and John Wilson
On a Presentment of the Grand jury for not keeping the Road whereof they are Overseers in repair
The Attorney of our Lord the King saith that he will not further prosecute of and upon the Premises It is therefore Ordered that this Presentment be discontinued

24 August 1761, p. 103
John Harrison is hereby Appointed Surveyor of the Highway from Volintine Seviers old place to Daniel Davisons And It is Ordered that with the Tithable Persons within Two Miles thereof he Clear and keep the same in repair According to Law

24 August 1761, p. 103
Daniel Davison is hereby Appointed Surveyor of the Highway from his House to John Stevensons and It is Ordered that with the Tithable Persons within Two Miles Thereof he Clear and keep the same in repair According to Law

24 August 1761, p. 104
Archibald Huston is hereby Appointed Surveyor of the highway from John Stevenson to James Beard and It is Ordered that with the Tithable persons within Two Miles thereof he Clear and keep the same in repair According to Law.

24 August 1761, p. 104
Ordered that James Trimble James Edmiston and William Holdman or any two of them being first Sworn Veiw the Nearest and Convenientest way from Thomas Paxtons by Harts bottom to the fork of Buffelow and make report thereof to the next Court

17 November 1761, p. 107
John Mills and David Looney are hereby Appointed Surveyors of the Highway On the South side of James River from the ferry and ford to Sloans Land above William Harbesons from thence on a Road formerly Opened to Archibald Grymes Land and that George Paris be

Surveyor of the Highway from thence to the Gap of the Mountain and It is Ordered that with the Adjacent Tithables they Clear and keep the same in repair According to Law

17 November 1761, p. 107
George Robinson is hereby Appointed Surveyor of the Highway from Grymes Land to the Great Licks and It is Ordered that with the Adjacent Tithables he Clear and keep the same in repair According to Law

17 November 1761, p. 107
William Hutcheson (Georges Son) is hereby Appointed Surveyor of the Highway from the Tinkling Spring to Mr Craig's and It is Ordered that with the Tithables as shall be Appointed him by Andrew Russell and Alexander Thompson he Clear and keep the same in repair According to Law

18 November 1761, p. 109
John Gilmore is hereby Appointed Surveyor of the Highway in the room of Francis McCown and It is Ordered that with the Tithable persons that Usally Worked Under the said Francis McCown he Clear and keep the same in repair According to Law

19 November 1761, p. 111
Silas Hart is hereby Appointed Surveyor of the Highway lately laid of by John M^{c}kam and Henry Smith from the said Harts to the Meeting House on Cooks Creek and It is Ordered that with the Adjacent Tithables he Clear and keep the same in repair According to Law

20 November 1761, p. 121
Alexander Walker and James Gay are hereby Appointed Surveyors of the Highway from the said Walkers to the painter Gap and It is Ordered that with the Adjacent Tithables they Clear and keep the same in repair According to Law

20 [21] November 1761, p. 145
Thomas Sheilds is Appointed Surveyor of the Highway in the room of John Campbell It is Ordered that with the Tithable persons that Usally worked under the said John Campbell he Clear & keep the same in repair According to Law

20 [21] November 1761, p. 146
Ordered that Robert Poage Sampson Mathews and Elijah McClenachan they being first sworn view the Most Convenient way from this Court to Robert McClenachan and make report thereof to the next Court

20 [21] November 1761, p. 150
Ordered that John Bryan and John Thomas they being first sworn view the Most Convenientest way from Thomas Mill to Thomas Harrisons and make report thereof to the next Court

20 [21] November 1761, p. 150

John Henderson is hereby Appointed Surveyor of the highway in the room of Joseph Gamble and It is Ordered that with the Tithable persons that Usally worked under the said John Henderson he clear and keep the same in repair According to Law

17 February 1762, p. 156
Ordered that John Poage George Anderson Audley Hamilton Charles Lewis and John Baskins they being first sworn Veiw the Most Convenient way from Carrs Shop to this Court House and make report thereof to the next Court

17 February 1762, p. 156
Robert Poage Sampson Mathews and Elijah McClenachan being Appointed to Veiw the Way from this Court House to Robert McClenachans made report that the old Road is the Most Convenient It is therefore Ordered that the said Road lie Established

18 February 1762, p. 162
Ordered that Jacob Nicholas Ludwick Francisco and Jacob Parsinger they being first sworn veiw the most Convenient way from Jone's Ford to John Scots and that Soloman Turpin and Daniel Ponder they being first sworn veiw the Most Convenient way from thence to Thomas Mill and make report thereof to the next Court

22 February 1762, p. 169
John Trimble and Sampson Mathews are hereby Appointed Surveyor of the Highway from this Court House to Trimbles ford and It is Ordered that with the Tithable persons as shall be Appointed them by Felix Gilbert Gent they Clear and keep the same in repair According to Law

23 February 1762, p. 196
Ordered that the Sherif of this County Imploy Workmen to repair the Causeway Over the Run below this Town and bring in his Charge at the Laying of the next County Levy

24 February 1762, p. 203
The King against James Lockart & John Wilson
On a Presentment of the Grand jury for not keeping the Road whereof he is Overseer in repair According to Law
The Attorney of our Lord the King saith that he will not further prosecute of and upon the Premises It is therefore Ordered that this Presentment be discontinued

18 May 1762, p. 208
William McGee is Appointed Surveyor of the Highway in the room of Zebulon Harrison and It is Ordered that with the Tithable persons that Usally worked under the said Zebulon Harrison he Clear and keep the same in repair According to Law

18 May 1762, p. 211
Jacob Goodman is hereby Appointed Surveyor of the Highway in the room of Andrew Vought and It is Ordered that he with the Tithable Persons that Usually worked Under the said Andrew Vought he Clear and keep the same in repair According to Law

18 May 1762, p. 211
William Martin is hereby Appointed Surveyor of the Highway in the room of John Davis and It is Ordered that he with the Tithable Persons that Usally worked Under the said John Davis he Clear and keep the same in repair According to Law

18 May 1762, p. 212
Thomas Conerly is hereby Appointed Surveyor of the Highway in the room of Henry Reaburn and It is Ordered that with the Tithable persons that Usally worked under the said Henry Reaburn he Clear and keep the same in repair According to Law

18 May 1762, p. 212
John Craven is Appointed Surveyor of the Highway in the room of Daniel Love and It is Ordered that with the Tithable Persons that Usally worked under the said Daniel Love he Clear and keep the same in repair According to Law

18 May 1762, p. 212
Mathew Black is Appointed Surveyor of the Highway in the room of Daniel Love and It is Ordered that with the Tithable persons that Usally worked under the said Daniel Love he Clear and keep the same in repair According to Law

18 May 1762, p. 212
William Beard is Appointed Surveyor of the Highway in the room of Andrew Davidson and It is Ordered that with the Tithable persons that Usally worked under the said Andrew Davidson he Clear and keep the same in repair According to Law

18 May 1762, p. 214
James Lasley is Appointed Surveyor of the Highway in the room of Archibald Hamilton and It is Ordered that with the Tithable persons that Usally worked Under the said Archibald Hamilton he Clear and keep the same in repair According to Law

18 May 1762, p. 214
Samuel McCutcheon is Appointed Surveyor of the Highway in the room of William McCutcheon and It is Ordered that with the Tithable Persons that Usally worked Under the said William McCutcheon he Clear and keep the same in repair According to Law

18 May 1762, p. 214
Thomas Berry is Appointed Surveyor of the Highway in the room of John Handley and It is Ordered that with the Tithable Persons that Usally Worked Under the said John Handley he Clear and keep the same in repair According to Law

18 May 1762, p. 214
Samuel Huston is Appointed Surveyor of the Highway in the room of John Fulton and It is Ordered that with the Tithable Persons that Usally worked Under the said John Fulton he Clear and keep the same in repair According to Law

19 May 1762, p. 215
John Hopkins and John Herdman are hereby Appointed Surveyors of the Highway from Ephraim Loves to James Waits and It is Ordered that with the Adjacent Tithables they Clear and keep the same in repair According to Law

19 May 1762, p. 216
Ordered that James Hamilton and Thomas Turk they being first sworn View the Most Convenient Way from the Stone Meeting House to Samuel Davidsons ford and make report thereof to the next Court

19 May 1762, p. 216
John Bryan is hereby Appointed Surveyor of the Highway from Daniel Smith to Rubin Harrisons Meadow and It is Ordered that with the Adjacent Tithables he Clear and keep the same in repair According to Law

19 May 1762, p. 216
Mathais Rader is Appointed Surveyor of the Highway in the room of Alexander Painter and It is Ordered that with the Tithables persons that Usally Worked Under the said Alexander Painter he Clear and keep the same in repair According to Law

19 May 1762, p. 218
James Davis is Appointed Surveyor of the Highway in the room of Patrick Young and It is Ordered that with the Tithable persons that Usally worked under the said Patrick Young he Clear and keep the same in repair According to Law

19 May 1762, p. 218
John Vance is Appointed Surveyor of the Highway in the room of Alexander Richey and It is Ordered that with the Tithable Persons that Usally worked Under the said Alexander Richey he Clear and keep the same in repair According to Law

21 May 1762, p. 229
Ordered that Ralph Laverty James M^ckoy and John Dickenson or any two of them being first Sworn Veiw the Most Convenient way from Doves to Captain John Dickenson and make report thereof to the next Court

21 May 1762, p. 229
Ralph Laverty and James Gay are hereby Appointed Surveyors of the Highway from the Panther Gap to Captain John Dickenson and It is Ordered that with the Tithables as shall be Appointed them by John Dickenson they Clear and keep the same in repair According to Law

22 May 1762, p. 234
Ordered that Stephen Rentfro James Rowland Bryan McDonall or any two of e'm being first sworn Veiw and Mark the Nearest and best way from Looneys ferry to the first ford of Catawbo and make report thereof the next Court

22 May 1762, p. 234
Robert McGomery and Joseph Robinson j^r. are hereby Appointed Surveyors of the Highway from Grahams Clearing to Catawbo and It is Ordered that with the Tithables as shall be Appointed them by David Cloyd and George Robinson they Clear and keep the same in repair According to Law

22 May 1762, p. 234
Ordered that Robert Neilly and George Pearis they being first sworn Veiw and Mark the Nearest and best way from Bedford Gap to the old road near John Neillys and make report thereof to the next Court

22 May 1762, p. 234
Jacob Nicholas is hereby Appointed Surveyor of the Highway from Jones ford to John Scots and It is Ordered that with the Tithable persons within Three Miles of the said road he Clear and keep the same in repair According to Law

22 May 1762, p. 235
Michael Warring is hereby Appointed Surveyor of the Highway from Shipays to Thomas Mill and It is Ordered that with the Tithable persons within Three Miles of the said road he Clear and keep the same in repair According to Law

22 May 1762, p. 235
James Neilly and William Graham are hereby Surveyors of the highway from Grahams Clearing by the Great Lick to Alexander Boyds and It is Ordered that with the Adjacent Tithables he Clear and keep the same in repair According to Law

22 May 1762, p. 236
Ordered that Felix Gilbert Gent Appoint and devide the Tithables in the Town of Staunton to work on the several roads Leading to the said Town

22 May 1762, p. 236
Ordered that William Lewis and Charles Lewis they being first sworn Veiw the Nearest and best way from this Court House to Christy's Creek and make report thereof to the next Court

22 May 1762, p. 236
Ordered that James Lockart and Patrick Martin Appoint the Tithables to work on the Road from Buchanans to Youngs Mill

24 May 1762, p. 250
John Poage Gent George Anderson Audley Hamilton and John Baskin who were Appointed to Veiw a Road from Carrs Shop to this Court House made their return that the said Road in their Opinion Ought to be Continued from the said Carrs Shop to Baskins ford thence up a Ridge between Daniel Denistons and John Poages from thence into the road from Robert Poages to this Town It is Ordered that the said Road be Established and John Baskin be Surveyor thereof and that with the Tithables as shall be Appointed him by John Poage he Clear and keep the same in repair According to Law

24 May 1762, p. 253
Ordered that Sampson Mathews and William Tees they being first sworn Veiw and Mark the Nearest and best way from Rockfish Gap to the old Road above Archibald Stewarts and make thereof to the next Court

17 August 1762, p. 281
George Poage and James Hamilton being Appointed to Veiw a Way from Davidsons ford to the stone Meeting House mad report that the most Convenient way is from the said Davidsons to Edward Rutledges and from thence to John Allisons ford near his feild and from thence by John Kerrs to the stone Meting House It is therefore Ordered that the said Road be Established and that Thomas Turk be Surveyor thereof from Davidsons ford to John Allisons ford and John Cockrance from thence to the Stone Meeting House and It is Ordered that with the Adjacent Tithables he Clear and keep the same in repair According to Law

17 August 1762, p. 282
William Bowyer is hereby Appointed Surveyor of the Highway from the Stone House to Bedford Line and It is Ordered that with the Tithables as shall be Appointed him by William Grymes and James Neilly he Clear and keep the same in repair According to Law

17 August 1762, p. 283
Sampson Mathews and William Tees being Appointed to Veiw a Road from Rockfish Gap to the old Road near Archibald Stewarts made report that the said Road Ought to Pass by Alexander

Stewarts It is therefore Ordered that the said Road be Established and that William Tees and Alexander Stewart be Surveyors thereof and that with the Tithables as shall be Appointed them by Thomas Stewart and Alexander Thompson they Clear and keep the same in repair According to Law

17 August 1762, p. 283
Ordered that Robert Armstrong and Alexander Crawford they being first sworn veiw and mark the Most Convenient way from the Drybranch Gap of the North Mountain to Archers Mill and make report thereof to the next Court

18 August 1762, p. 285
Henry Pickle is hereby Surveyor of the Highway from Henry Stones to Silas Hart and that It is Ordered that with the Tithable persons from Nicholas Havener's up the South fork of Potowmack he Clear and keep the same in repair According to Law

20 August 1762, p. 296
On the motion of Peter Hog. John Harvie Gent is Appointed to Apply to the Court of Amherst for Persons to Veiw a way from the New Gap of Rockfish to the line of Albemarle and so to the Road that leads over the Secretary ford

20 August 1762, p. 296
Ordered that Michael Waring and Solomon Turpin they being first sworn Veiw the Most Convenient way from the said Waring to John Scots and It is Ordered that they be Surveyors thereof and that with the Adjacent Tithables they Clear and keep the same in repair According to Law

25 August 1762, p. 355
Ordered that the Overseer of the road from Jening's Gap work on the Road to the turn of the Calf Pasture Waters

19 November 1762, p. 392
Robert McClenachan is hereby Appointed Surveyor of the Highway from Staunton to Buchanans Mill Creek on the Road Leading to William Longs Mill And It is Ordered that with the Tithables in Staunton and the Adjacent Tithables he Clear and keep the same in repair According to Law

22 November 1762, p. 441
Ordered that John Thompson Henry Ferguson and Hugh Mills or any two of them being first sworn Veiw the Nearest and best way from the Stone House to Bedford Line and make report thereof to the next Court

23 November 1762, p. 448
Ordered that the Road be turned from the Corner of Grimes Land by Captain Breckenridges House leaving his little feild on the Left hand and thence into the main Road and that John Neilly

with the tithables that worked under John Robinson the former Overseer he Clear and keep the same in repair According to Law

15 February 1763, p. 450
Ordered that James Lockart Joseph Martin and Thomas Brown they being first sworn Veiw the best and Most Convenient Way from this Court House to the North Mountain Meeting House and make report thereof to the next Court

15 February 1763, p. 451
Ordered that Thomas Gardner and Nathan Gilliland they being first sworn Veiw the Most Conveint way from the Gry [Guy?] branch Gap to Buchanans Mill and Make report thereof to the next Court

15 February 1763, p. 452
On the Petition of John Patrick and Others seting forth that they are not only obliged to work on the Mountain at Woods Gap but on Several other Roads It is Ordered that they be Exempted from working on any Roads and they only keep the Pass over Woods Gap in repair

17 February 1763, p. 471
The Persons Appointed to Veiw a Road from Staunton to the North Mountain Meeting House having made their report It is therefore Ordered that the Road Petitioned for be Established and that James Lockart and Nathan Gilliland they being first sworn mark the same and Israel Christian and Thomas Fulton be Surveyors thereof and that they with the Tithables that Usually worked on the old Road Clear and keep the same in repair According to Law

18 February 1763, p. 477
Ordered that Andrew Russell with Two Tithables William Palmer William Martin Alexander McDonald William Thompson Alexander Thompson John Thompson George Caldwell and his two Sons William Henderson and John Wallace work under the Several Overseers of the Road from Christians Creek to Rock Fish Gap

19 February 1763, p. 486
Ordered that Edward Garwin and James McCown they being first sworn Veiw a way from the Stone House to James M^cafees or James McCowns on Catapo and make report thereof to next Court

Book VIII, 1763-1764

21 February 1763, p. 23
On the Motion of Sampson Mathews for leave to turn the Road Through his Plantation It is Ordered that William Lewis and Robert Poage they being first sworn veiw the Ground and make report thereof to the next Court

21 February 1763, p. 23
Ordered that Audley Hamilton and William Tees they being first sworn veiw and mark the most Convenient way from Mathews Plantation to the New Road that Leads to Rockfish Gap and make report thereof to the next Court

19 April 1763, p. 24
David Cuningham and James Callison are Appointed Surveyors of the Highway in the room of John Wilson and James Lockart and It is Ordered that with that with the Tithable persons that Usally worked under the said John Wilson and James Lockart they Clear and keep the same in repair According to Law

19 April 1763, p. 24
Joseph Waughul and John Ramsey are Appointed Surveyors of the Highway in the room of Archibald Armstrong and It is Ordered that with the Tithable persons that Usally worked under the s^d Archibald Armstrong they Clear and keep the same in repair According to Law

19 April 1763, p. 25
John Davidson is Appointed Surveyor of the Highway in the room of Robert Brown and It is Ordered that with the Tithable persons that Usally worked under the said Robert Brown he Clear and keep the same in repair According to Law

21 April 1763, p. 40
On the Motion of Robert McClanachan leave is given him to Cut a Road from his House to the Road that leads to the Tinkling Spring at his own Cost provided it doth not go tho' the Lands of David Stewart

22 April 1763, p. 45
Ordered that a Road be Cleared from Walkers Place to the Warm Springs and that Thomas Feemster be Surveyor of the Road from Walkers place to Charles Lewis's and John Lewis be Surveyor of the Road from Charles Lewis to the Warm Springs and that the Inhabitants of the Cow Pasture the Inhabitants on back Creek in the Calfpasture and the Inhabitants from the Falling Springs upwards on Jacksons River and the Inhabitants from Hance Harpers downwards in the Bull Pasture they Clear and keep the same in repair According to Law

23 April 1763, p. 49
On the Petition of Sundry the Inhabitants seting forth that the Road turned by Israel Christian round his Meadow fence is Inconvenient It is Ordered that Robert McClenachan Sampson Mathews Thomas Poage and Daniel Deniston or any three of them being first sworn do Veiw and make report whether the old or New Road is Most Convenient to the next Court

23 April 1763, p. 51
William Grymes James Neilly and William Robinson be Overseers of the Road from Grymes Clearing to the head of the Run above Madisons Plantation and that John Craig be Overseer of the Road from thence to New River on the Lands of John Buchanan Gent and Alexander and

William Sayers be Overseers from thence to Fort Chiswell and that William Preston Gent devide their precints and appoint the Tithables as far as Fort Lewis and William Thompson from thence to Fort Chiswell and It is Ordered that the Several Overseers with the Tithables as shall be Appointed them by they keep the several Roads in Repair According to Law

23 April 1763, p. 51
On the Motion of James McDowell Praying to have the Road turned round his feild that runs tho' his Plantation It is Ordered that James Trimble and William Paxton they being first sworn veiw the same and make report thereof to the next Court

26 April 1763, p. 93
Robert Poage and William Lewis having been Appointed to Veiw a way thro' the Plantation of Sampson Mathews made their report that the Road by him petitioned for was the most Convenient It is therefore Ordered that the same be Established he Clearing the same at his own Expence

26 April 1763, p. 101
William Preston Gent is hereby Appointed Surveyor of the Highway from Grymes Clearing to Catapo and It is Ordered that with the Adjacent Tithables he Clear and keep the same in repair According to Law

26 April 1763, p. 102
Ordered that David Ball Thomas Poage and William Tees they being first sworn Veiw and Mark the Most Convenient way from Mathews's Plantation to the New Road that leads to Rockfish Gap and make report thereof to the next Court

21 June 1763, p. 107
Ordered that John Bowyer and Archibald Alexander Gent the Tithables to work on the Road whereof Moses McClure and David Dryden are Overseers

22 June 1763, p. 115
The Person Appointed to Veiw the Road round James McDowells Plantation having returned that the road Petitioned for is Convenient It is Ordered that it be Established

22 June 1763, p. 115
On the Petition of Robert Scot and Others for a Road from the South River above Joseph Hanahs Over Coles Foard to Mathew Thompsons It is Ordered that Joseph Hanah Robert Shankland and Robert Frazier or any two of them being first sworn do Veiw the same and make report thereof to the next Court

22 June 1763, p. 116
Ordered that Felix Gilbert and William Crow devide and Appoint the Tithable Inhabitants of Staunton to Work on the Several Roads that Lead to the s^d Town

22 June 1763, p. 116
Ordered that Joseph Lapsley and Robert Erwin Appoint the Tithables to work on Carrs Creek Roads and the Main Roads that Leads from Poages to Paxtons

22 June 1763, p. 116
James McDowell is Appointed Surveyor of the Highway in the room of James Greenlee and It is Ordered that with the Tithable person that Usally worked under the said James Greenlee he Clear and Clear and keep the same in repair According to Law

22 June 1763, p. 117
William Ward is hereby Appointed Surveyor of the Highway from Evans Run to David Moore and It is Ordered that with the Adjacent Tithables he Clear and keep the same in repair According to Law

22 June 1763, p. 119
Thomas Berry is Appointed Surveyor of the Highway in the room of John Davis and It is Ordered that with the Tithable persons that Ussally worked under the said John Davis he Clear and keep the same in repair According to Law

23 June 1763, p. 128
The Persons Appointed to Veiw the Road turned by Israel Christian Gent round his Meadow fence made report that the same is more Convenient than the old Road It is therefore ordered that the same be Established

24 June 1763, p. 133
On the Motion of John Robinson It is Ordered that William Robinson he being first sworn veiw a Road from English's to Madisons Plantation and make report thereof to the next Court

25 June 1763, p. 205
Ordered that Patrick Shirkey and George Patterson they being first sworn Veiw the Nearest and best way from the ford of Catabo to John M^{c}farrons and make report thereof to the next Court

25 June 1763, p. 206
William Preston and John Armstrong are hereby Appointed Surveyors of the Highway from Bryan McDaniels to James M^{c}afees and It is Ordered that with the Adjacent Tithables they Clear and keep the same in repair According to Law

23 September 1763, p. 251
John Madison is hereby Appointed Surveyor of the Highway from Givens Mill to the forks of the River and It is Ordered that with the Tithable persons from Givens Mill on the Middle River and from Christian Clemons's to the said Madisons on the South River he Clear and keep the same in Repair According to Law

23 September 1763, p. 251
John Madison is hereby Appointed Surveyor of the Highway from the Forks of the South River to William Fraziers and It is Ordered that with the Tithable persons within Three Miles on Each side of the Main River he Clear and keep the same in repair According to Law

23 September 1763, p. 251
Frances Kirtley Gent is hereby Appointed Surveyor of the Highway from William Fraziers to the Mountain at Swift Run Gap and It is Ordered that with the Tithables that Usually worked under John Early and Henry Long together with the Convenient Tithables he Clear and keep the same in repair According to Law

23 September 1763, p. 252
Ordered that Robert Belshire John Richey and John McMahon they being first sworn do Veiw and Mark the Most Convenient Way from William Beards to the Stone Meeting House and make report thereof the next Court

26 September 1763, p. 321
David Bell Thomas Poage and William Tees the persons Appointed to Veiw a Road from Mathewses Plantation to the new Road that Leads Over Rockfish Gap and having reported that the same is Convenient It is Ordered that the said Road be Established and that George Mathews be Surveyor thereof and that with the Tithable persons as shall be Appointed him by John Poage Gent he Clear and keep the Same in repair According to Law

26 September 1763, p. 322-3
[Grand Jury Presentments]

The King against Joseph Gamble
On a Presentment of the Grand Jury for not keeping the Road whereof he is Overseer in repair
The Defendant being Summoned and not Appearing It is Considered that for the said Offence he make his fine with our Lord the King by the Paiment of fifteen Shillings and that he pay the Cost of this Prosecution & May be taken &
Cost   Tobacco

* * *

The King against The Surveyors of the Highway from the Stone Meeting House to Thomas Connerleys
On a Presentment of the Grand Jury
The Sherif having returned that the Surveyors was not found in his [blank]   It is Ordered that this Presentment be discontinued

26 September 1763, p. 324
George Skillern is hereby Appointed Surveyor of the Highway On the Left of CoL° Lewis's from Staunton to John Grymes and It is Ordered that with the Adjacent Tithables he Clear and keep the same in repair According to Law

9 November 1763, p. 326
[Trial of slave, Tom, convicted of murdering his master John Harrison and sentenced to hang; ordered that after his death:]his head be Severed from his body and Affixed on a Pole on the Top of the Hill near the Road that Leads from this Court House to Edward Tars

16 November 1763, p. 332
John Huston is hereby Appointed Surveyor of the Highway from Timber Ridge to Providence Meeting House and It is Ordered that with the Tithable persons as shall be Appointed him by Samuel McDowell Gent he Clear and keep the same in repair according to Law

16 November 1763, p. 332
On the Motion of John Buchanan It is Ordered that the Tithables within Three Miles of Each side of the Road whereof he is Overseer work on the same

16 November 1763, p. 333
John Summers is hereby Appointed Surveyor of the Highway from Joseph Long Mill to the Great Road near Thompsons and It is Ordered that with the Tithable persons within four Miles of the said Road he Clear and keep the same in repair According to Law

17 November 1763, p. 342
William Beard is hereby Appointed Surveyor of the highway from John Stevensons to the Top of the Ridge by the Feild of John Harrison Junr. deceased and that Alexander Buchanan be Surveyor of the Highway from the Top of the Ridge to the Line of this County and It is Ordered that with the Tithable persons within four Miles on Each side of the said Road they Clear and keep the same in repair According to Law

17 November 1763, p. 342
Ordered that John Smith William Grymes James Nealey and Israel Christian or any three of them being first sworn Veiw the Roads that Leads from Vauses Over the New River on the Lands of John Buchanan and Likewise by Inglesses Ferry to the Lead Mines and make report of the Conveniences and Inconveniennces of Each Road to the next Court

17 November 1763, p. 342
Ordered that Jacob Archenbright and Jacob Nicholas they being first sworn Veiw the Most Convenient way from Capt Kirtleys to the Top of the Ridge at Swift Run Pass and make report thereof to the next Court

17 November 1763, p. 342 [Note: both sides of page numbered 342]
George Mathews is hereby Appointed Surveyor of the highway from his Mill to Francis Alexanders and that Francis Alexander by Surveyor of the Highway from his House to the new Road that Leads to Rockfish Gap and It is Ordered that with the Tithable persons as shall be Appointed them by John Poage and George Skilleren they Clear and keep the same in repair According to Law

20 March 1764, p. 387
James Hughes is Appointed Surveyor of the Highways from this Court House to Robert Poages in the room of Robert Poage and It is Ordered that with the Tithable persons that Usally worked under the said Robert Poage he Clear and keep the same in repair According to Law

20 March 1764, p. 389
On the Petition of Sundry of the Inhabitants for a road from John Kings Mill on Naked Creek to John Kings Mill on the Middle River and from thence to Staunton It is Ordered that John King and James Young they being first sworn veiw the road Petitioned for and make report thereof to the next Court

20 March 1764, p. 391
Ordered that the Sherif Imploy a Workman to build a bridge Over the Run near Robert Poages and to make a Sufficient Causeway and bring in his Charge at the Laying of the next County Levy

20 March 1764, p. 391
Ordered that James Lockart John Tate and David Doage they being first sworn veiw the most Convenient way from the North Mountain Meeting House to John Tates Mill and make report thereof to the next Court

20 March 1764, p. 392
On the Petition of Jacob Nicholas praying that he may not be Compelled to Clear the Road whereof he is Overseer According to Law is rejected

20 March 1764, p. 392
Robert Shanklin is hereby Appointed Surveyor of the Highway from Shanklins Run to Stoney Run and It is Ordered that with the Adjacent Tithables he Clear and keep the same in repair According to Law

21 March 1764, p. 394
Ordered that John Anderson John Francis and James Bell they being first sworn Veiw the most Convenient way for turning the Road that Leads from Jenning's Gap to Swift Run at that part at the Long Glade and make report thereof to the next Court

21 March 1764, p. 394
John Thomas is hereby Appointed Surveyor of the Highway from his Mill to Thomas Brians and It is Ordered that with the Adjacent Tithables he clear and keep the same in repair According to Law

21 March 1764, p. 395
John Bryan is hereby Appointed Surveyor of the Highway from Smiths Bridge to the forks of the Road near John Harrisons and It is Ordered that with the Adjacent Tithables he Clear and keep the same in repair According to Law

21 March 1764, p. 395
Ordered that Daniel Lyle William Ramsey and James Simpson they being first sworn Veiw the most Convenient way from the Ford of the North branch of James River to James Stinsons on Buffelow and make report thereof to the next Court

21 March 1764, p. 395
Ordered that James Trimble James Magavock John Gilmore and John Summers lay of the several districts and Appoint the Tithables to work on the Several Roads in the forks of James River

21 March 1764, p. 395
Ordered that Daniel Price John Burk and Thomas Burk they being first sworn Veiw the most Convenient way from Lord Fairfax's Line to the Road that Leads over Swift Run Pass and make report thereof to the next Court

22 March 1764, p. 406
William Preston Gent is Appointed Surveyor of the Highway from the Widow McDaniels to William Harbisons and It is Ordered that with the Adjacent Tithables he Clear and keep the same in repair According to Law

22 March 1764, p. 406
James Rowland is Appointed Surveyor of the highway from Stephen Rentfroes to John Millers Mill and It is Ordered that with the Adjacent Tithables he Clear and keep the same in repair According to Law

22 March 1764, p. 406
Bryan McDaniel is Appointed Surveyor of the Highway from Fort William to the Market Road and It is Ordered that with the Adjacent Tithables he Clear and keep the same in repair According to Law

22 March 1764, p. 406
James Neelley is Appointed Surveyor of the Highway from Fort Lewis to the Great Lick and It is Ordered that with the Adjacent Tithables he Clear and keep the same in repair According to Law

22 March 1764, p. 406
David Bryans is Appointed Surveyor of the Highway from the Great Lick to the County Line and It is Ordered that with the Adjacent Tithables he Clear and keep the same in repair According to Law

22 March 1764, p. 411
Ordered that that the former persons who were Appointed to Veiw the Road now Established from Mathewses Mill to Tees's Gap they being first sworn Veiw the Nearest and best way tho' the Plantation of Francis Alexander and make report thereof to the next Court

23 March 1764, p. 413
William Ward is Appointed Surveyor of the Highway from his House to Bordens Patent Line and It is Ordered that with the Adjacent Tithables he Clear and keep the same in repair According to Law

24 March 1764, p. 474
On the Petition of William Crow It is Ordered that Sampson Mathews Robert McClenachan and James Huston they being first sworn Veiw the Ground from the Rocks below this Town to Elizabeth Moores and make report thereof to the next Court

15 May 1764, p. 494
The Persons Appointed to Veiw a Way from Lord Fairfax's Line to the Road that leads Over the Swift Run Pass having made their report It is Ordered that the said Road be Established and that Michael Coger and Daniel Price be Surveyors thereof and that with the Convenient Tithables he Clear and keep the same in repair According to Law

19 June 1764, p. 494
Robert Scot is Appointed Surveyor of the Highway formerly Veiwed from Joseph Hannahs to Mathew Thompsons and It is Ordered that with the Tithable persons within Two Miles on Each side of the said Road he Clear and keep the same in repair According to Law

19 June 1764, p. 495
Ordered that George Skillern and John Finley Imploy a Workman to build a bridge and Causeway Over the Long Meadow where the Road Crosses it that Leads from Francis Alexanders to William Tees's and bring in his Charge at the Laying of the next County Levy

19 June 1764, p. 495
James Lockart and John Tate being Appointed to Veiw the Most Convenient way from the North Mountain Meeting House to John Tates Mill returned that the Road formerly Cleared is the Most Convenient It is Ordered that the said Road be Established and that James Lockart David Doage

be Surveyors thereof and It is Ordered that with the Tithable persons within Two Miles on Each side of the said Road they Clear and keep the same in repair According to Law

19 June 1764, p. 496
James Gilmore is Appointed Surveyor of the Highway from Poage Run to Robert Renix's Plantation and It is Ordered that with the Adjacent Tithables he Clear and keep the same in repair According to Law

19 June 1764, p. 497
Ordered that Samuel Steel John Tate and David Doage they being first sworn Veiw the Nearest and best way from Beverly Mannor line to the Forks of the Road near Hugh Fultons and make report thereof to the next Court

20 June 1764, p. 505
John Philips is Appointed Surveyor of the Highway in the room of Alexander Buchanan and It is Ordered that with the Tithable persons that Usually worked under the said Alexander Buchanan he Clear and keep the same in repair According to Law

21 June 1764, p. 512
Ordered that John Poage and George Mathews Imploy Workmen to make a Causeway in the Lane near his House and Cut Down the side of a Hill near it and bridge a Hollow near the same and bring in their Charge at the Laying of the next County Levy

Book IX, 1764-1765

22 June 1764, p. 56
Ordered that William Lewis and Andrew Russell they being first sworn Veiw the Most Convenient way from this Town to Christians Creek and make report thereof to the next Court

22 June 1764, p. 60-3
[Grand Jury Presentments]

The King against John Baskins
On a Presentment of the Grand jury for not keeping the road whereof he is Overseer in repair According to Law
The Defendant being Summoned and not Appearing It is Considered that for the said Offence he make his fine with our Lord the King by the Paiment of fifteen Shillings and that he pay the costs of this Prosecution and may be taken &c
Cost   Tobacco

The King against John Madison
On a Presentment of the Grand jury for not keeping the Road whereof he is Overseer in repair According to Law

The Defendant being Summoned and not Appearing It is Considered that for the said Offence he make his fine with our Lord the King by the Paiment of fifteen Shillings and that he pay the Cost of this Prosecution and may be taken &c
Cost   Tobacco

The King against Felix Gilbert Gent
On a Presentment of the Grand jury for not keeping the Road whereof he is Overseer in repair According to Law
The Defendant being Summoned and not Appearing It is Considered that for the said Offence he make his fine with our Lord the King by the Paiment of fifteen Shillings and that he pay the Cost of this Prosecution and may be taken &c
Cost   Tobacco

The King against Henry Murray
On a Presentment of the Grand jury for not keeping the Road whereof he is Overseer in repair According to Law
The Attorney of our Lord the King saith that he will not further prosecute of and upon the Premises It is therefore Ordered that this Presentment be dismised

The King against Patrick Crawford
On a Presentment of the Grand jury for not keeping the Road whereof he is Overseer in repair According to Law
The Defendant being Summoned and not Appearing It is Considered that for the said Offence he make his fine with our Lord the King by the Paiment of fifteen Shillings and that he pay the Cost of this Prosecution and may be taken &c
Cost   Tobacco

* * *

The King against Samuel Wallace
On a Presentment of the Grand jury for not keeping the Road whereof he is Overseer in repair According to Law
The Attorney of our Lord the King saith that he will not further prosecute of and upon the Premises It is therefore Ordered that this Presentment be dismised

The King against William Beard
On a Presentment of the Grand jury for not keeeping the Road whereof he is Overseer in repair According to Law
The Summons against the said William Beard being returned not Executed on the Motion of his Majestys Att° an Alias Summons is Awarded against him returnable here the next Court

* * *

The King against Jacob Nicholas
On a Presentment of the Grand jury for not keeping the Road whereof he is Overseer in repair According to Law
The Defendant being Summoned and not Appearing It is Considered that for the said Offence he make his fine with our Lord the King by the Paiment of fifteen Shillings and that he pay the Cost of this Prosecution and may be taken &c

Cost   Tobacco

* * *

The King against James Givens
On a Presentment of the Grand jury for not keeping his Mill Dam and Bridge in Repair According to Law
The Defendant being Summoned and not Appearing It is Considered that for the said Offence he make his fine with our Lord the King by the Paiment of Twenty Shillings and that he pay the Cost of this Prosecution and may be taken &c
Cost   Tobacco

The King against William Campbell and David Doage
On a Presentment of the Grand jury for not keeeping the Road whereof he is Overseer in repair According to Law
The Attorney of our Lord the King saith that he will not Further Prosecute of and upon the premises It is therefore Ordered that this ~~suit~~ presentment be discontinued

* * *

The King against The Surveyor of the Highway from Jenings's Gap to the Long Glade
On a Presentment of the Grand jury
The Sherif having returned that the Surveyors was not found in his Bailiwick on the Motion of the Attorney of our Lord the King It is Ordered that this Presentment be discontinued

22 June 1764, p. 64
John Brown is Appointed Surveyor of the Highway in the room of Samuel Wallace and It is Ordered that with the Tithable persons that Usually worked under the said Samuel Wallace he Clear and keep the same in repair According to Law

22 June 1764, p. 64
John Henderson is Appointed Surveyor of the Highway from Staunton to Christians Creek in the room of Felix Gilbert and It is Ordered that with the Tithable persons that Usually worked under the said Felix Gilbert he Clear and keep the same in repair According to Law

17 June [probably 17 July] 1764, p. 65
Thomas Lewis Gent is Appointed Surveyor of the Highway from the Mouth of the South River to James Fraziers and It is Ordered that with the Tithables of Gabriel Jones Peachey Ridgway Gilmore John Madison Jacob Miller and his Own he Clear and keep the same in repair According to Law and It is further Ordered that the Tithables of the said Madison be Exempted from Working on any Other Road

17 June [probably 17 July] 1764, p. 65
Ordered that William Robinson and William Inglis Imploy Workmen to make a Causeway a Cross Madisons Meadow at Vauses in the Most Convenient Place which they are hereby Ordered to Veiw and Appoint and bring in their Charge at the Laying of the next County Levy

21 August 1764, p. 66
On the Motion of Bryce Russell leave is granted him to Clear a Road from his House to the Main Road near John Reaburns

22 August 1764, p. 71
William Paxton is Appointed Surveyor of the Highway from Buffelow Creek to the ford of the North River and It is Ordered that with the Adjacent Tithables he Clear and keep the same in repair According to Law

22 August 1764, p. 75
Ordered that William Lewis Robert McClenachan and Alexander Thompson they being first sworn Veiw the Most Convenient way from Staunton to Christian Creek and make report thereof to the next Court

22 August 1764, p. 78
Nathaniel Evans is Appointed Surveyor of the Highway from Buffelow Creek to Edward Sharps and It is Ordered that with the Adjacent Tithables he Clear and keep the same in repair According to Law

23 August 1764, p. 85
The Persons Appointed to Veiw a Road from the North Branch of James River to Buffelow reported that by turning the Road by One Abraham Browns it would be nearer and better but for reasons Appearing to the Court It is Ordered that the Road from John Paxtons be Established

23 August 1764, p. 87
Ordered that William Carwin and John McNeil they being first sworn Veiw the best way from the Stone House to Fort Lewis and make report of the Conveniances and Inconveniances to the next Court

24 August 1764, p. 91
Ordered that John Poage Gent Appoint the Tithables to work on the Road from this Town to Robert Poages

24 August 1764, p. 99
Ordered that Zachariah Smith John Hutchison Junr. and George Mathews they being first sworn Veiw the Ground between Christians Creek and Tees's and make a report wether or not a better way can be had than the road now Established to the next Court

20 November 1764, p. 156

Peachy Ridgeway Gilmore is Appointed Surveyor of the Highway in the room of Jacob Nicholas and It is Ordered that with the Tithables that Usually worked under the said Jacob Nicholas he Clear and keep the same in repair According to Law

20 November 1764, p. 159-60
[County Levy]

To John Poage for Makeing a Causeway 2880

* * *

To Joseph Gamwell and William Patton for Cuting down the side of a Hill and makeing a Causeway and bridgeing a hollow 8160

* * *

To the Trustees for Opening a Road Over Rockfish Gap £ 100 24000

To William Robinson for makeing a Causeway at Vauses Plantation £ 50 12000

21 November 1764, p. 161
Ordered that Samuel Lyle and Daniel Lyle they being first sworn Veiw the Nearest and best Way from William Davis's to Timber Ridge Meeting House and make a report of the Conveniances and Inconveniances to the next Court

21 November 1764, p. 162
The Persons Appointed to Veiw the Most Convenient way from Staunton to Christians Creek made their report the Old Road to be the best It is therefore Ordered that the same be Established

21 November 1764, p. 162
James Wait is Appointed Surveyor of the Highway in the room of Mathew Black and It is Ordered that with the Tithable persons that Usually worked under the said Matthew Black he Clear and keep the same in repair According to Law

22 November 1764, p. 171
William Ward is Appointed Surveyor of the Highway from where the Road Crosses the run above his House to Bordens Patent line and It is Ordered that with the Adjacent Tithables he Clear and keep the same in repair According to Law

22 November 1764, p. 172
David Dryden is hereby Appointed Surveyor of the Highway from the North branch of James River to Edward Tarrs old Shop on said Road and It is Ordered that with the Adjacent Tithables he Clear and keep the same in repair According to Law

23 November 1764, p. 211
Robert Reed is hereby Appointed Surveyor of the Highway in the room of John Henderson and It is Ordered that with the Tithable persons that Usually worked under the said John Henderson he Clear and keep the same in repair According to Law

23 November 1764, p. 211
Ordered that Felix Gilbert and Daniel Smith Gent^n Appoint the Tithables to work on the Roads between the said Smiths and Gilberts

24 November 1764, p. 218
William Preston and George Poage are Appointed Surveyors of the Highway from Ramseys Cabbin to John Crawfords and It is Ordered that with the Adjacent Tithables he Clear and keep the same in repair According to Law

24 November 1764, p. 218
Thomas Moore is Appointed Surveyor of the Highway in the room of Alexander Buchanan and It is Ordered that with the Tithable persons that Usually worked under the said Alexander Buchanan he Clear and keep the same in repair According to Law

24 November 1764, p. 230
Robert Breckinridge Gent is Appointed Surveyor of the Highway from Crosby's feild to Bedford Line and It is Ordered that with the Adjacent Tithables he Clear and keep the same in repair According to Law

24 November 1764, p. 230
Ordered that the Sherif pay Andrew Lewis and Peter Hog Gent who are Appointed Trustees for agreeing with the Undertakers for Clearing a Road Over Rockfish Gap One Hundred Pounds Levied for that Use and that the said Trustees be Impowered to Contract for a further sum of Money not exceeding fifty Pounds for Purposes aforesaid

24 November 1764, p. 230
Ordered that Fifty Pounds levied for William Robinson remain in the Sherifs hands until the Causeway he has made at Vauses be by the Persons Impowered to let the same taken of his hands

19 March 1765, p. 234
Ordered that Daniel Lyle and Samuel Lyle devide the Precints and Appoint the Tithables to Work Under the Overseers of the Road from the North River to John Bowyers

19 March 1765, p. 235
William Carvin and John McNeil the persons Appointed to Veiw the most Convenient way from the Stone House to Fort Lewis made their report It is Ordered that the said Road be Established and that Peter Evans be Surveyor thereof and that with the Convenient Tithables he Clear and keep the same in repair According to Law

19 March 1765, p. 235
Robert Wiley is Appointed Surveyor of the Highway in the room of James Gamble and It is Ordered that with the Adjacent Tithables he Clear and keep the same in repair According to Law

19 March 1765, p. 235
On the Motion of Samuel Lyle leave is granted him to Clear a Road at his Own Expence from his House thro' William Taylors Land to the County Road as it shall be laid of by Isaac Taylor:

19 March 1765, p. 235
Hugh Hays is Appointed Surveyor of the Highway from John Montgomeries to Robert Steels and It is Ordered that with the Adjacent Tithables he Clear and keep the same in repair According to Law

20 March 1765, p. 236
Ordered that Silas Hart Gent Appoint the Tithables to work on the Road from the Duck Ponds to Alexander Blairs

20 March 1765, p. 237
Ordered that John Maxwell John Poage and James Simpson they being first sworn Veiw the Nearest and best Way from John Poages to Audley Pauls and make report of the Conveniences and Inconveniences thereof to the next Court

20 March 1765, p. 239
Ordered that the Tithables in a list Mentioned work on the Road from the Tinkling Spring to Rockfish Gap

20 March 1765, p. 244
John Davis is Appointed Surveyor of the Highway in the room of Ludwick Waggoner And It is Ordered that with the Tithable persons that Usually worked under the said Ludwick Waggoner he Clear and keep the same in repair According to Law

20 March 1765, p. 244
George Spears is Appointed Surveyor of the Highway in the room of John Thomas from Thomas Bryans to Thomas's Mill and It is Ordered that with the Tithable persons that Usually Worked under the said John Thomas he Clear and keep the same in repair According to Law

21 March 1765, p. 247
On the Petition of Thomas Barnes James Mckeachy and Others to prevent the Establishing a road lately Veiwed from the Stone House to Fort Lewis is rejected

21 March 1765, p. 247
Ordered that James Bruister John Stevenson and Joseph English they being first sworn do Veiw the Nearest and best Way from John Stevenson to Thomas Rutherfords and make a report of the Conveniances and Inconveniances to the next Court

21 March 1765, p. 248
Ordered that Robert McClenachan David Stewart and John Buchanan or any two of them being first sworn Veiw the Nearest and best Way from Staunton to the Glebe and make a report of the Conveniances and Inconveniances thereof to the next Court

21 March 1765, p. 251
Ordered that William Robinson James Neelley and William Bryans they being first sworn Veiw the Ground from Vauses by Inglis's ferry to Peak Creek and report the Conveniances or Inconveniances to the next Court

21 March 1765, p. 251
Ordered that the Persons formerly Appointed to Veiw the Way from Vauses to Fort Chiswell be Summoned to Shew Cause why they have not Compiled with the said Order

21 March 1765, p. 251
Ordered that Nicholas Harplore Paul Shaver and Jacob Wees they being first sworn Veiw the Ground on North Mill Creek from the Upper Tract to the County line below Jacob Peterson and make a report of the Conveniances and Inconveniances thereof to the next Court

22 March 1765, p. 253
Daniel Smith Felix Gilbert and Francis Kirtley Gent are Appointed to devide the Tithables to work on the several Roads below the North River

22 March 1765, p. 253
Ordered that John Frazier John Richey and Robert McMahon they being first sworn Veiw the most Conveniant Way from Patrick Fraziers to the Stone Meeting House and make a report of the Conveniances and Inconveniances thereof to the next Court

22 March 1765, p. 254
Ordered that John Lyle and Daniel Lyle they being first sworn Veiw the Ground from Samuel McDowells by Matthew Lyles to James M^ckees and make a report of the Conveniances and Inconveniances thereof to the next Court

23 March 1765, p. 255
James Bruister is Appointed Surveyor of the Highway from John Stevensors to William Beards and It is Ordered that with the Adjacent Tithables he Clear and keep the same in repair According to Law

23 March 1765, p. 258

John Bowyer Gent is Appointed Surveyor of the Highway in from the the North Branch of James River to Buffalo and It is Ordered that with the Adjacent Tithables he Clear and keep the same in repair According to Law

23 March 1765, p. 258
James Simpson is Appointed Surveyor of the Highway from Buffelo to James Gilmores and It is Ordered that with the Adjacent Tithables he Clear and keep the same in repair According to Law

23 March 1765, p. 258
James Gilmore is Appointed Surveyor of the Highway from his House to Renix's old Place and It is Ordered that with the Adjacent Tithables he Clear and keep the same in repair According to Law

25 March 1765, p. 312
Ordered that William Crow and Sampson Mathews Appoint the Tithables in the Town of Staunton to work on the Roads leading thereto

26 March 1765, p. 333
Ordered that John Trimble Thomas Fulton and Hugh Allen Veiw the Bridge Built and Causeway made by John Brown and report whether or not the same is done in a Workmanlike Manner if so to receive the same of the said Brown and also Value the same and make a report of the Value thereof to the next Court

21 May 1765, p. 342
William McCutcheon (Merchant) is Appointed Overseer of the Road from Charles Campbells Long Meadow branch by Joseph Kanady's to Beverley Mannor Line and It is Ordered that with the Adjacent Tithables he Clear and keep the same in repair According to Law

21 May 1765, p. 343
John Buchanan Gent is Appointed Surveyor of the Highway from Renix's to Jame River at his House and It is Ordered that with the Convenient Tithables he Clear and keep the same in repair According to Law

21 May 1765, p. 343
Henry Black is Appointed Surveyor of the Highway from Abraham Smiths to the foot of the Mountain at Briery Branch Gap and It is Ordered that with the Convenient Tithables he Clear and keep the same in repair According to Law

21 May 1765, p. 344
John Lyle and Daniel Lyle the Persons Appointed to Veiw the Ground from Samuel McDowells by Matthew Lyles to James M^{c}kees made report that the Road by Matthew Lyles is best It is therefore Ordered that the same be Established

21 May 1765, p. 344

James Montier is Appointed Surveyor of the Highway in the room of James Lockart and It is Ordered that with the Tithable persons that usually worked under the said James Lockart he Clear and Keep the same in repair According to Law

21 May 1765, p. 344
William Reah is Appointed Overseer of the Road in the room of James Buchanan deceased and It is Ordered that with the Tithables that Usually Worked under the said James Buchanan he Clear and keep the same in repair According to Law

22 May 1765, p. 345
Mark Swatley is Appointed Surveyor of the Highway from Michael Props To Conrod Goods and It is Ordered that with the Adjacent Tithables he Clear and keep the same in repair According to Law

22 May 1765, p. 345
John Trimble Thomas Fulton and Hugh Allen the Persons Appointed to Veiw And Value the Causeway and Bridge built by John Brown made their report that the same is of the Value of Forty one Pounds Eleven Shillings and three pence

22 May 1765, p. 347
James Bruister is Appointed Surveyor of the Highway of the Way lately Veiwed from John Stevensons to Thomas Rutherfords and It is Ordered that with the Convenient Tithables he Clear and keep the same in repair According to Law

22 May 1765, p. 347
John Gratton and Francis Green are Appointed Surveyors of the Highway from Edward Shanklins to Widow Thomases Old Place near Brocks Gap and It is Ordered Archibald Hopkins and Daniel Smith Gent. devide their districts and Appoint the Tithables and that the said Gratton and Green with the Tithables as shall be Appointed them they Clear and keep their districts in repair According to Law

22 May 1765, p. 347
William Mathews is Appointed Surveyor of the Highway from Mossey Creek to William Anderson and It is Ordered that with the Convenient Tithables he Clear and keep the same in repair According to Law

22 May 1765, p. 347
David Trimble is Appointed Surveyor of the Highway from William Andersons to the Town of Staunton and It is Ordered that with the Convenient Tithables he Clear and keep the same in repair According to Law

22 May 1765, p. 352
John Coulton is Appointed Surveyor of the Highway from Stewarts Run to Murrays Place in the room of James Alexander and It is Ordered that with the Tithables that Usually Worked under the said James Alexander he Clear and keep the same in repair According to Law

22 May 1765, p. 353
Samuel Love is Appointed Surveyor of the Highway from CoL° Pattons Mill Place to the Tinkling Spring Meeting House in the room of Robert Cuningham and It is Ordered that with the Tithables that Usually Worked under the said Robert Cuningham he Clear and keep the same in repair According to Law

22 May 1765, p. 353
The Persons Appointed to Veiw the Nearest and best Way from Staunton to the Glebe having not proceeded According to Law It is Ordered that John Christian John Poage James Bell John Brownlee and James Sayers or any three of them being first sworn Veiw the said Road and make a report thereof to the next Court.

22 May 1765, p. 354
Joseph Rutherford Sen[r]. is Appointed Surveyor of the Highway in the room of Solomon Turpin and It is Ordered that with the Tithables that Usually Worked under the said Soloman Turpin he Clear and keep the same in repair According to Law

22 May 1765, p. 354
Samuel Monsey is Appointed Surveyor of the Highway from the forks of the Road below John Harrisons to the Upper End of Reubin Harrisons Meadow and It is Ordered that with the Convenient Tithables he clear and keep the same in repair According to Law

22 May 1765, p. 354
Reubin Harrison is Appointed Surveyor of the Highway from the Upper End of his Meadow to Daniel Smiths Bridge and It is Ordered that with the Conveniant Tithables he Clear and keep the same in repair According to Law

22 May 1765, p. 354
Ordered that John Christian Gent Appoint the Tithables to work on the Roads whereof James Bell and John Coulter are Surveyors

22 May 1765, p. 355
William Bryan and Israel Christian Gent are Appointed Surveyors of the Highway from the Stone House to Fort Lewis in the room of Peter Evans and It is Ordered that with the Tithables that shall be Appointed them by Robert Breckenridge Gent they clear and keep the same in repair According to Law

23 May 1765, p. 355
Isaac Taylor is Appointed Surveyor of the Highway from Fort Lewis to Vauses and It is Ordered that with the Tithables as shall be Appointed him by Israel Christian Gent he Clear and keep the same in repair According to Law

23 May 1765, p. 356
William Curruthers is Appointed Surveyor of the Highway in the room of Moses McClure and It is Ordered that with the Tithables that Usually Worked under the said Moses McClure he Clear and keep the same in repair According to Law

23 May 1765, p. 356
William Kennady is Appointed Surveyor of the Highway in the room of James McCrorey and It is Ordered that with the Tithables that Usually Worked under the said James McCrorey he Clear and keep the same in repair According to Law

23 May 1765, p. 356
Ordered that Andrew Lockridge and Thomas Hugart they being first sworn Veiw the Most Convenient Way from Samuel Hodges to Jennings's Gap and make a report of the Conveniances and Inconveniances thereof to the next Court

24 May 1765, p. 363
Ordered that David Robinson be Appointed in the room of William Robinson deceased and that he being first sworn together James Neelley and William Bryans who were formerly Appointed for that purpose do Veiw the Ground from Vauses by Ingleses ferry to Peak Creek and report the Conveniances or Inconveniances thereof to the next Court

24 May 1765, p. 370
Loftus Pullen is Appointed Surveyor of the Highway in the room of Richard Bodkin and It is Ordered that with the Tithable Persons that Usually Worked under the said Richard Bodkin he Clear and keep the same in repair According to Law

24 May 1765, p. 373
Ordered that William Lewis Robert McClenachan William Fleming and William Bowyer or any two of them Imploy Workmen to repair the Bridge below this Town near William Duncans

25 May 1765, p. 430-2
[Grand Jury Presentments]

The King against James Hughes
On a Presentment of the Grand jury for not keeping the Road whereof he is Overseer in repair The Attorney of our Lord the King saith that he will not further Prosecute of and upon the Premises It is therefore Ordered that this Presentment be dismised

* * *

The King against Alexander Stewart

On a Presentment of the Grand jury for not keeping the Road whereof he is Overseer in repair According to Law
The Defendant being Summoned and not Appearing It is Considered that for the said Offence he make his fine with our Lord the King by the Paiment of fifteen Shillings and that he pay the Costs of this Prosecution and may be taken &c
Costs   Tobacco

The King against William Tees
On a Presentment of the Grand jury for not keeping the Road whereof he is Overseer in repair According to Law
The Defendant being Summoned and not Appearing It is Considered that for the said Offence he make his fine with our Lord the King by the Paiment of fifteen Shillings and that he pay the Cost of this Prosecution and May be taken &c
Costs   Tobacco

The King against John Baskins
On a Presentment of the Grand jury for not keeping the Road whereof he is Overseer in repair According to Law
The Defendant being Summoned and not Appearing It is Considered that for the said Offence he make his fine with our Lord the King by the Paiment of fifteen Shillings and that he pay the Cost of this Prosecution and May be taken & c
Costs   Tobacco

* * *

The King against William Beard
On a Presentment of the Grand jury for not keeping the Road whereof he is Overseer in repair According to Law
The Defendant being Summoned and not Appearing It is Considered that for the said Offence he make his fine with our Lord the King by the Paiment of fifteen Shillings And that he pay the Costs of this Prosecution and may be taken & c
Cost   Tobacco @15/

* * *

The King against John Henderson
On a Presentment of the Grand jury for not keeping the Road whereof he is Overseer in repair According to Law
The Attorney of our Lord the King saith that he will not further prosecute of and upon the Premises It is therefore Ordered this Presentment be dismised

* * *

The King against William Beard
On a Presentment of the Grand jury for not keeping the Road whereof he is Overseer in repair According to Law
The Sherif having returned on the Summons against the said Defendant not Executed on the Motion of his Majestys Attorney an Alias Summons is Awarded against him returnable here the next Court

20 August 1765, p. 437
Thomas Frame is Appointed Surveyor of the Highway in the room of John Cochran deceased and It is Ordered that with the Tithables persons that Usually worked Under the said John Cochrane he Clear and keep the same in repair According to Law

20 August 1765, p. 439
Ordered that the Sherif of this County pay Major John Brown Forty Six Pounds Eleven Shillings and three pence for Building the Bridge and Causeway near his House

20 August 1765, p. 441
On the Motion of John McCreary It is Ordered that he be for the future Exempted from Working on the Roads

20 August 1765, p. 443
Robert Bratton and Thomas Hugart are Appointed Surveyors of the Highway from the Widow Gays to Samuel Hodges and It is Ordered that with the Adjacent Tithables they Clear and keep the same in repair According to Law

20 August 1765, p. 444
Ordered that David Robinson and James Robinson they being first Sworn Veiw the Hill whereon Fort Lewis Stands from the East to the West End and make a report of the Conveniances and Inconveniances of turning the Road Round the said Hill to the next Court

21 August 1765, p. 445
On the Motion of David Nelson It is Ordered that he be for the future Exempted from Working on the Roads

21 August 1765, p. 445
Robert Armstong is Appointed Surveyor of the Highway from the turns of the Waters in Jenning's Gap in the room of Henry Murray and It is Ordered that with the Tithables that Usually Worked under the said Henry Murray he Clear and keep the same in repair According to Law

21 August 1765, p. 451
James Robertson is Appointed Surveyor of the Highway from Vauses to Fort Lewis and It is Ordered that with the Tithable Persons that shall be Appointed him by William Preston Gent he Clear and keep the same in repair According to Law and It is further Ordered that such Tithables as shall be Appointed to Work on the Warwick Road as low as the Great Lick be Exempted from Working on any Other Road

21 August 1765, p. 451
Henry Cartmill and Samuel Gibson are Appointed Surveyors of a Bridle Way from the Widow Longs to Henry Kirkhams and It is Ordered that with the Tithables and their Perceints that shall

be Appointed them by John Buchanan and Richard Woods Gent (the Tithables not Exceeding Twenty) they Clear and keep Each their Perceint in repair According to Law

21 August 1765, p. 451
Henry Hoffman is Appointed Surveyor of the Highway in the room of Charles Wilson and It is Ordered that with the Tithables that Usually Worked Under the said Charles Wilson he Clear and keep the same in repair According to Law

22 August 1765, p. 453
Ordered that Michael Hogshead Robert Trimble George Moffett James Bell and Benjamin Harrison or any three of them being first sworn Veiw the Most Conveniant Way from Jennings's Gap to Barnat Man's and make a report of the Conveniances and Inconveniances thereof to the next Court

23 August 1765, p. 468
Ordered that John Risk William McCutcheon and Thomas Berry or any two of them they being first sworn Veiw the Most Conveniant Way from John Risks Mill to Providence Meeting House and make a report of the Conveniances and Inconveniances thereof to the next Court

23 August 1765, p. 469
George Mathews having Informed this Court that there is in his hands Seven Pounds which is the ballance of the Money Lodged in his hands for Building a Bridge on the Road that leads to Rockfish Gap from his House It is therefore Ordered that he pay the same to Francis Alexander in part of his Account against this County for Building a Bridge Over the Long Meadow Run

23 August 1765, p. 469
James Alexander is Appointed Surveyor of the Highway from Staunton by John Hutchisons to the Old Road Leading from Mathew's Mill to John Ramseys in the Room of George Skillern Gent and It is Ordered that with the Tithables within two Miles thereof he Clear and keep the same in repair According to Law

24 August 1765, p. 529
Ordered that William Lewis Gent Appoint the Tithables to work on the Road from Staunton to Christians Creek whereof John Henderson is Surveyor

24 August 1765, p. 529
James Gay is Appointed Surveyor of the Highway from the Painter Gap to Captain Dickinsons and It is Ordered that with the Adjacent Tithables he Clear and keep the same in repair According to Law

24 August 1765, p. 529
John Christian James Bell John Poage and John Brownlee four of the Persons Appointed to Veiw the Nearest and best way from Staunton to the Glebe made a report that a Way leading by the

Widow Youngs to be the Nearest Notwithstanding which for reasons Appearing to the Court It is Ordered that the Road leading by Major Browns be Established

24 August 1765, p. 529
On the Motion of Samuel Cowden leave to Cut a Road from the Glebe to the Town of Staunton at his Own Expence is Granted him

Book X, 1765-1767

15 October 1765, p. 5
William Lourey is Appointed Surveyor of the Highway from the Wilderness Bridge to Beverley Mannor Line in the room of John Wardlaw and It is Ordered that with the Tithables that Usually Worked under the said John Wardlaw he Clear and keep the same in repair According to Law

15 October 1765, p. 6
John Risk and Thomas Berry are Appointed Surveyors of the Highway from Risks Mill to Providence Meeting House and It Ordered that with the Tithables that shall be Appointed them by James Ewing they Clear and keep the same in repair According to Law

16 October 1765, p. 10
Ordered that John Madison Thomas Lewis Francis Kirtley and Felix Gilbert Gentlemen or any three of them agree with some person or persons for the Clearing Mending and Repairing the Road that goes Over Swift Run Gap and make a report of their Proceedings to this Court

16 October 1765, p. 14
Alexander Walker is Appointed Surveyor of the Highway from Hayses Gap to Captain Cultons and It is Ordered that with the Adjacent Tithables he Clear and keep the same in repair According to Law

18 October 1765, p. 24
Ordered that John Looney and Absolom Looney they being first sworn do Mark a Bridle Way from Buchanans Ferry to the Top of the Blew Ridge Joinning Bedford Line and make a report of the Conveniances and Inconveniances thereof to the next Court

18 October 1765, p. 24
Ordered that James Cathey and David Bryans they being first sworn veiw and Mark a Road from the Great Lick to Bedford Line to the Road that Leads to Captain Rentfroes and make report of the Conveniences and Inconveniances Thereof to the next Court

18 October 1765, p. 24
Ordered that George Poage and John Crawford they being first sworn Veiw and Mark a Road from the Mouth of Craigs Creek to Fort Young and make report of the Conveniances and Inconveniances thereof to the next Court

19 October 1765, p. 33
Ordered that William Black John Hicklen and John Estill they being first sworn Veiw a Road from Estills Mill in the Bull Pasture to George Lewises in the Cow Pasture and make a report of the Conveniances and Inconveniances thereof to the next Court

19 October 1765, p. 39
Charles Lewis is Appointed Surveyor of the Highway in the room of Thomas Feemster and It is Ordered that with the Tithables that Usually Worked under the said Thomas Feemster he Clear and keep the same in repair According to Law

19 October 1765, p. 39
John McClanachan is Appointed Surveyor of the Highway in the room of John Lewis and It is Ordered that with the Tithables that Usually Worked Under the said John Lewis he Clear and keep the same in repair According to Law

19 October 1765, p. 40
William Black is Appointed Surveyor of the Highway from George Lewis's to Robert Halls and It is Ordered that with the Tithables that shall be Appointed him by Charles Lewis he Clear and keep the same in repair According to Law

19 October 1765, p. 40
John Estill is Appointed Surveyor of the Highway from the turn of the Waters of the Cow Pasture River to Robert Halls and It is Ordered that with the Adjacent Tithables he Clear and keep the same in repair According to Law

19 October 1765, p. 40
John Greenlee is Appointed Surveyor of the Highway from John Mathews Junior deceased to the Top of the Mountain at Sinclars Gap and It is Ordered that with the Tithables that shall be Appointed him by James Greenlee he Clear and keep the same in repair According to Law

19 October 1765, p. 40
Thomas McFarron is Appointed Surveyor of the Highway from Catawbo to the Pedler Foard on James River in room of William Preston Gent and It is Ordered that with the Tithables that shall be Appointed him by the said William Preston he Clear and keep the same in repair According to Law

19 October 1765, p. 44
William Long and Robert Christian are Appointed Surveyors of the Highway from William Longs to Caldwells Creek and It is Ordered that with the Adjacent Tithable persons they Clear and keep the same in repair According to Law

19 October 1765, p. 45
Benjamin Hawkins G^t. is Appointed Surveyor of the Highway from James Montgomerys to the foot of the Mountain towards Craigs Creek and It is Ordered that with the Adjacent Tithables he Clear and keep the same in repair According to Law

19 October 1765, p. 45
George Poage is Appointed Surveyor of the Highway from the Pedler Foard on James River up the said River Eight Miles and It is Ordered that with the Adjacent Tithables he Clear and keep the same in repair According to Law

19 October 1765, p. 45
William Gallespy and James Beard are Appointed Surveyors of the Highway from Eight Miles above the Pedlar Foard on James River to Captain Dickinsons and It is Ordered that with the Tithables that shall be appointed them by the said Dickinson they Clear and keep the same in repair According to Law

19 October 1765, p. 45
John Potts is Appointed Surveyor of the Highway from the Mouth of Johns Creek to the top of the Gap next Montgomerys and It is Ordered that with the Adjacent Tithables he Clear and keep the same in repair According to Law

19 October 1765, p. 47
John Burnsides is Appointed Surveyor of the Highway from the Stone Meeting House to Shanklins Place and It is Ordered that with the Adjacent Tithables he Clear and keep the same in repair According to Law

21 October 1765, p. 89
John Bowen is Appointed Surveyor of the Highway from Colonel Buchanans on the North Side of James River to the Pedlar Foard and It is Ordered that with the Tithables that shall be Appointed him by John Buchanan Gent he Clear and keep the same in repair According to Law

22 October 1765, p. 142
James Cloyd is Appointed Surveyor of the Highway from David Cloyds Juniors to the ~~Plantation~~ of John Bowyer G^t Plantation on James River and It is Ordered that with the Tithables that shall be Appointed him by John Bowyer he clear and keep the same in repair According to Law

22 October 1765, p. 143-4
[County Levy]

To Samuel Cowdon for Makeing a bridge and Causeway Thirty Pounds   7200

* * *

For Clearing the Road Over Rockfish Gap Fifty Pounds Nine Pounds Eighteen Shillings and three pence to be paid to Israel Christian Gent by him advanced and the remainder to David Kinkead   12000

* * *

For Clearing of Swift Run Gap Seventy Pounds   16000

22 October 1765, p. 145
Ordered that Gabriel Jones Gent pay the Money in his Hands the Property of this County to the Persons Appointed to agree with Workmen to Clear Swift Run Gap

22 October 1765, p. 145
Andrew McClure is Appointed Surveyor of the Highway in the room of George Skillern And It is Ordered that with the Tithables that Usually worked under the said George Skillern he Clear and keep the same in repair According to Law

22 October 1765, p. 147
David Robinson and James Robertson the Persons Appointed to Veiw the Hill whereon Fort Lewis Stands from the East to the West End whether or not the Road may be Conveniently turned made a report that the same Road may be Conveniently turned as the Ground is more even Through it will be Longer by about Twenty Poles It is therefore Ordered that the said Road be Established and that the Overseer of the former Road Clear and keep the same in repair According to Law

20 May 1766, p. 151
John Ramsey is Appointed Surveyor of the Highway in the room of Andrew McClure and It is Ordered that with the Tithable Persons that Usually worked under the said Andrew McClure he Clear and keep the same in repair According to Law

20 May 1766, p. 151
James Patterson is Appointed Surveyor of the Highway in the room of Francis Erwin and It is Ordered that with the Tithable persons that Usually worked under the said Francis Erwin he Clear and keep the same in repair According to Law

20 May 1766, p. 153
James McCampbell is Appointed Surveyor of the Highway in the room of William Davis and It is Ordered that with the Tithables that Usually worked under the said William Davis he clear and keep the same in repair According to Law

20 May 1766, p. 154
James Cloyd is Appointed Surveyor of the Highway from the Lower End of John Bowyers Plantation on James River by Seder Bridge to Mathews's Road and It is Ordered that with the Tithables of Christopher Vinyard John Hall William Hall John Logan James Skidmore George Wilson John Berry John Jones James McClure Matthew Hair John Bowyer George Skillern and Conrod Wall he Clear and keep the same in repair According to Law

20 May 1766, p. 155
Thomas Wilson is Appointed Surveyor of the Highway in the room of William Ward and It is Ordered that with the Tithable persons that Usually worked under the said William Ward he Clear and keep the same in repair According to Law

21 May 1766, p. 190
William Kinkead is Appointed Surveyor of the highway from the Widow Gays to the Deviding of the Waters in Jenningses Gap and It is Ordered that with the Tithables that shall be Appointed him by Andrew Hamilton he Clear and keep the same in repair According to Law

21 May 1766, p. 190
John McPheetters and William McPheetters Junior are Appointed Surveyors of the Highway in the room of John Trimble and Robert Campbell and It is Ordered that with the Tithable persons Usually Worked under the said John Trimble and Robert Campbell they Clear and keep the same in repair According to Law

21 May 1766, p. 192
John Lyle Junior is Appointed Surveyor of the Highway from the Second branch between M^r. Browns and John Houston to the Great Road by the Widow Lyles and It is Ordered that with the Tithable persons that shall be Appointed him by Samuel McDowell Gent he Clear and keep the same in repair According to Law

21 May 1766, p. 193
John Findley is Appointed Surveyor of the Highway from the Middle River to Staunton in the room of John Trimble deceased and It is Ordered that with the Tithables that Usually Worked under the said John Trimble he Clear and keep the same in repair According to Law

21 May 1766, p. 193
Alexander Gibson is Appointed Surveyor of the Highway in the room of John Henderson and It is Ordered that with the Tithables that Usually Worked under the said John Henderson he Clear and keep the same in repair According to Law

21 May 1766, p. 193
Ordered that Daniel Smith Joseph Dickton William Gragg and James McGill they being first Sworn Veiw the Most Convenient Way from Bernerd Manns to Edward Erwins Juniors and make report of the Conveniances and Inconveniances thereof to the next Court

21 May 1766, p. 193
Archibald Hamilton is Appointed Surveyor of the Highway from Kerrs Shop to the Main Road near Poages and It is Ordered that with the Adjacent Tithables he Clear and keep the same in repair According to Law

19 August 1766, p. 198
William Mathews is Appointed Surveyor of the Highway in the room of Nathaniel Evans and It is Ordered that with the Tithable persons that Usally Worked under the said Nathaniel Evans he Clear and keep the same in repair According to Law

19 August 1766, p. 200
William Fulton is Appointed Surveyor of the Highway in the room of Thomas Berry and It is Ordered that with the Tithable Persons that Usually worked under the said Thomas Berry he Clear and keep the same in repair According to Law

19 August 1766, p. 200
Samuel Lyle is Appointed Surveyor of the Highway in the room of David Dryden and It is that with the Tithable persons that Usually worked under the said David Dryden he Clear and keep the same in repair According to Law

19 August 1766, p. 201
Gawin Leeper is Appointed Surveyor of the Highway in the room of John Burnsides and It is Ordered that with the Tithable Persons that Usually worked under the said John Burnsides he Clear and keep the same in repair According to Law

20 August 1766, p. 205
Ordered that John Dickinson Gent and William Hugart take an Account of the Tithables and Devide the Road from within Eight Miles of the Pedler Foard to Captain Dickinsons whereof William Galespy and James Beard are Surveyors and make report thereof to the next Court

20 August 1766, p. 205
Alexander Walker is Appointed Surveyor of the Highway from James Beards to the Stone Meeting House and It is Ordered that with the Adjacent Tithables he Clear and keep the same in repair According to Law

20 August 1766, p. 206
John Hannah is Appointed Surveyor of the Highway in the room of John Summers and It is Ordered that with the Tithable persons that Usually worked under the said John Summers he Clear and keep the same in repair According to Law

21 August 1766, p. 217
Ordered that David Robinson Robert Breckenridge and John Buchanan Gentlemen View the Causeway made by William Robinson deceased at Vauses and make a report thereof to the next Court whether the same is done According to Contract

21 August 1766, p. 217
The Persons formerly Appointed to Veiw a Way from Vauses Over Inglis's Ferry to Peak Creek having made their report on Consideration of which the Court are of Opinion that it is not made According to Law and that the same be rejected

21 August 1766, p. 218
Ordered that the Persons Mentioned in a List delivered in by John Finley work on the Road whereof he is Surveyor

21 August 1766, p. 218
William Black John Hicklen and John Estill the Persons Appointed to Veiw a Road from Estills Mill in the Bull Pasture to George Lewises in the Cow Pasture made their report that a good Way may be had It is therefore Ordered that the said Road be Established and that John Estill be Surveyor thereof and that with the Convenient Tithables he Clear and keep the same in repair According to Law

21 August 1766, p. 225
Ordered that the Sheriff pay Sixty six Pounds thirteen Shillings and four pence the Money levied for Clearing Swift Run Gap to Felix Gilbert and that he also pay him Three Pounds Seven Shillings and Eight pence out of the Depositum in his Hands

22 August 1766, p. 229
Ordered that Silas Hart James Hogshead John Hogshead and John Hopkins or any three of them being first sworn Veiw the old Road together with the new Road lately Marked that goes from Jennings Gap to Edward Erwin Junior and make a report which is most Convenient to the next Court

22 August 1766, p. 233
John Gum is Appointed Surveyor of the Highway in the room of Alexander Herron and It is Ordered that with the Tithable persons that Usually Worked under the said Alexander Herron he Clear and keep the same in repair According to Law

22 August 1766, p. 239
Ordered that John Davis Jacob Nicholas Benjamin Harrison and Daniel Love they being first sworn Veiw the New Marked Way from Edward Erwins to the Market Road that Leads to Swift Run and that they likewise Veiw the Old Road that leads from Jenningses Gap to Swift Run Gap and make report of the Conveniances there and Inconveniances of Each Road to the next Court

25 August 1766, p. 289

Andrew Lewis Gent is Appointed Surveyor of the Highway in the room of John Henderson deceased and It is Ordered that with the Tithable persons that Usually worked under the said John Henderson he Clear and keep the same in repair According to Law

25 August 1766, p. 290
Ordered that John Bowyer Gent Joseph Lapsley Peter Wallace and John Moore or any three of them being first Sworn Veiw the Most Convenient Way from the North Branch of James River round the Poplar Hills to Buffalo Creek and make a report of the Conveniances and Inconveniances thereof to the next Court

25 August 1766, p. 292
Ordered that John Bowen and John Crawford they being first sworn Veiw the Nighest and best Way from CoL° Buchanans to the Pedlar Foard on James River on the North side and make a report of the Conveniences and Inconveniances thereof to the next Court

16 September 1766, p. 330
Silas Hart Gent John Hogshead and James Hogshead three of the Persons Appointed to Veiw the Old Road together with the new Road lately Marked that Leads from Jenningses Gap to Edward Erwin Juniors and to make a report which is the Most Convenient made their report that the New Marked way is much the Leavelest Clearest of Stones and the Straightest It is therefore Ordered that the said Road be Established and George Moffett Gent be Surveyor of the said Road from Jenningss Gap to William Flemings and Edward Erwin be Surveyor from the said Flemings to his House and that all the Tithables between the North and Middle River from Jennings Gap as far down as John Young and from the said Youngs to Joseph Reaburns and from thence to Edward Erwins and from thence to Margaret Ramseys work On the said Road and that Silas Hart and James McGill devide the Tithables between the Overseers and that they then keep the said Roads in Repair According to Law

16 September 1766, p. 331
Daniel Love Jacob Nicholas John Davis and Benjamin Harrison the Persons Appointed to Veiw the New Marked Way from Edward Erwins to the Markett Road that Leads to Swift Run and likewise to Veiw the Old Road that Leads from Jenninges Gap to Swift Run and make a report of the Conveniances and Inconveniances of Each Road to this Court made their report that they had Veiwed the Old Market Road from Edward Erwins to the fork below Jacob Nicholases and look on the Cheif Part of the same to be Very bad and hilly The new Road Mentioned in above Order not being all Marked as we could find out we have take all Possible Care to Veiw the Ground for the Most Convenient Way and found only One Inconvenience Viz^t from John Fowlers Still House to the East End of Shanklins (about a Mile) it leaves the Straitest Course considerably Nevertheless we reckon it may be made the best Way the Ground will Afford between Edward Erwins and said Forks below said Nicholas's to begin at said Edward Erwins leaving William Currys on the right Hand and Edward Erwins Junr. on the Left thence down the old Road to said Fowlers Still House thence passing thro Edward Shanklins Lane the most direct Course to David Nellsons thence to Join with the South Branch Road at Houstons Meadow and thence to aforesaid Forks below Jacob Nicholas's It is therefore Ordered that the said Road be Established

and that James Magill be Surveyor of the said Road from Erwins to Edward Shanklins and that John Cravens be Surveyor of the said Road from Edward Shanklins to the forks Below Nicholases and that all the Tithables within four Miles on Each side the said Road work thereon and that the said Surveyors with the s^d Tithables as they shall be devided to them by Felix Gilbert Gent and Edward Shanklin clear and keep their Roads in repair According to Law

18 November 1766, p. 335
John Lyle Senior is Appointed Surveyor of the Highway in the room of Daniel Lyle and It is Ordered that with the Tithable persons that Usually worked under the s^d. Daniel Lyle he Clear and keep the same in repair According to Law

18 November 1766, p. 337
John Young is Appointed Surveyor of the Highway in the room of John Vance and It is Ordered that with the Tithable persons that Usually worked under the said John Vance he clear and keep the same in repair According to Law

18 November 1766, p. 338
Ordered that David Robinson James Robinson John Buchanan and William Thompson or any three of them Veiw the Road and Causeway made by William Robinson deceased at Vauses whether the same is done According to Contract and the Value thereof to this Court

18 November 1766, p. 338
John Buchanan Gent David Robinson and William Thompson three of the Persons Appointed to Veiw the Road and Causeway made by William Robinson deceased at Vauses whether the same is done According to Contract and the Value thereof made there report that the same is of the Value of Forty Pounds which sum It is Ordered that the Late Sheriff pay unto Margaret Robinson his Widow Out of the Money levied for that Purpose

19 November 1766, p. 339
Ordered that Robert Dunlap William Elliott and Alexander Hamilton they being first sworn Veiw the Most Convenient way from William Elliots to McCutcheons Mill and from thence thro Buffaloe Gap and make a report of the Conveniances and Inconveniances thereof to the next Court

19 November 1766, p. 340
Ordered that Joseph Carpenter Senior and William Whooley are Appointed Surveyors of the Highway in the Fort Defiance to Handleys Mill and It is Ordered that with Peter Wright Soloman Carpentor Thomas Carpentor Nathaniel Carpentor John Umpris Thomas Carpenter Zophar Carpenter Ezekel Johnson Edward McMullin John McMullin James Williams Joseph Soper John Frelen William Whooley Christian Whooley Peter Whooley William McMurry Thomas Wright Robert Galespy Patrick Carrigan and Joseph Carpenter Junior and their Tithables they Clear and keep the same in repair According to Law

19 November 1766, p. 340

Hugh Crockett is Appointed Surveyor of the Highway from the Head of Meadow Creek to the Causeway at Vauses and It is Ordered that with the Adjacent Tithables he Clear & keep the same in repair According to Law

19 November 1766, p. 341
Matthew Patton Gent and Mark Swatley are Appointed Surveyors of the Highway from Michael Props to the head of the South fork of Potomack and It is Ordered that with the Adjacent Tithables he Clear and keep the same in repair According to Law

21 November 1766, p. 356
Benjamin Harrison is Appointed Surveyor of the Highway in the room of John Gratton and It is Ordered that with the Tithable persons that usually worked under the said John Gratton he Clear and keep the same in repair According to Law

21 November 1766, p. 356
John Stevenson is Appointed Surveyor of the Highway from Kings Mill or Naked Creek to Patrick Hamiltons and Robert Young from thence by John Poages Mill to the Staunton Road and It is Ordered that with the Tithables that shall be Appointed them by John Poage and George Moffett Gent they Clear and keep the same in repair According to Law

21 November 1766, p. 357
Ordered that Abraham Bird John Bryan and Reuben Harrison they being first sworn Veiw the most Convenient way from Hites Mines to the Road that leads to Swift Run Gap and make a report of the Conveniences and Inconveniences thereof to the next court

21 November 1766, p. 357
Ordered that Hugh Duglass James Duglass and Abraham Smith they being first sworn Veiw the most Convenient way from Abraham Smiths to the Road that leads to Swift Run Gap and make a report of the Conveniences and Inconveniences thereof to the next Court

22 November 1766, p. 359
Sampson Mathews Gent is Appointed Surveyor of the Highway in the room of Andrew Lewis Gent and It is Ordered that with the Tithable Inhabitants Liveing on this side of Christians Creek from the Road down the Creek as far as George Hutchinsons deceased by CoL° Lewis's Includeing the Tithables in Staunton and from thence by Colonel Stewarts Stephens Loys and Andrew Scotts and thence to Christians Creek two Miles above the Road he Clear and keep the same in repair According to Law

25 November 1766, p. 454-7
[Grand Jury Presentments]

The King against William Beard
On a Presentment of the Grand jury for not keeping the Road whereof he is Overseer in repair According to Law

The Defendant being Summoned and not Appearing It is Considered that for the said Offence he make his fine with our Lord the King by the Paiment of fifteen Shillings and that he pay the Costs of this Prosecution and may be taken &ᶜ
Costs 159 Tobacco @ 151

* * *

The King against John Baskins
On a Presentment of the Grand jury for not Grubing the Road whereof he is Overseer According to Law
The said John Baskins not being an Inhabitant of this Colony the Attorney of our Lord the King saith that he will not further Prosecute of and upon the premises It is therefore Ordered that this presentment against him be dismised

The King against The Surveyor of Highway throˢ Jennings's Gap
On a Presentment of the Grand jury for not keeping the Road in repair According to Law
Thomas Armstrong the Surveyor being Summoned and not Appearing It is Considered that for the said Offence he make his fine with our Lord the King by the Paiment of fifteen Shillings and that he pay the Cost of this Prosecution and may be taken &ᶜ
Costs 144 Tobacco @ 151

The King against The Surveyor of the Highway from the Long Glade to the North River Commonly known by the Name of Swift Run
On a Presentment of the Grand jury for not keeping the Road in repair According to Law
The Attorney of our Lord the King saith that he will not further prosecute of and upon the Premises It is therefore Ordered that this Presentment against him be dismised

The King against The Surveyor of the Streets of Staunton
On a Presentment of the Grand jury for not keeping the Streets in repair According to Law
The Attorney of our Lord the King saith that he will not further prosecute of and upon the premises It is therefore Ordered that this Presentment against him be dismised

The King against The Surveyor of the Highway from James Beards foard to the Stone Meeting house
On a Presentment of the Grand jury for not keeping the Road in repair According to Law
Thomas Connerly the Surveyor being Summoned and not Appearing It is Considered that for the said Offence he make his fine with our Lord the King by the Paiment of fifteen Shillings and he pay the Costs of this Prosecution and may be taken &ᶜ
Costs 144 Tobacco @ 151

The King against The Surveyors of the Highway from John Davisons to the Stone Meeting House
On a Presentment of the Grand jury for not keeping the Road in repair According to Law
John Davison the Surveyor being Summoned and not Appearing It is Considered that for the said Offence he make his fine with our Lord the King by the Paiment of fifteen Shillings and he pay the Costs of this Prosecution and may be taken &ᶜ
Costs 144 Tobacco @ 151

The King against The Surveyors of the Highway from John Fowlers foarding to the Stone Meeting House

On a Presentment of the Grand jury for not keeping the Road in repair According to Law Alexander Kile the Surveyor not being an Inhabitant of this Colony the Attorney of our Lord the King saith that he will not further prosecute of and upon the Premises It is therefore Ordered that the Presentment against him be dismised

The Order of Court for Summoning John Smith Israel Christian Gent William Grymes and James Neelley for not Veiwing the Roads that Lead from Vauses Over the New River on the Land of John Buchanan and likewise by Ingleses Ferry to the Lead Mines is dismised

25 November 1766, p. 460
Ordered that Ten Pounds the remainder of fifty Pounds that was formerly levied for William Robinson for making a Causeway at Vauses be by the Sheriff paid to Israel Christian Gent and Philip Love who are Appointed to Imploy Workmen to repair the same

20 January 1767, p. 462
Ordered that John Wilson John Tate Alexander M^{c}elroy they being first sworn Veiw a way round the Plantation of Margaret Clark and make a report whether or not the Road she turned which Leads from Risks Mill to Providence be Convenient or Inconvenient to the next Court

17 March 1767, p. 463
William McCutcheon (Merchant) is Appointed Surveyor of the Highway in the room of John Stewart and It is Ordered that with the Tithable Person that Usually Worked under the said John Stewart he Clear and keep the same in repair According to Law

17 March 1767, p. 464
Samuel Wilson is Appointed Surveyor of the Highway from his House to Wallace Estills and It is Ordered that with the Tithables from Estills up the Bull Pasture River to Black Thorn and from James Gwinns up the Cow Pasture they Clear and keep the same in repair According to Law

17 March 1767, p. 467
Robert Dunlap William Elliot and Alexander Hamilton the Persons Appointed to Veiw the most Convenient way for a Road from William Elliotts to McCutcheons Mill and from thence thro^g the Buffalo Gap and report the Conveniances and Inconveniances thereof made their Report that they had Veiwed the within Mentioned Road and finds it Sufficient It is Ordered that the said Road be Established and that Alexander Hamilton and Robert Dunlap be Surveyors thereof and that with the Adjacent Tithables they Clear and keep the same in repair According to Law

18 March 1767, p. 475
Malcom Allen is Appointed Surveyor of the Highway from William Lawrances to the Ferry on James River It is Ordered that he with the Tithables from James Arbuckles on both sides of the River to the ferry he Clear and keep the same in repair According to Law

18 March 1767, p. 477
On the Petition of Frederick Stern, Isaac Job, Thomas Grayon John Bell, Henry Skaggs, Joseph Hix John Draper, George Baker, Joseph Howe, Levy Smith, Erasmus Noble, Samuel Pepper, James Condon Edmund Vansell, Humphrey Baker, Anthony Bledsoe, James Newell and Alexander Page for a Road from Vauses by Ingleses ferry to Peak Creek on the North side of the New River It is Ordered that James Neelley Philip Love William Christian and William Bryans or any three of them being first sworn do Veiw the same and make a report of the Conveniances and Inconveniances thereof to the next Court

18 March 1767, p. 477
Hugh Douglass James Douglass and Abraham Smith Gent the persons Appointed to Veiw the Most Convenient Way from Abraham Smiths to the Road that Leads to Swift Run Gap made a report that after Reveiwing we find a Straight and a good Road by James Douglasses and Crossing Dry River above James McClure's feild and Cross Cooks Creek between William Snodons and Alexander Herons Meadow fence and to the Left hand of Edward Shanklins to the Main Road that Leads to Swift Run Gap It is therefore Ordered that the said Road be Established and that Hugh Douglas be Surveyor thereof and that with the Convenient Tithables he Clear and keep the same in repair According to Law

18 March 1767, p. 477
It is Ordered that the Tithables within four Miles of the Road whereof John Estill is Overseer work the same

18 March 1767, p. 478
On the Petition of Wallis Estill Hugh Miller John Davidson Loftus Pullen John Carlile James Bodkin James Byrnsides John Miller Thomas Hambleton John Miller William Martin Dawson Wade Richard Bodkin John Bodkin James Freelan William Blanton Hugh Bodkin Robert Duffield Robert Carlile and Samuel Givens for a Road from Hicklens in the Bull Pasture to Thomas Feemsters in the Cow Pasture is rejected

18 March 1767, p. 478
On the Petition of William Wilson Ralph Laverty Robert Bratton David Frame William Laverty Robert Barnett George Skillern William Givens Duncan M^{c}farling Robert M^{c}farling Alexander M^{c}farling Stephen Wilson John Davis and Thomas Lewis for a Road from William Wilsons Mill into the New Layed out Road at the foot of the Bull Pasture and thence into the Branch Near Feemsters It is Ordered that William Givens John Wilson Stephen Wilson and John Hicklen or any three of them being first sworn Veiw the same and make a report of the Conveniances and Inconveniances thereof to the next Court

19 March 1767, p. 482
On the Petition of Samuel Woods Thomas Goodson John Richards William Ward, Hugh Crockett, Jacob Kent Robert Crockett Philip Love and Joseph Crockett for a road from Vauses to Samuel Woods's It is Ordered that Hugh Crockett Samuel Woods and Jacob Kent they being first sworn Veiw the same and make a report of the Conveniances and Inconveniances thereof to the next Court

19 March 1767, p. 485
William Mcbride is Appointed Surveyor of the Highway from John Poages by William M^{c}brides Shop to the Main Road between Baileys and Browns It is Ordered that with the Tithables within two miles of the said Road he Clear and keep the same in repair According to Law

21 March 1767, p. 493
Samuel Hamilton is Appointed Surveyor of the Highway from Captain Dickinsons to the Main Road between Captain Lewis's and the Warm Springs and It is Ordered that with the Tithables from Thomas Galespies down the Cow Pasture to Alexander Clarks he Clear and keep the same in repair According to Law

21 March 1767, p. 493
Ordered that James Gamwell John Anderson Junior and Isaac Carson they being first sworn Veiw the Most Convenient way for a Road from John Archers Mill to Robert Fowlers and make a report of the Conveniances and Inconveniances thereof to the next Court

21 March 1767, p. 499
[Grand Jury Presentment]

The King against John Estill
On a Presentment of the Grand jury for not keeping the Road whereof he is Overseer in repair According to Law
The deft being Summoned and not Appearing It is Considered that for the said Offence he make his fine with our Lord the King by the paiment of fifteen Shillings and that he pay the Costs of this prosecution and may be taken &
Costs   Tobacco @ 151

Book XI, 1767-1768

23 March 1767, p. 32
On the Petition of John Henderson and others It is Ordered that Samuel McCune Andrew McClure and James Galespie they being first sworn Veiw the Most Convenient way from John Patricks to Rockfish Gap and make a report of the Conveniances and Inconveniances thereof to the next Court

19 May 1767, p. 64
John Graham is appointed Overseer of the road in the room of Ja^s. Alexander

19 May 1767, p. 64
Walter Stewart is appointed Overseer of the road in the room of John Buchanan

19 May 1767, p. 64
Isaac White is Appointed Overseer of the road in the room of Jn° Ramsey

19 May 1767, p. 64
John Beard is appointed Overseer of the road in the room of Jn° Findlay

19 May 1767, p. 64
James Leard is appointed Overseer of the road in the room of Wm Beard

19 May 1767, p. 64
Thomas Bryans is appointed Overseer of the road in the room of George Spears

19 May 1767, p. 65
Ordered that Mich^l. Warren George Shoemaker & John Bryans Veiw the most Convenient way from Adam Readers Mines to Isaac Robinsons from thence to the Widow Wrights and from thence to Thomas Harrisons and make a report thereof to the next Court

19 May 1767, p. 65
John Patterson is appointed Overseer of the road from John Andersons Meadow to Mathews's Mill and that the Tithable within two Miles of the road work thereon

20 May 1767, p. 72 [Second of two pages numbered 72]
John Poage is appointed Overseer of the Road from Pedler Ford to Lapsleys Run & that the Tithables within three Miles on each side of the road work thereon

20 May 1767, p. 78
Michael Dickey is appointed Overseer of the road from Thomas Wattersons field to John Davis Mill and that the tithables within three miles on each side of the road work thereon & It is Ordered that he Clear & keep the same in repair According to Law

21 May 1767, p. 82
John McMahen is appointed Overseer of the road from John Richeys old place on the North River to the Stone Meeting House and that the Tithables within three Miles on each side of the road work thereon & It is Ordered that he with the said Tithables Clear and keep the same in repair According to Law

21 May 1767, p. 82
George Baxter is Appointed Surveyor of the Highway in the room of John Thomas and It is Ordered that with the hands that usually worked under the said John Thomas he Clear and keep the same in Repair According to Law

21 May 1767, p. 85
William Christian, Phillip Love and William Bryan three of the Persons appointed to View the most Convenient way from Vauses on Roanoake by English's ferry to Peak Creek on the north side of New River and make report of the Conveniences and Inconveniences to this Court Made their Report that they had Viewed the Ground from Vauses Plantation to Peak Creek by English's ferry and found that a good and Convenient road may be had as we have marked it if Properly Cleared to which John Buchanan Gent by his Attorney Objected for that the said Report was Defective and not made according to Law in not setting forth the Conveniences and Inconveniences Attending the same and further the part of the road Petitioned for is on the Lands of the Western Waters and that it was Contrary to his Majestys Proclamation to grant any order for Clearing any Road thereon which said Objections was Overrulled by the Court and it was therefore Ordered that the said Road be Established.
From which said Order the said John Buchanan prayed an Appeal to the sixth day of the next General Court and having given security of Prosecution According to Law his Appeal is Allowed.

21 May 1767, p. 86
Thomas Bredshaw is appointed Surveyor of the High way in the room of David Trimble and It is Ordered that with the hands that Usually worked under the said David Trimble he Clear and Keep the same in repair According to Law

21 May 1767, p. 86
Charles Donerly is appointed Surveyor of the High Way from Painter Gap to James Gays and It is Ordered that with Tithables within three miles on each side of the road he Clear and keep the same in repair According to Law

21 May 1767, p. 87
John Robinson and John Henderson are appointed Surveyors of the Highway from the Head of the north fork of Roanoake to Capt. John Robinson Mill's and Its ordered that with the Tithables within five miles on each side of the road they Clear and keep the same in Repair According to Law

21 May 1767, p. 88
Isaac Robinson is appointed Overseer of the road in the room of Mathias Rider and It is Ordered that with with the hands that usually worked under the said Mathias Rider he Clear and Keep the same in repair According to Law

21 May 1767, p. 88
George Carpenter is appointed Surveyor of the High way in the room of James Bruister and It is Ordered that with the hands that Usually worked under the said Ja^s. Bruister he Clear and Keep the same in Repair According to Law

22 May 1767, p. 92
Jacob Persenger is appointed Surveyor of the High Way In the room of Ludwick Francisco and It is Ordered that with the hands that Usually worked under the said Ludwick Francisco he Clear and Keep in repair According to Law

22 May 1767, p. 94
It's Ordered that Matthew Patton and John Davis View the Road round John Bennets Plantation and report thereof to the next Court

25 May 1767, p. 164
[Grand Jury Presentments]
The King Against Loftus Pullings
On a Presentment of the Grand Jury for not Keeping the road Whereof he is Overseer in repair According to Law
This Day Came the Attorney for our Lord the King and the said Defendant being duly Summoned and not Appearing It is Considered by the Court that our said Lord the King recover against the said Loftus Pullings fifteen Shillings or one hundred and fifty Pounds of Tobacco to the use of the Parish of Augusta and that he pay the Costs of this Prosecution and may be taken &c--Costs 134 Tob° @ 151

25 May 1767, p. 186
Alexander Herron is appointed Surveyor of the High Way from Robert Cravens to the ford at the North River at John Fowlers in the room of John Cravens and It is Ordered that with the hands that Usually Worked under the said Cravens he Clear and keep the same in repair According to Law

18 August 1767, p. 215
Robert Allen is Appointed Surveyor of the Highway in the room of Isaac White and It is Ordered that with the Tithable persons that Usually worked under the said Isaac White he Clear and keep the same in Repair According to Law

18 August 1767, p. 215
Robert Gragg is Appointed Surveyor of the Highway from the Duck Ponds to the Middle River and It is Ordered that With the Tithables formerly worked under him he Clear and Keep the same in repair According to Law

18 August 1767, p. 215
Ordered that John Poage and George Moffett Gent lay of and Appoint the Tithables to work on the road from Staunton to Jennings Gap.

18 August 1767, p. 217
Samuel Henderson is appointed Surveyor of the High Way from John Madisons to Givens Mill and that with the Tithables from James Craigs up the Middle River to James Givens and with the

Tithables On the South River from William Pattersons to Christian Clemons he Clear and Keep the same in repair According to Law

18 August 1767, p. 217
John Madison is Appointed Surveyor of the high Way from his house to Jones Ford and that with the Tithables on the Middle River from James Craigs Downwards and on the South River from William Pattersons Downwards and as low as the said Madisons he Clear and Keep the same in repair According to Law

18 August 1767, p. 217
Andrew Fought is Appointed Surveyor of the High Way in the room of Archibald Huston and It is Ordered that with the hands that Usually Worked under the said Archibald Huston he Clear and Keep the same in Repair According to Law

18 August 1767, p. 218
John Anderson and William Ralston are Appointed Surveyors of the High Way from the Duck Ponds to the Middle river in the room of Roberts Gregg and It is Ordered that Abraham Gent Divide their Tithables and Precints--

18 August 1767, p. 218
On the Petition of [blank in book] and Others It is Ordered that James Craig, Robert Frazier, and Christian Clements being first Sworn View the Most Convenient way from Craigs Mills to the Mouth of the South river and from the Mills to the Great road Leading to Staunton and report to the next Court the Conveniences and Inconveniences that Attends the same

18 August 1767, p. 219
John Robinson is Appointed Surveyor of the High Way from his Mill by the Den to County road Leading to Warwick and that Israel Christian Gent Appoint the Tithables to work thereon.

19 August 1767, p. 220
John Beard and James Sayers jun^r. is appointed Surveyors of the high Way in the room of Robert Armstrong and that George Moffett Gent Divide their Tithables and Precints

19 August 1767, p. 220
Hugh Allen is appointed Surveyor of the High Way from James Givens Mill by his house to the Stone Meeting house and that Samuel Hinds Hugh Allen, Andrew Lockart, William Kerr, William McClure, John Burnside John Stewart, Robert Stevenson, Samuel McKee, John Campbell James Allen, James Searight James Allen, Samuel Bell, Thomas Storey and Jno Anderson and there Tithables work on the said Roads

19 August 1767, p. 225
Aaron Hughes is appointed Surveyor of the High Way in the room of Jn° Phillips and It is Ordered that with the Tithables that Usually Worked under the said Jn° Phillips he Clear and keep the same in repair According to Law

19 August 1767, p. 230
Thomas Hicklen jun^r. is appointed Overseer of the road in the room of John Estill and It is Ordered that with the Tithables that Usually worked under the said Thos Hicklen he Clear & keep the same in repair According to Law.

19 August 1767, p. 230
John Dailey is appointed Overseer of the road from the North River to the south River and that Archibald Alexander & Samuel McDowell Gent Appoint the Tithables to work thereon

19 August 1767, p. 230
Walter Smiley is appointed Overseer of the road in the room of Willm Kennady and It is Ordered that with the Tithables that Usually Worked under the said William Kennady he Clear and keep the same in Repair According to Law

21 August 1767, p. 239
Ordered that Joseph McMurty and George M^{c}afee they being first Sworn View a Way from McMurtys Mill through McAfees Gap to the Waggon road and report the Conveniences and Inconveniences to the next Court--

21 August 1767, p. 239
James McAfee Senior and Bryan McDonald are Appointed Surveyors of the High way from fort William to the head of Catawbo and that William Preston Gent Appoint the Tithables to work thereon

21 August 1767, p. 239
Patrick Shirley and William Watkins are Appointed Surveyors of the high Way from James Montgomerys at Catawbo to the side of Craigs Creek Mountain where John Potts Quit Clearing and It is Ordered that with the Tithables that will be Appointed by William Preston Gent they Clear and Keep the same in repair According to Law

21 August 1767, p. 239
James Cloyd is appointed Surveyor of the High Way from Grahams Clearing to James Johnstons in the room of William Preston and It is Ordered that with the Tithables that Usually Worked under the said William Preston he Clear and keep the same in repair According to Law

21 August 1767, p. 239
Samuel McRoberts is appointed Surveyor of the High Way from James Johnstons to Josiah Ramseys Cabbain in the room of William Preston and It is Ordered that with the Tithables that

usually worked under the said Wm Preston and It is Order that with the Tithables that usually worked under the said Wm Preston he Clear & Keep the same in repair According to Law

21 August 1767, p. 240
Michael Cloyd is appointed Surveyor of the high Way from his house to the branch below James Moores Junior and that with the Tithables that shall be appointed him by William Preston Gent he Clear and Keep the same in repair According to Law

21 August 1767, p. 240
Ordered that Henry Dooley and John Thompson they being first Sworn View the Most Convenient Way from the Welshmans run to the Bedford Line and report the Conveniency and Inconveniency to the next Court

21 August 1767, p. 240
Israel Christian Gent is appointed Surveyor of the High Way from the Great Lick to Grahams Clearing in the room of William Graham and It is Ordered that with the Tithables that Usually worked under the said William Graham he Clear and Keep the same in repair According to Law

21 August 1767, p. 241
Ordered that James Trimble, John Maxwell and William McClenachan being first Sworn View the Old and New Roads from McClenachans Mill to William Holdmans and report the Conveniences and Inconveniences of each road to the next Court

21 August 1767, p. 241
Robert Thompson is Appointed Surveyor of the High Way in the room of Alexander Thompson and It is Ordered that with the Tithables that Usually worked under the said Alexander he Clear and Keep the same in repair According to Law

21 August 1767, p. 241
Henry Keffman is appointed Surveyor of the High Way in the room of Charles Willson and It is Ordered that with the Tithables that Usually Worked under the said Charles Willson he Clear and Keep the same in repair According to Law

22 August 1767, p. 252
Francis Erwin Junr. is appointed Surveyor of the High Way from Charles Campbells run to John Davis's Mill in the room of Michael Dickey and It is Ordered that with the Tithables that Usually worked under the said Mich^l Dickey he Clear and Keep the same in repair According to Law

24 August 1767, p. 313
William Bryans is appointed Surveyor of the High Way from Fort Lewis to Peters Creek and It is Ordered that with the Tithables that shall be Appointed him by William Preston Gent he Clear and Keep the same in repair According to Law

24 August 1767, p. 313
Thomas Barnes is appointed Surveyor of the High Way from Peters Creek to Tinker Creek and It is Ordered that with the Tithables that shall be Appointed him by William Preston Gent he Clear and keep the same in repair According to Law

24 August 1767, p. 313
John M^{c}adoo and John Thompson are Appointed Overseers of the High Way from Tinker Creek to the County Line and It is Ordered that with the Tithables that shall be Appointed by William Preston Gent he Clear and Keep the same in repair According to Law

17 November 1767, p. 338
Hugh Donaho is Appointed Surveyor of the high Way from Thomas Connellys House to James Beards ford in the room of Alexander Walker and It is Ordered that with the Tithables that Usually Worked under the said Alexander Walker he Clear and Keep the same in repair According to Law

17 November 1767, p. 341
Joseph Bell is Appointed Surveyor of the High Way from James Lesslys to the fork of the road leading to Staunton and It is Ordered that with the Tithables that Usually Worked under the said Archibald Hamilton he Clear and Keep the same in repair According to Law

17 November 1767, p. 342
James Craig Robert Frazier and Christian Clements the persons Appointed to View the Most Convenient way from Craigs Mill to the Mouth of the south River and from the Mills to the great Road leading to Staunton this day made their report that the same was Conveninent. It is therefore Ordered that the said Road be Established agreeable to the said Report and James Craig and Robert Frazier are Appointed Surveyors of the said Road & that with the Adjacent Tithables within three Miles of the road they Clear and Keep the same in repair According to Law

17 November 1767, p. 343
James Davis is Appointed Surveyor of the high Way in the room of John Hanna and It is Ordered that with the Tithables that Usually Worked under the said Jno Hanna he Clear and Keep the same in Repair According to Law

17 November 1767, p. 344
John White and John Hall is Appointed Surveyors of the High Way from George Campbells to William McClenachans Mill and that the Tithables mentioned in a Petition work thereon

18 November 1767, p. 345
James Simpson is Appointed Surveyor of the High Way from the Cow Pasture to Gilmers Gap and the Inhabitants from W^m. Doughertys Down the River to Capt. Christians work thereon

18 November 1767, p. 345
Ordered that Abraham Smith and Silas Hart Appoint the Tithables to Work under John Gum and Ephraim Love

18 November 1767, p. 347
On the Petition of Sundry the Inhabitants It is Ordered that Thomas Tosh Daniel McNeill and Francis Grymes they being first Sworn View and Mark the most Convenient from the Stone house to Evanses Mill and report to the next Court the Conveniences and Inconveniences that Attends the same

18 November 1767, p. 347
David Campbell and Samuel Downey is appointed Overseers of the road from John McCreerys to James Moffetts in the room of James Callison and David Cunningham and It is Ordered that with the Tithables that Usually Worked under the said James Callison and David Cuninngham they Clear and Keep the same in repair According to Law

18 November 1767, p. 347
John Bowen is appointed Overseer of the road from the ferry On James River to the Warm Springs Oppisite to John McClures and that the Adjacent Tithables within two Miles of the said Road work thereon

18 November 1767, p. 348
Ordered that Alexander McClenachan Jones Henderson and Michael Bowyer or any three of them being first Sworn View the Most Convenient Way from this Town to the Glebe and report to the next Court the Conveniences and Inconveniences that Attends the same

18 November 1767, p. 349
John Colter is appointed Surveyor of the high Way from Benjamin Stuarts branch to the Courthouse road and that with the Tithables that Usually worked under him he Clear and Keep the same in Repair According to Law

19 November 1767, p. 352
John Seewright is Appointed Surveyor of the High Way from the Stone Meeting house to Naked Creek

19 November 1767, p. 352
Gawin Leeper is Appointed Surveyor of the High Way from Grattons Store to Naked Creek

19 November 1767, p. 352
Felix Gilbert and Joseph Dickton are Appointed Surveyors of the High Way in the room of John Cravens and It is Ordered that with the Tithables that Usually worked under the said John Cravens they Clear and Keep the same in repair According to Law

19 November 1767, p. 352
Ordered that Felix Gilbert, Peter Hog Samuel Erwin and James Allen or any three of them being first Sworn View the Most Convenient way from Joseph Dickensons to the Stone Meeting house, and report to the next Court the Coveniences and Inconveniences that Attends the same

19 November 1767, p. 358
William McCutcheon is Appointed Surveyor of the High Way in the room of John Risk and It is Ordered that with the Tithables that Usually worked under the said John Risk he Clear and Keep the same in repair According to Law

19 November 1767, p. 360
Joseph McMurty and George M^{c}afee the persons Appointed to View the Most Convenient Way from McMurtys Mill thro' M^{c}afees Gap to the Waggon road and make report of the Conveniences and Inconveniences to this Court made a report that they had viewed the road and believe it Practicable to make a Waggon road through the Gap but are of Opinion that there not hands enough Convenient to do more than Clear it for Carrying Loads on horseback untill the Country is better Settled It is therefore Ordered that the said Road be Established and that Joseph McMurty and James M^{c}afee jun^r. be Surveyors thereof and that with the Tithables on Craigs Creek and Its Branches from Gathives up and on Catabo from Alexander Smiths up they Clear and Keep the same in repair According to Law

19 November 1767, p. 361
Jacob Pence is Appointed Overseer of the road in the room of Jacob Parsenger and It is Ordered that with the Tithables that Usually worked under the said Jacob Parsenger he Clear and Keep the same in repair According to Law.

19 November 1767, p. 361
Michael Shirley is appointed Surveyor of the highway in the room of Nich^s. Null and It is Ordered that with the Tithables that Usually worked under the said Nicholas Null he Clear and keep the same in repair According to Law

19 November 1767, p. 361
Zebulon Harrison is appointed Surveyor of the high Way in the room of John Phillips and It is Ordered that with the Tithables that Usually worked under the said John Phillips he Clear and Keep the same in repair According to Law

19 November 1767, p. 362
William Black is Appointed Surveyor of the High Way in the room of John Black and It is Ordered that with the Tithables that Usually worked under the said John Black he Clear and Keep the same in repair According to Law

20 November 1767, p. 366
the Persons Appointed to View a road from John Archers Mill to Robert Fowlers made their report that the same was Convenient It is therefore Ordered that the said Road be Established According thereto and John Blair and John Young are Appointed Surveyors thereof and It is Ordered that with the Tithables within three Miles on each side of the road they Clear and Keep the same in repair According to Law

21 November 1767, p. 371
Ordered that Samuel McDowell Jn° Lyle James McDowell & Daniel Lyle or any three of them being first Sworn View the Old and New Road from Timber Ridge Meeting house Isaac Taylors and report to the next Court the Conveniences and Inconveniences that Attends the same

23 November 1767, p. 432
Andrew Greer is Appointed Surveyor of the High Way from John Harrisons at the big Spring to the County Line and It is Ordered that with the Adjacent Tithables within three Miles On each side of the said Road he Clear and Keep the same in repair According to Law

23 November 1767, p. 441
Archibald Gilkison is appointed Surveyor of the High Way in the room of George Moffett and It is Ordered that with the Tithables that shall be Appointed him by the said George Moffett and John Archer Gent. he Clear and Keep the same in repair According to Law

24 November 1767, p. 483
On the Petition of Sundry the Inhabitants It is Ordered that John Patrick, John Ramsey, and Samuel Steel they being first Sworn View the Most Convenient way from James Craigs Mill up the South river to John Patricks and report to the next Court the Convenience and Inconveniences that Attends the same

15 March 1768, p. 493
Ordered that John Campbell, James Campbell, John Henderson, William Tees Robert Allen Senr. John Steel Andrew Steell James Bell, John Henderson Lazarus Inman Isaac White John Finley, Robert Finley, William Finley, James Ramsey John Ramsey, John Galespie, John Patrick and James Gillespy and their Tithables work on the road whereof Robert Allen Junr. is Overseer and that they be Exempted from working on any other road whatever

15 March 1768, p. 495
James Blair Junior is appointed Surveyor of the high Way in the room of John Stevenson and It is Ordered that with the Tithables that usually worked under the said John Steven he Clear and Keep the same in repair According to Law--

15 March 1768, p. 495
David Erwin is Appointed Surveyor of the high Way from Thomas Wattersons to the Stone Meeting house in the room of Jn° Stevenson It is Ordered that with the Tithables that usually worked under the said John Stevenson he Clear & Keep the same in repair According to Law

15 March 1768, p. 496
William Alexander is Appointed Surveyor of the high Way in the room of William Lowrey and It is Ordered that with the Tithables that Usually under the said William Lowry he Clear and Keep the same in repair According to Law

15 March 1768, p. 496
Robert Fowler is appointed Surveyor of the high Way in the room of James McGill and It is Ordered that with the Tithables that Usually worked under the said James McGill he Clear and Keep the same in repair According to Law

15 March 1768, p. 496
James Crockett is appointed Surveyor of the high way from the Painter Gap to Samuel Hodges and It is Ordered that with the Tithables within one Mile on Each Side of the road he Clear and Keep the same in repair According to Law

15 March 1768, p. 497
Thomas Connelly is Appointed Surveyor of the high Way in the room of Hugh Donaho and It is Ordered that with the Tithables that usually worked under the said Hugh Donaho he Clear and Keep the same in repair According to Law

16 March 1768, p. 504
Ordered that Peter Wallace, Samuel Wallace James McNabb and Halbert McClure or any three of them being first Sworn do Veiw the most Convenient Way from William Halls Mill to William McKees and report to the next Court the Conveniences and Inconveniences that Attends the same

16 March 1768, p. 506
The Persons appointed to View a road from Welshmans run to the Bedford Line this day made their report that the same is Convenient It is Therefore Ordered that the said Road be Established According thereto and that Henry Dooley be Surveyor thereof and he with the Adjacent Tithables within three Miles on each side of the road he Clear and Keep the same in repair According to Law

17 March 1768, p. 508
John Bodkin is Appointed Surveyor of the high Way in the room of John Estill from James Givens to the head of the Cowpasture River and that the Tithables from the said Givens up work thereon and It is Ordered that With the said Tithables he Clear and Keep the same in repair According to Law

Book XII, 1768

21 March 1768, p. 92
Ordered that the Overseer of the road from the Stone house to Tinker Creek with the Assistance of Robert Breckenridge and David Robinson make a small alteration on the road three Quarters of a Mile from the Old ford to the same and that he Open and Keep the Same in repair According to Law and that Israel Christian Gent Clear out the ford at his own Expence

21 March 1768, p. 94
Robert Armstrong is Appointed Surveyor of the High Way from Archers Mill to the Dry branch Gap and It is Ordered that with the Tithables within four Miles on each side side of the said Road he Clear and Keep the same in repair According to Law

22 March 1768, p. 127
[Grand Jury Presentments]

The King Against Walter Stewart
On the Presentment of the Grand Jury for not Keeping the road whereof he is Overseer In repair According to Law
The Defendant being Summoned and not Appearing It is Considered that for the said Offence he make his fine with our Lord the King by the Paiment of fifteen Shillings and that he Pay the Cost of this Prosecution and may be taken &c
Costs   Tobacco   @ 15/

The King Against Walter Smiley
On a Presentment of the Grand Jury for not keeping the road whereof he is Overseer in repair According to Law
The Attorney for our Lord the King saith that he will not further Prosecute of and upon the Premises It is therefore Ordered that this suit Against him be Discontinued

The King Against The Surveyors of the Highway from the forks Betwixt the Widow Steels and James Bells
On a Presentment of the Grand Jury for not keeping the road in repair According to Law
John Brownlee the Surveyor being Summoned and not Appearing It is Considered that for the said Offence he make his fine with our Lord the King by the Payment of fifteen Shillings and that he Pay the Costs of this Prosecution and may be taken &c
Costs 144 Tob° @15/

* * *

The King Against The Surveyors of the Highway from Lord Fairfax line to William Beards
On the Presentment of the Grand Jury for not Keeping the road in repair According to Law
The Attorney for our Lord the King saith that he will not further Prosecute in and upon the Premises It is therefore Ordered this Presentment against him be Dimissed

* * *

The King Against John Cravens

On a Presentment of the Grand Jury against him for not Keeping the road whereof he is Overseer In repair According to Law
The Attorney for our Lord the King saith that he will not further Prosecute in and upon the premises It is Therefore Ordered this Presentment against him be Dismissed

The King Against The Surveyors of the Highway from John Grattans to the Stone Meeting House
On a Presentment of the Grand Jury for not Keeping the said Road in repair According to Law
The Attorney for our Lord the King saith that he will not further Prosecute in and upon the Premises It is therefore Ordered that this Presentment against him be Dismissed

The King against Alexander Walker
On a Presentment of the Grand Jury for not Keeping the road whereof he is Overseer in repair According to Law
The Attorney for our Lord the King saith that he will not further Prosecute of and upon the Premises It is therefore Ordered that this Presentment again him be Dismissed

* * *

The King Against Francis Alexander
On a Presentment of the Grand Jury for not Keeping the Road whereof he is Overseer in repair According to Law
The Defendant being Summoned and not Appearing therefore It is Considered that he make his fine with our Lord the King by the paiment of fifteen Shillings and that he pay the Costs of this Prosecution and may be taken &^{c}
Costs   Tobacco @ 15/

22 March 1768, p. 131
Samuel Frazier is Appointed Surveyor of the Highway from the Long Meadow Bridge to Rockfish Gap Road in the room of Francis Alexander and It is Ordered that the Tithathables that Usually worked under the said Fra^s. Alexander he Clear & Keep the same in repair According to Law

19 [17?] May 1768, p. 141
James Phillips is Appointed Surveyor of the High Way in the room of Thomas Bradshaw and It is Ordered that with the Tithables that Usually worked under the said Thomas Bradshaw he Clear and keep the same in repair According to Law

19 [17?] May 1768, p. 142
Joseph Bosart is Appointed Surveyor of the Highway in the room of Andrew Faught It is Ordered that with the Tithables that Usually worked under the said And^w Faught he Clear and Keep the same in repair According to Law

19 [17?] May 1768, p. 142

Thomas Willson ^{CH}[?] is Appointed Surveyor of the Highway in the room of Thomas Willson & It is ordered that with the Tithables that Usually worked under the said Thomas Willson (Chestnut Hill) he Clear and keep the same in repair According to Law

19 [17?] May 1768, p. 143
Ordered that James Robinson, Hugh Crocket, and Philip Love they being first Sworn View a road James Montgomerys Lower Line to the Old County Line Leading from Catawbo to the New River and make report of the Conveniences and Inconveniences that Attends the same to the next Court

18 May 1768, p. 153
Alexander Walker Junr. is appointed Surveyor of the Highway in the room of John McMahon and It is Ordered that with the Tithables that Usually worked under the said John McMahon he Clear and Keep the same in repair According to Law

19 May 1768, p. 160
Francis Stuart is appointed Surveyor of the High Way in the room of Alexander Herron and It is Ordered that with the Tithables that Usually worked under the said Alexander Herron he Clear and keep the same in repair According to Law

19 May 1768, p. 162
Ordered that James Bell, James McGill and Charles Campbell ~~view~~ they being first Sworn view the road turned round the Plantation of James Hendersons by him whether the Alteration is Convenient or Inconvenient to the next Court

20 May 1768, p. 167
William Hutchinson is Appointed Surveyor of the High way in the room of George Mathews and It is Ordered that with the Tithables that Usually worked under the said George Mathews he Clear and keep the same in repair According to Law

20 May 1768, p. 168
John Patterson is Appointed Surveyor of the High Way from John Andersons Meadow to George Mathews and It is Ordered that with the Tithables within two miles on each side the road he Clear and Keep the same in repair According to Law

20 May 1768, p. 168
Ordered that John Bowyer, Abraham Brown, John Paxton and Samuel Wallace or any three of them being first sworn View the most Convenient way from the North branch of James River round the Poplar Hill to Buffalo Creek and make report of the Conveniences and inconveniences Attending the same to the next Court

20 May 1768, p. 168
Ordered that Jonathan Smith, Walter Stuart, and John Mills they being first Sworn View the most Convenient way from Walter Stewarts to the best foard on James River between the ferry and Col^o. Buchanans and from thence to the main road Leading to John Mills's and make report of the Conveniences and Inconveniences Attending the same to the next Court

20 May 1768, p. 168

Ordered that John McClung, James Greenlee, James Cowdon, and James McDowell, or any three of them (being first Sworn) View the Most Convenient Way from David Moores to Capt. Saml McDowell and make report of the Conveniences and Inconveniences Attending the same to the next Court

23 May 1768, p. 254
The Order for to View a Road from this Town to the Glebe Alexander McClenachan Elijah McClenachan and Michael Bowyer three of the Persons Appointed made their Report that the new Road by Youngs Mill to be the Nearest and most Convenient Way. It is Ordered that the said Road be Established and that Joseph Henderson and John Handley be Overseers thereof and that the Tithable within three Miles on each side of the Road Work Thereon and that the old Road by Browns bridge be Discontinued

24 May 1768, p. 309
Ordered that Robert McClenachan Gent make a Foard ACross the Creek near Daniel Kidds and bring in his Charge at the Laying of the next County Levy

18 [16?] August 1768, p. 314
James Gamwell Is Appointed Overseer of the road in the room of John Anderson and It is Ordered that with the Tithables that usually worked under the said John Anderson he Clear and Keep the same in repair according to Law

18 [16?] August 1768, p. 314
Robert McMahon is appointed Surveyor of the High Way from John Seewrights Mill to Thomas Connerlys and it is ordered that with the Tithables mentioned in a Petition he Clear and Keep the same in repair According to Law

17 [19?] August 1768, p. 317
The persons appointed to View a Road from William M^ckees to William Halls mill this day made their report that the same is Convenient It is therefore Ordered that the said Road be Established and William M^ckee is appointed Surveyor of the said Road and It is Ordered that with the Tithables within two miles on each side of the Road he Clear and Keep the same in repair According to Law

18 [20?] August 1768, p. 333
John McClure is appointed Surveyor of the high Way in the room of John Bowen and It is Ordered that with the Tithables that usually worked under the said John Bowen he Clear and Keep the same in repair According to Law

18 [20?] August 1768, p. 335
Ordered that ~~Samuel~~ Weer Samuel Steel and Robert Steell (Miller) they being first Sworn do view the most Convenient way from Steels mill to James Telfords and make report of the Conveniences and Inconveniences Attending the same to the next Court

20 [22?] August 1768, p. 352
John Hogshead is Appointed Surveyor of the High Way in the room of James Sayers Junr. and It is Ordered that with the Tithables that Usually worked under the said James Sayers jr he Clear and keep the same in repair According to Law

22 [24?] August 1768, p. 444
Ordered that John Shanklin Charles Callachan & John Hopkins View the Road from Thomas Gordons to Aron Olivers and make report of the Conveniances and Inconveniances to the Next Court

23 [25?] August 1768, p. 450
John Black is appointed Overseer of the Road in the room of Robert Reed and Ordered that he with the usuall Tithables that worked thereon he Clear & keep the same in repair According to Law

23 [25?] August 1768, p. 466
Ordered that the Tithables in Staunton work on no other road but the road from Staunton to Christians Creek whereof Sampson Mathews is Surveyor

23 [25?] August 1768, p. 466
David Bell is appointed Surveyor of the road in the room of John Anderson & Ordered that he with the usuall Tithables Clear & keep the same in repair According to Law

23 [25?] August 1768, p. 466
Ordered that James M^{c}kearny Peter Evans & Thomas Tosh they being first sworn View a road from said Toshes to the road cleared by Richard Doggett to the Bedford line and make report of the Conveniences and Inconveniences to the next Court

15 November 1768, p. 472
Thomas Rowland is appointed Surveyor of the Road in the room of Samuel McRoberts and Ordered that he with the Tithables that usually worked thereon he Clear & keep the same in Repair According to Law

15 November 1768, p. 473
Cornelious Ruddle is appointed Surveyor of the Old Road from Ruders Mines to Michael Warings and It is Ordered that the Tithables with in two Miles each side of the Road work thereon, and that he with the same Clear & keep it in Repair According to Law

15 November 1768, p. 473
John Crawford is Appointed Surveyor of the road in the room of George Poage from Pedler foard to Bulletts Springs and Ordered that he with the Tithables that usually worked thereon he clear & keep the same in repair According to Law

15 November 1768, p. 473
Ordered that James Ewing John Tate and John Wilson they being first sworn view the road from Patrick Martins to Browns Meeting House and make report of the Conveniances and Inconveniances at the next Court also report the Alterations made thereon by Margaret Clark

16 November 1768, p. 475
John Miller is appointed surveyor of the road in the room of Loftus Pullin from Wallace Estills to Tinchers & Ordered that he with the usual Tithables Clear & keep the same in repair According to Law

16 November 1768, p. 483
Ordered that the Sheriff pay Robert McClenachan Three Pounds Ten Shillings for repairing the Bridge near Daniel Kidds

16 November 1768, p. 487
The Persons appointed to View a Road from James Tedfords to Steeles Mill made report and Ordered that the same be Established and that Moses Moore be Surveyor thereof and that he with the Tithables within two Miles each side of the said Road he Clear & keep the same in repair According to Law

17 November 1768, p. 490
Henry Ervin is appointed Surveyor of the Road in the room of Benjamin Harrison from Linvells Creek to Mole Hill Draft and ordered that he with the Tithables that usually worked thereon he Clear & keep the same in repair According to Law

17 November 1768, p. 494
Robert Belshee is appointed Surveyor of the road in the room of Samuel Monsey and Ordered that he with the Tithables that usually Worked thereon he Clear & keep the same in repair According to Law

18 November 1768, p. 494
Moses McElwain is appointed Surveyor of the Road in the room of William Renix and Ordered that he with the Tithables that usually worked thereon he Clear & keep the same in repair According to Law

18 November 1768, p. 495
John Wilson William Givens and John Hicklen three of the Persons appointed to View a Road from William Wilsons Mill to the new Road near John Hicklens made report that the same is Convenient. It is Therefore Ordered that the said Road be Established and that John Wilson be

Surveyor thereof and that he with the tithables from Jacksons Land to the head of Jacksons River Clear and keep the same in repair According to Law

18 November 1768, p. 495
Ordered that John Summers James Gilmore and Moses Colier View the most Convenient way for a Road from George Gibsons at the House Mountain to John Hannas Mill and make report of the Conveniences and Inconveniences at the next Court

Book XIII, 1768-1769

21 November 1768, p. 45
John McCreery is appointed Surveyor of the road from Captain Charles Lewis's to where Dickinsons road joins the road leading from Staunton to Warm springs and Ordered that he with the Tithables from John Dickensons to William Blacks on the Cow Pasture and Stuarts Creek Clear and keep the same in repair According to Law in the room of John McClenachan

21 November 1768, p. 45
John Hamilton is appointed Surveyor of the road from the Warmsprings to the forks of the road leading to Captain John Dickinsons And Ordered that with the tithables on Jacksons River from William Manns to Duncan M^{c}farlands and the Tithables on back Creek clear and keep the same in repair According to Law in the room of John McClenachan

22 November 1768, p. 48
Sampson Mathews and William Bowyer Gentlemen are Appointed Surveyors of the Streets of Staunton and Ordered that they with the Tithables in the said Town Clear & keep the same in repair According to Law

22 November 1768, p. 61
Ordered that Robert Brown and James Sawyers Junior they being first sworn view the nearest and most Convenient way from thro' Buffalo Gap to the road leading to Staunton and make report of the Conveniences and Inconveniences at the next Court

22 November 1768, p. 61
Ordered that Thomas Hughart and Andrew Hamilton (they being first sworn) view the most Convenient way from John Hodges to the Buffalo Gap road and make report of the Conveniances and Inconveniances at the next Court

21 March 1769, p. 80
Ordered that Archibald Hamilton Hugh Allen & Matthew Robertson they being first sworn View the most Convenient way from the Stone meeting House to James Kerrs and make report of the Conveniances and Inconveniences at the next Court

21 March 1769, p. 83
John Finley is Appointed surveyor of the road in the Room of Robert Allen and Ordered that he with the tithables that usually Worked thereon clear & keep the same in repair According to law

21 March 1769, p. 83
On the Motion of Malcolm Allen It is Ordered that John Clark be Summoned to appear here the next Court to shew cause why he did not execute several precipts put into his hands on persons fined for not working on the road whereof the said Allen is Surveyor of

21 March 1769, p. 83
Ordered that Walter Trimble & William Bell View the most Convenient way from Buffalo Gap to the road leading to Staunton and make report at the next Court

21 March 1769, p. 84
Robert Hamilton is appointed Surveyor of the road in the room of John Gilmore and It is Ordered that he with the Tithable that usually worked thereon clear & keep the same in repair According to law

21 March 1769, p. 84
John Hays is appointed Surveyor of the road in the room of Jacob Anderson and Ordered that he with the Tithables that usually worked thereon clear & keep the same in repair According to Law

22 March 1769, p. 87
John Paxton is appointed Surveyor of the Road in the room of John Bowyer and Ordered that he with the Tithables that usually worked under him clear & keep the same in repair According to Law

22 March 1769, p. 89
Joseph Robinson is appointed Surveyor of the Road from Major Breckenridges to the Great Lick and Ordered that he with the Tithables that usually worked thereon, clear and keep the same in repair According to Law

22 March 1769, p. 90
On the Petition of Sundry of the Inhabitants It is Ordered Ordered that Silas Hart George Moffitt and James Bell they being first sworn View a road from the Dry Gap to John Archers Mill and make a report whether the same will be useful or not at the next Court

22 March 1769, p. 96
Ordered that Joseph Culton Samuel Steel and William Porter they being first sworn view the Old Road from Alexander Walkers by James Moores to Andrew Hays's and the new Road from Alexander Walkers by Charles Hays's to Andrew Hays's and make report of the Conveniances and Inconveniances at the next Court

22 March 1769, p. 96
The Persons appointed to View a Road round the Plantation of Margaret Clark made report that the same is not Inconvenient. It is Ordered that the road round the fence be Established

23 March 1769, p. 100
Ordered that Robert Armstrong and John Boller they being first sworn view the way from the little Warm springs to the fork of the road on Dunlaps Creek and make report of the Conveniances and Inconveniances to the next Court

23 March 1769, p. 107
Ordered that John Moore Joseph Walker and Andrew Hall they being first sworn View the most Convenient way from James Thompsons by John Allisons Ferry on the North River to John Paxtons and make a report of the Conveniances and Incoveniances at the next Court

23 March 1769, p. 107
Ordered that John Fulton James Henry Patrick Campbell and John Tate or any three of Them they being first sworn View the most Convenient Way from Samuel McDowells to James Cowdons Store to Samuel Brawfords and make a report of the Conveniances and Inconveniances to the next Court

24 March 1769, p. 108
Ordered that James Steel James Bell and Hugh McClure they being first sworn View view the road from John Coulters by Benjamin Stuarts Mill to William Tees's and Make a report of the Conveniances and Inconveniances at the next Court

24 March 1769, p. 113
Felix Gilbert and Michael Shirley is appointed Surveyors of the Road from Jacob Nicholas's to Hance Magots and It is Ordered that they with the Tithables within three Miles on each side of the Road Clear & keep the same in repair According to Law

25 March 1769, p. 125
Charles Donnerly and John McCreery is appointed Surveyors of the road from Captain Charles Lewis's to the fork of Dickinson Road and Charles Lewis to divide the same & Tithables and Ordered that they with the s^d. Tithables clear and keep the same in repair According to Law

27 March 1769, p. 169
Ordered that Henry Pauling Joseph Murty and John Potts they being first sworn View a Road from Joseph Murtys House down Craigs Creek and Pattersons Creek into the main Road from John Crawfords to the stone House and make report of the Conveniances and Inconveniances thereof at the next Court

28 March 1769, p. 195
Thomas Bowyer Robert Reed William Bowyer and Sampson Mathews is appointed Overseers of the Streets of Staunton and Ordered that they with the Tithables in Staunton keep the same in repair According to Law

20 June 1769, p. 199
Thomas Reed is appointed Overseer of the Road in the room of Malcom Allen And It is Ordered that he with the Tithables that usually worked thereon clear & keep the same in repair According to Law

20 June 1769, p. 199
The Persons appointed to View the Road from the Stone Meeting House to James Kerrs made a report that the same is Conveniant It is Ordered that the said road be Established and that Mathew Kinny be Surveyor thereof and that he with the Tithables within two miles on each side of the same clear and keep the same in repair According to Law

20 June 1769, p. 200
John Buchanan is appointed Overseer of the Road in the room of Samuel McCutcheon and Ordered that he be Summoned to be sworn into the said Office According to Law

20 June 1769, p. 204
Henry Stone is appointed overseer of the road in the room of Henry Pickle and It is Ordered that he with the Tithables that usually worked under Pickle clear and Keep the same in repair According to Law

21 June 1769, p. 210
Ordered that Jonathan Smith and George Skillern appoint the Tithables to work on the road whereof John McClure and Thomas Reed are Surveyors of

21 June 1769, p. 210
The Persons appointed to View a Road from the Dry Gap to M^r. John Archers Mill whether the same would be usefull or not made a report that the said is not usefull It is Ordered that the said road be set aside

21 June 1769, p. 212
Thomas Moore is appointed Overseer of the road from the County line to the fork of the road by John Harrisons in the room of Andrew Greer and It is Ordered that he with the Tithables that usually worked thereon clear & keep the same in repair According to Law

21 June 1769, p. 218
Ordered that Robert Armstrong Henry Cresswell & James Bell they being first sworn View the most Conveniant way from Buffalo gap to Staunton & make report of the Conveniances and Inconveniances at the next Court

22 June 1769, p. 220
Ordered that Aron Hughes John Moore Thomas Moore and Jacob Woodley or any three of them they being first sworn do View the road from Hughs's lane by M^r. Matthew Harrisons Mills to the County line and make a report whether the alteration would be Conveniant or Inconveniant at the next Court

22 June 1769, p. 220
Ordered that Ruben Harrison Michael Warren Aron Hughes and John Ray or any three of them they being first sworn View a road from M^r. Matthew Harrisons Mills to the road leading to swift run Gap and make report of the Conveniances and Inconveniances at the next Court

22 June 1769, p. 227
George Baxter is Appointed Surveyor of the Road in the room of John Thomas and It is Ordered that he with the Tithables that usually worked under him he Clear & keep the same in repair According to Law

23 June 1769, p. 228
Ordered that John Herdman Junior Nehemiah Harrison Samuel Hemphill and Robert Cravens or any three of them they being first sworn View the most Conveniant way from Hopkins Mill to the road leading to Swift run Gap Road and make report of the Conveniances & Inconveniances at the next Court

23 June 1769, p. 234
William Herrin is appointed Overseer of the road in the room of Benjamin Harrison and It is Ordered that he with the Tithables that usually worked thereon he clear and keep the same in repair According to Law

27 June 1769, p. 313
William Armstrong is appointed Surveyor of the Road from Thomas Armstrongs to the Calfpasture Waters in the room of John Hogshead

27 June 1769, p. 313
John Dean is Appointed Surveyor of the road from the forks of Lewis and Dickinsons road to the Warmsprings in the room of John Hamilton

27 June 1769, p. 313
Ordered that Thomas Feemster Charles Donnerly and John McCreary (they being first sworn) do View the most Convenient way from Davis's Cabben to the Warmsprings and make report of the Conveniances & Inconveniances at the next Court

27 June 1769, p. 315
[Grand Jury Presentment]

The King vs The overseer of the road from Nathan Gillilans to Staunton Alias Summons

27 June 1769, p. 315
John Logan is appointed overseer of the road from the foard on James River Called Buchanans to the main Road already established over Cedar Bridge and Ordered that the Tithables within three miles on each side of the same work under him

27 June 1769, p. 316
John Black is appointed Overseer of the Road in the room of Robert Reed

15 August 1769, p. 316
Matt Arbuckle is appointed Surveyor of the Road in the room of William Gillispy

15 August 1769, p. 316
John Hogshead is appointed Surveyor of the Road in the room of William Armstrong

15 August 1769, p. 316
The Persons appointed to View a Road from Samuel McDowells by James Cowdens Store House to Samuel Braffords having made their report It is the Opinion of the Court that the report made by the viewers is Insufficient & Therefore It is Ordered that the Old road be Established & Confirmed

15 August 1769, p. 317
Ordered that Jonathan Smith John Miller Reece Bowen William Bowen and James Skidmore or any three of them they being first sworn View the most Convenient way from James River a Cross the mountain to the Bedford line and make a report thereof to the next Court

15 August 1769, p. 317
Alexander Hundley is appointed Surveyor of the Road in the room of James Simpson

16 August 1769, p. 320
William Dougherty is appointed Surveyor of the road in the room of James Beard

17 August 1769, p. 324
The Persons appointed to View a road from Hughes lane by Mr. Harrisons Mill made report that the same is Convenient It is Ordered that the said Road be established and that Matthew Harrison be Surveyor thereof & Ordered that the Tithables that worked on the Old Road work under him

17 August 1769, p. 324
The Persons appointed to View a road from Mr. Matthew Harrisons Mills to the road leading to Swift run Gap made a report that the same is Convenient Ordered that the same be Established and that Jacob Woodley be Surveyor thereof & that he with the Tithables within three Miles on each side of the road work thereon

17 August 1769, p. 325
James Fraizer is appointed Surveyor of the Road from Hance Magotts to Fraziers Old Place in the room of Henry Long

17 August 1769, p. 325
Ordered that Daniel Price Michael Kelly & John Seller they being first sworn View a road from John Coutts to Cross Shanando River by Henry Longs into the new Road leading Massenutting and make report of the Conveniences and Inconveniences at the next Court

17 August 1769, p. 334
The persons appointed to View a road from Buffalo Gap to Staunton having made their report that the same is Convenient It is Ordered that the same be Established & that James Bell and Henry Cresswell be overseers thereof and that the Tithables within three Miles on each side of the road work thereon

Index

This index is arranged by subject: Bridges and Causeways; Ferries and Fords; Land Features; Meetings Houses, Churches and Glebes; Mills and Mill Dams; Mines; Miscellaneous subjects; Personal Names; Rivers, Runs, Springs; Creeks, and other Water Features; and Roads

Bridges and Causeways

Brown's bridge, 44, 52, 145
bridge near/built/repaired by John Brown, 59, 72, 75, 77, 110, 111
causeway built by John Brown, 110, 111
bridge near (and built by) Maj. John Brown, 115
causeway near (and built by) Maj. John Brown, 115
Cedar bridge, 153
[NOTE: see also Seder bridge]
bridge below the Court House, 74
causeway over the marsh between the Court House and the Tinkling Spring, 52
bridge made by Samuel Cowdon, 120
causeway made by Samuel Cowdon, 120
James Given's bridge and mill dam, 104
bridge near Daniel Kidd's, 147
Lewis Creek bridge, 74
Long Meadow bridge, 16, 101, 116, 143
Long Meadow causeway, 101
Madisons Meadow causeway, 105, 106
Col. Patton's bridge, 10
bridge near John Poage's, 102
causeway near John Poage's, 102
bridge near Robert Poage's, 99
causeway near Robert Poage's, 99
bridge on the road from George Mathew's to Rockfish Gap, 116
Seder Bridge, 121
Smith's Bridge, 100
Daniel Smith's Bridge, 112
bridge below Staunton, 113
causeway over the run below the town [Staunton], 87
Timber Broge [bridge?], 7

causeway at Vause's, 106, 107, 123, 125, 126, 128
Wilderness Bridge, 70, 117

Ferries and Fords

John Allison's ferry, 8, 150
John Allison's ford, 91
Baskin's ford, 91
James Beard's ford, 63, 127, 137
first ford above Bell's land, 5
Bingaman's ferry, 53
Brush Bottom ford, 26
Buchanan's ferry, 117
Buchanan's ford on James River, 153
Buffallow Creek ford, 79
Buffalo ford, 81
Gilbert Campbell's ford, 13
Catabo Creek ford, 96
first ford on Catabo Creek, 12, 30, 90
lower ford on Catabo Creek, 6, 39
Cherry tree bottom ford, 30
Chester's ford, 41
Cole's ford, 95
Davidson's ford, 91
Samuel Davidson's ford, 89
English's ferry, 132
[NOTE: see also Ingleses ferry]
John Fowler's fording, 128
Ingleses/Inglis's ferry, 98, 109, 113, 123, 128, 129
James River ferry, 76, 129, 138
James River ferry & ford, 85
best James River ford, 144
ford on north branch of James River, 100
second ford on Jenning's Branch, 56
Jones' ford, 87, 90, 134

ford near Daniel Kidd's, 145
Looney's ferry, 21, 90
Looney's ford, 5
North River ford, 79, 105, 133
North River wagon ford, 76
Paxton's ford, 77
Pedlar ford (on James River), 118, 119, 122, 124, 131, 147
ford near Esther Robinson's, 47
Secretary ford, 92
Old ford on Tinker Creek, 142
Trimble's ford, 87

Land Features (Mountains, Gaps, etc.)

[NOTE: "Ridge" and "Blue Ridge" may be used interchangeably; check both references]

Armer's Gaps, 48
Bedford Gap, 90
Beverley's Big Meadows, 23, 24
Blew/Blue Ridge, 1, 2, 6, 14, 17, 21, 22, 23, 29, 31, 33, 38, 41, 117
Blue Ledge, 14
Samuel Braford's meadow, 41
Brock's Gap, 47, 74, 79, 84, 111
Buffalo/Buffaloe Gap, 125, 128, 148, 149, 151
dividing ridge of Catapo, 40
Cherry tree bottom, 30
James Cowan's meadow, 55
Craig's Creek Mountain, 135
Dry Branch Gap, 142
Dry Gap, 149, 151
Dry River Gap, 77, 79
Eagle bottom, 5
James Fulton's meadow, 50
Gilmer's Gap, 137
Graham's Clearing, 90, 135, 136
Great Lick, 90, 101, 115, 117, 136, 149
Great Licks, 86
Gry [Dry? Guy?] Branch Gap, 93

Grymes' Clearing, 94, 95
Hands meadow, 47
Rubin Harrison's meadow, 89
Hart's bottom, 85
Hays's Gap, 117
Hill near the Road from the Court House to Edward Tarr's, 98
House Mountain, 148
Jenings's/Jennings's/Jennings'es Gap, 1, 2, 15, 22, 34, 37, 43, 62, 82, 84, 92, 100, 104, 113, 115, 116, 121, 123, 124, 127, 133
Kingkade's Gap, 77
King's Gap, 26
Lewis's great bottom, 22
Long/Longs Glade, 34, 43, 57, 62, 100, 104, 127
[NOTE: may also refer to Long Glade Creek]
Long Meadow, 101
Madison's Meadow, 105
Massenutting, 154
McAfee's/Mcafee's Gap, 135, 139
Mole Hill, 147
Gap near Montgomery's, 119
the Mountain/the Mountains, 9, 31, 32, 53, 54
Mountain by William King's, 1, 11
Mountain Near Alexander Thompson's, 4
Mountain near Craigs Creek, 119
North Mountain, 3, 4, 7, 8, 9, 19, 20, 21, 40, 42, 72, 75, 82, 84, 92, 93, 99, 101
    South side of, 82
North Mountain Gap, 47
the old Gap, 55
Painter Gap, 83, 86, 116, 132, 141
Panther Gap, 76, 90
Peaked Mountain, 7, 8
Poplar Hill, 77, 144
Poplar Hills, 81, 124
the Ridge, 1, 2, 9, 10, 14, 58, 71, 77, 99
Ridge above Tobias Bright's, 6
Ridge adjoining to Lunenburg County, 4
Ridge between Daniel Deniston's and John Poage's, 91

Ridge by John Harrison Jr.'s,. deceased, 98
Ridge Leading to Louisa [County], 8
dividing ridge between New River and the South Branch of Roan Oak, 5, 6
dividing Ridge beween Wood's River and the South Fork of Roan Oak, 20
dividing ridge between the waters of Roan oak and Mississippi, 14
Ridge near John Terrald's, 7
Rockfish/Rock Fish/Rock-Fish Gap, 8, 48, 84, 91, 93, 94, 95, 97,99, 106, 107, 108, 120, 130, 143
   New, 92
Sinclar's Gap, 118
South Mountain, 8, 9, 68, 84
Swift/Swit Run Gap/Pass, 6, 9, 23, 24, 30, 31, 32, 34, 35, 36, 41, 44, 46, 47, 58, 71, 77, 97, 99, 100, 101, 117, 120, 123, 126, 129, 152, 153
Gap at Tavern Spring, 64
Tees's Gap, 101
Thorn's Gap, 3, 11, 32, 33
Timber Ridge, 26, 29, 60, 69, 82, 98, 106, 140
Warwick Gap, 64
John Willson's Gap, 76
Woods's Gap, 8, 16, 17, 58, 77, 79, 84, 93
   New Cleared/New Gap, 26, 39
   Old pass, 21

Meeting Houses, Churches and Glebes

Brown's Meeting House, 41, 147
Church (to be built), 10
Dunkers, 6
Fork Meeting House, 50
Glebe/Glebe Land, 41, 44, 52, 109, 112, 117, 138, 145
the Meeting House, 6, 11, 19, 36
Lower Meeting house, 4, 9, 13, 14, 17
Meeting House on Cook's Creek, 83, 86
New Meeting House, 18

North Mountain Meeting House, 15,19, 20, 21, 42, 72, 75, 93, 99, 101
Parish of Augusta, 133
Providence Meeting House, 20, 35, 43, 60, 98, 116, 117
Stone Meeting House, 16, 23, 24, 29, 32, 36, 41, 54, 56, 63, 76, 79, 80, 89, 91, 93, 97, 109, 119, 122, 127, 128, 131, 134, 138, 139, 141, 143, 148, 151
Timber Ridge Meeting House, 29, 69, 82, 106, 140
Tinkling Spring Meeting house, 10, 75, 76, 112

Mills and Mill Dams

Benjamin Allen's mill, 1
Archer's mill, 92, 142
John Archer's mill, 130, 140, 149, 151
Buchanan's mill, 38, 40, 92, 93
John Buchanans mill, 26
Carter's mill, 7
James Carter's mill, 5
Coburn's mill, 22, 29
Craig's mill/mills, 134, 137
James Craig's mill, 140
Davis's mill, 61
David Davis's mill, 1
John Davis's mill, 26, 41, 131, 136
James Edmondson's mill, 50
Wallace Estell's mill, 29, 44
Estill's mill, 118, 123
Evans's mill, 138
Givens's mill, 41, 97, 133
James Givens's mill, 39, 104, 134
James Givens's mill dam, 104
Hall's mill, 76
William Hall's mill, 141, 145
Handley's mill, 125
John Hanna's mill, 148
Harrison's mill, 153
Mathew Harrison's mills, 152, 153
Frederick Hartsaw's mill, 54

Hays's mill, 43, 69, 82
Hays's fulling mill, 29
Adrew Hays's mill, 68
John Hays's mill, 20
Hopkins's Mill, 152
Calop Jones's mill, 7, 15
Kenaday's mill, 43, 70
Joseph Kenaday's mill, 47
King's mill, 76, 79, 126
John King's mill, 99
John King's mill on Middle River, 99
John King's mill on Naked Creek, 99
Long's saw mill, 82
Joseph Long's mill, 40, 98
William Long's mill, 14, 38, 92
Robert Looney's mill, 64
Mathews's Mill, 101, 116, 131
George Mathews' mill, 99
McClenachan's mill, 136
William McClenachan's mill, 137
McCutcheon's mill, 125, 128
Robert McCutcheon's mill, 34
McMurty's mill, 135, 139
John Miller's mill, 100
Moore's Mill, 19, 21
David Moore's mill, 30, 65
North mill, 109
Nutt's mill, 36, 65
Col. Patton's mill place, 112
Patton's mill, 25, 29
Pickens's grist mill, 56
Pickens's mill, 9, 14, 17, 36
John Poage's mill, 126
Robert Poage's mill place, 30
Ramsay's mill, 76
Peter Reed's mill, 39
Risk's Mill, 44, 60, 117, 128
John Risk's mill, 52, 116
Capt. John Robinson's mill, 132
John Robinson's mill, 134
Rufner's mill, 42
Rusk's mill, 75
the saw mill, 84
Alexander Sayers's mill, 53

John Seewright's mill, 145
Sivers' mill, 79
John Staly's mill, 21
Steel's mill, 146, 147
Benjamin Stuart's mill, 150
Tate's mill, 81
John Tate's mill, 72, 99, 101
Thomas's mill, 86, 87, 90, 108
John Thomas's mill, 100
William Wilson's mill, 44, 129, 147
Wright's mill, 32
Young's Mill, 38, 91, 145
James Young's mill, 8, 40

Mines

Hite's, 126
Lead, 98, 128
Adam Reader's, 131
Ruder's, 146

Miscellaneous

Beverley/Beverly Manor line, 13, 35, 68, 70, 72, 102, 110, 117
Black Thorn, 128
Borden's (patent) line, 20, 72, 101, 106
Burden's Tract, 32
Campbell's school house, 52
Carr's shop, 87, 91
Chestnut Hill, 143
Clerk's Office, 3
Court House, 1 2, 3, 4, 5, 7, 8, 9, 10,11, 13, 15, 16, 17, 18,19,21, 26, 27, 31, 34, 36, 40, 41, 42, 43, 44, 45, 46, 49, 51, 52, 57, 62, 63, 64, 65, 66, 67, 78, 79, 83, 84, 86, 87, 91, 93, 98, 99
Cowan's line, 70
James Cowan's line, 69
James Cowden's store house, 153
James Cowdon's store, 150
the Den, 134
Lord Fairfax's Line, 100, 101

Fort Chiswell, 95, 109
Fort Defiance, 125
Fort Lewis, 95, 101, 105, 107, 108, 112, 113, 115, 118
Fort William, 100, 135
Fort Young, 118
John Fowler's still house, 124
Fredericksburg, 8, 34
Gratton's store, 138
William Hamilton's fenced ground, 76
Kerr's shop, 122
William Mcbride's shop, 130
James Montgomery's lower line, 144
New Providence, 26
Pennsylvania, 84
Providence, 128
the race paths, 79
Alexander Richey's smiths shop, 38
the rocks below the town [Staunton], 101
the smith's shop near Jacob Roger's, 18
Staunton, town of [this town], 54, 72,74, 79, 87, 91, 92, 93, 96, 98, 101, 102, 104-106, 109, 110, 111, 112, 113
[NOTE: see also entries for Court House]
Stone House, 91-93, 105, 107, 108,112, 138, 142, 150
Tarr's Shop, 61, 62
Edward Tarr's old shop, 106
Thomas Teat's shop, 44
Timber Broge, 7
Timber Grove, 10, 15
Warwick, 38, 134

Other Counties, County Lines, etc.

Albemarle County
    County line, 21, 92
    Court/Court House, 21
Amherst County Court, 92
Bedford County line, 91, 92, 107, 117, 136, 141, 146, 153
Bounds of Brunswick County, 2
County line, 3, 7, 15, 21, 22, 77, 79, 82, 101, 137, 140, 151, 152
old County Line, 144
County line below Jacob Peterson's, 109
Culpeper County
    Court/Justices, 18, 41
    County Line, 18, 41
Frederick County line, 15, 18, 31, 41
Hampshire County line, 69, 74
Louisa [county line], 8
Lunenburg (Luninburg/Luningsburgh)
    County line, 4, 16, 20
    Court/Court House, 4, 16, 20
Orange County Court, 2, 8, 9, 25, 58

Personal Names
[NOTE: Names may be spelled several different ways; all spelling variants should be checked]

George, the Tinker, 5
Tom (slave), 98
Acres
    Thomas, 51
    Uriah, 51
Akres
    Simon, 2
Akers
    William, 51
Akry
    William, 40, 44
Alcorn
    Robert, 20
Alexander
    Archabald/Archibald, 30, 35, 61,62, 69, 77, 79, 81, 84, 95, 135
    Francis, 99, 101, 116, 143
    Gabriel, 38
    James, 14, 22, 32, 33, 38, 77, 112, 116, 130
    William, 27, 141
Alkin
    Manis, 39
Allen
    Benjamin, 1
    Hugh, 110, 111, 134, 148
    James, 9, 17, 31, 32, 79, 134, 139
    Malcolm/Malcom, 129, 149, 151

Robert, 133, 149
Robert, Jr., 140
Robert, Sr., 140
Allison
    John, 8, 52, 71, 75, 76, 91, 150
    Robert, 73
    Samuel, 52
Anderson
    George, 78, 87, 91
    Isaac, 69
    Jacob, 29, 58, 60, 69, 82, 149
    James, 27, 71, 83
    John, 2, 9, 17, 18, 19, 29, 31, 36, 48,
        66, 69, 76, 78, 100, 131, 134, 144, 145, 146
    John, Jr., 57, 130
    John, Sr., 63
    William/Wm, 5, 9, 36, 38, 45, 71, 111
Andrews
    Adam, 51
Anglen
    James, 28
Arbuckle
    James, 129
    Matt, 153
Archenbright
    Jacob, 99
Archer
    _____, 92, 142
    John, 5, 71, 130, 140, 149, 151
    Sampson, 5, 34, 62, 82
Armer
    _____, 48
Armstong
    Robert, 62, 115
Armstrong
    Archibald, 70, 94
    Black James, 14
    James, 3, 14
    John, 96
    Robert, 1, 2, 5, 56, 92, 134, 142,
        150, 151
    Thomas, 34, 82, 127, 152
    William/Wm, 19, 28, 51, 84, 152,
        153

Arnold
    Stephen, 50, 52
    Steven, 50
Baggs
    Alexander, 52
    James, 56
    Thomas, 74
Bailey
    _____, 130
Baird
    James, 75
Baker
    George, 129
    Humphrey, 6, 51, 129
Baley
    James, 50
Ball
    David, 95
    James, 71, 75
Balley
    James, 31
Ballon
    Henry, 20
Bane
    James, 51
Bard
    Thomas, 5
Barnes
    Thomas, 108, 137
Barnett
    Robert, 129
Bartley
    James, 34
    John, 4, 40, 44
Barton
    Thomas, 40
Baskin
    _____, 91
    Andr, 39
    John, 87, 91, 102, 114, 127
    William, 9, 17, 19
Bats
    James, 40
Baxter

George, 131, 152
Bealey
    James, 52
Bean
    James, 6
    John, 49
Beard
    James, 7, 8, 16, 18, 24, 63, 67, 70, 80, 85, 119, 122, 127, 137, 153
    John, 35, 131, 134
    Thomas, 45
    William/Wm, 23, 26, 88, 97, 98, 103, 109, 114, 127, 131, 142
Beggs
    Alexander, 50
Belay
    Edward, 50
Bell
    _____, 5
    David, 63, 68, 76, 97, 146
    James, 4, 5, 17, 22, 32, 33, 38, 44, 70, 100, 112, 116, 117, 140, 142, 144, 149, 150, 151, 154
    John, 129
    Joseph, 39, 137
    Samuel, 134
    William/Wm, 9, 17, 39, 44, 58, 149
    William, Jr., 9, 61
Belon
    Richard, 50
Belshee
    Robert, 147
Belshire
    Robert, 80, 97
Bennet
    John, 133
Bens
    William, 6
Berkley
    James, 41
Berriford
    John, 50, 52
Berry
    George, 44
    John, 40, 121
    Thomas, 89, 96, 116, 117, 122
    William, 70
Bethell
    William, 42
Beverley
    _____, 13, 23, 24, 35, 110, 117
Beverly
    _____, 68, 70, 72, 102
Bigam
    John, 71
Bigham
    John, 40, 42, 46, 67
Bingaman
    _____, 53
    John, Jr., 53
    John, Senior, 53
Bird
    Abraham, 82, 126
    Andrew, 13
Bishop
    Edward, 50, 52
Black
    _____, 35, 78
    Anthony, 14, 38
    Henry, 110
    James, 67
    John, 5, 38, 40, 42, 46, 75, 139, 146, 153
    Mathew/Matthew, 88, 106
    Samuel, 61, 67
    William, 118, 123, 139, 148
Blair
    Alexander, 69, 72, 108
    James, Jr, 140
    John, 14, 140
Blanton
    William, 129
Bledsoe
    Anthony, 129
Bodkin
    Hugh, 129

James, 129
John, 129, 141
Richard, 28, 61, 113, 129
Bohanon
   Williams, 74
Boil
   William, 50
Bollen
   Edmond, 26
Boller
   John, 150
Bomgardner
   John, 7
Borden
   _____, 20, 42, 72, 101, 106
   Benjamin/Benja, 9, 12, 13, 21, 28, 29, 30, 35
   Widow, 42
Bosart
   Joseph, 143
Bowen
   John, 119, 124, 138, 145
   Reece, 153
   William, 153
Bowyer
   John, 76, 95, 107, 110, 119, 121, 124, 144, 149
   Michael, 138, 145
   Thomas, 151
   William, 91, 113, 148, 151
Boyd
   Alexander, 90
   Thomas, 82
Boyn
   John, 5
Brackenridge
   Robert, 75
Bradshaw
   Thomas, 143
   William, 52
Brady
   William, 5
Brafford
   Samuel, 153

Braford
   Samuel, 41
Braham
   John, 11
Bratton
   Robert, 56, 58, 84, 115, 129
Brawford
   Samuel, 150
Brealey
   Daniel, 5
Breckenridge
   Captain, 92
   George, 50
   Rob, 66
   Robert, 46, 55, 59, 77, 112, 123, 142
Breckeridge
   Major, 149
Breckinridge
   Robert, 107
Bredshaw
   Thomas, 132
Brian
   Thomas, 100
Briant
   John, 11
Bright
   Erick, 40
   George, 6
   Tobais/Tobias, 6, 37, 39, 40, 53
Brock
   _____, 74, 79, 84
Brocke
   _____, 34
Brown
   _____, 41, 44, 52, 77, 78, 130, 145, 147
   Abraham, 76, 105, 144
   Abram, 50
   Francis, 27
   Henry, 6, 50, 62
   Henry Jr, 51
   Henry, Sr, 51
   Jacob, 6, 14, 40, 53, 54
   James, 18, 42, 45

John, 4, 11, 40, 41, 59, 72, 75, 77, 104, 110, 111, 115
Major, 117
Mr., 121
Robert, 26, 80, 94, 148
Samuel/Saml, 6, 14
Thomas, 93
William/Wm, 8, 26, 40, 64, 72, 80

Brownlee
Alexander, 49, 50, 59, 60, 70, 72
John, 11, 112, 117, 142

Bruister
James/Jas, 109, 111, 132

Bryan
John, 51, 86, 89, 100, 126
Thomas, 108
William, 49, 51, 112, 132
William, Jr., 51

Bryans
David, 101, 117
John, 131
Thomas, 131
William, 109, 113, 129, 136

Bryant
John, 26

Buchanan
_____, 38, 91-93, 117, 153
Alexander, 98, 102, 107
Col., 119, 124, 144
James, 25, 111
Colo John, 8
John, 4, 7, 23, 26, 38, 40, 46, 53, 59, 66, 74, 76, 84, 95, 98, 109, 110, 116, 119, 123, 125, 128, 131, 132, 151
Samuel, 39, 70, 73
William, 4

Buchannan
Colo John, 14
John, 10

Bullett
_____, 147

Burden
_____, 32

Burger
Steven Hans, 33

Burk
James, 6
John, 100
Thomas, 7, 100
William, 7, 33

Burnside
John, 134

Burnsides
John, 119, 122

Burt
William, 52

Burton
Richard, 5, 16, 21, 52

Byers
William, 52

Byran
William, 49

Byrnsides
James, 129

Cadwell
James, 36

Cain
Nicholas, 69

Caldwell
_____, 119
George/Geo, 4, 10, 25, 55, 66, 75, 93
James, 14, 46, 50, 65

Callachan
Charles, 146

Callison
James, 38, 94, 138

Cambell
Charles, 38
Patrick, 38

Campbell
_____, 52
Charles, 8, 9, 26, 29, 38, 39, 45, 48, 50, 57, 62, 63, 65, 110, 136, 144
David, 138
George, 42, 137

Gilbert, 13
Hugh, 26, 34
James, 6, 8, 10, 14, 19, 38, 40, 49, 51, 56, 60, 64, 140
John, 4, 14, 19, 27, 38, 40, 42, 44, 46, 65, 81, 86, 134, 140
Malcome, 51
Patrick, 11, 55, 69, 150
Robert, 23, 24, 26, 34, 44, 121
William, 75, 104

Canaday
    Joseph, 29
Canady
    Joseph, 12
Cannaday
    Joseph, 15
Caphon
    _____, 27
Caravan
    _____, 56
Carlile
    James, 47, 60
    John, 28, 44, 50, 60, 61, 129
    Robert, 28, 44, 129
    William, 28
Carlock
    Conrod, 51
    David, 51
    Frederick, 20, 51
    George, 51
    H[illegible], 39
Carpenter
    George, 132
    Joseph, 32, 37
    Joseph, Jr, 126
    Joseph, Sr, 125
    Thomas, 125
    Zophar, 125
Carpentor
    Nathaniel, 125
    Soloman, 125
    Thomas, 125
Carr
    _____, 87, 91, 96
    David, 34, 45, 59
    James, 16
    John, 40
Carravan
    William, 51
Carrigan
    Patrick, 126
Carroll
    Terrance, 26
    William, 27, 35
Carscaden
    Robert, .26
Carson
    Isaac, 130
Carter
    _____, 7
    James, 1, 5
Cartmill
    Henry, 116
Caruthers
    Hugh, 53
Carvin
    _____, 63
    William, 49, 63, 107
Carwin
    _____, 53
    William, 105
Castle
    Jacob, 6, 20
Cathey
    James, 117
Cave
    James, 20
Chiswell
    _____, 95, 109
Chittam
    _____, 74
Christian
    _____, 14, 16, 25, 45, 51, 78, 79, 81, 102, 104, 105, 106, 116, 126, 146
    Capt, 25, 137
    Israel/Israil, 16, 22, 31, 32, 44, 45, 46, 51, 54, 57, 77, 83, 93, 94,

    96, 98, 112, 113, 120, 128,
    134, 136, 142
  John, 14, 25, 31, 112, 117
  Robert/Robt, 14, 77, 119
  William/Wm, 9, 10, 13, 14, 46, 82,
    84, 129, 132
Christy
  _____, 46, 91
Clanie
  Michael, 6
Clark
  Alexander, 130
  James, 4, 40, 44, 52
  James, Jr., 44
  John, 44, 149
  Margaret, 128, 147, 150
Clayman
  Christians, 16
Claypole
  James, 34
  Willm, 34
Clements
  Christian, 134, 137
  Jacob, 60
Clemons
  Christian, 97, 134
Clendening
  Chas., 5
Clighorn
  Wm, 38
Cloyd
  David, 64, 90
  David, Junior, 119
  James, 119, 121, 135
  Michael, 136
Cober
  Jacob, 7
Coburn
  _____, 22, 29
Cochran
  John, 115
Cochrane
  John, 115
Cockmill
  John, 7
Cockrance
  John, 91
Coe
  Timothy, 51
Coffey
  Hugh, 7
Coger
  Jacob, 12, 16, 33
  Michael, 101
Coile
  James, 4
Cole
  _____, 95
Colett
  Abrahm, 9
Colhoon
  James, 6
  Patrick, 5
  William, 5
Colhouns
  Ezekiel, 20
Colier
  Moses, 148
Collet
  Abraham, 35
Collett
  _____, 8
Collier
  John, 40
Collins
  Duke, 29
Colter
  John, 138
Combs
  Andrew, 27
  Mason, 26
Condon
  James, 129
Conerly
  Thomas, 88
Coningham
  Adam, 26

Robert, 25
Conley
　James, 20
　John, 20
Connelly
　Thomas, 137, 141
Connerley
　Thomas, 97
Connerly
　Thomas, 127, 145
Cook
　_____, 83, 86
　Henry, 53
　Patrick, 4, 7, 9
Cooper
　John Finlas, 2
Coulter
　John, 112, 150
Coulton
　John, 112
　Joseph/Jos, 8, 12, 15, 35, 69
　Joseph, Capt., 29
Counce
　Martin, 51
Coutt
　John, 154
Cowan
　_____, 70
　Andrew, 21, 38, 40, 72
　James, 48, 49, 54, 55, 57, 69, 72
Cowden
　James, 153
　Samuel, 117
Cowdon
　James, 145, 150
　Samuel, 120
Cox
　Andrew, 51
　Charles, 7
Craig
　_____, 30, 53, 54, 61, 118, 119, 134, 135, 137, 139, 150
　Alexander, 69
　James, 133, 134, 137, 140
　John, 18, 22, 23, 94
　Mr, 86
　Robert, 35, 83
Craige
　Alexander, 73
　John, 30
Craven
　_____, 3
　John, 88, 125, 133, 142
　Peter, 51
　Robert/Robt., 3, 10, 17, 23, 31, 64, 44, 133
　William, 74
Cravens
　John, 138
　Robert, 11, 22, 152
Crawford
　Alexander, 5, 52, 92
　George, 9
　Gilbert, 40
　John, 107, 118, 124, 147, 150
　Patrick, 34, 61, 63, 81, 103
Cresswell
　Henry, 151, 154
Crestwell
　Henry, 4
Crim
　Philip, 7
Crisp
　William, 20
Crocket
　_____, 26
　Hugh, 144
　Joseph, 20
Crockett
　Hugh, 126, 130
　James, 141
　Robert, 130
Crosby
　_____, 107
Cross
　Charles, 33
Crouch
　John, 47

Crow
- William, 84, 96, 101, 110

Crump
- Edmond, 52

Crunk
- Richard, 3

Cuin
- Nicholas, 56

Culton
- Captain, 117
- Joseph, 149

Cuningham
- Adam, 7
- David, 94
- John, 42, 45, 46, 47, 54, 55
- Robert, 22, 112

Cunningham
- David, 138

Curruthers
- William, 113

Curry
- William, 124

Dailey
- John, 135

Daley
- Charles, 12

Dalton
- Robert, 48

Daniel
- Deniston, Jr., 9

Davids
- Samuel, 10

Davidson
- _____, 91
- Andrew, 88
- John, 94, 129
- Samuel, 79, 89

Davies
- Robert, 10

Davis
- _____, 61, 152
- David, 1, 8, 23, 32
- James, 30, 43, 51, 53, 89, 137
- John, 4, 6, 26, 32, 41, 42, 63, 75, 88, 96, 108, 123, 124, 129, 131, 133, 136
- Patrick, 23, 24, 37
- Robert, 4, 5, 11, 12, 40, 44
- Samuel, 77
- Walter, 66, 75
- William, 106 120

Davison
- Daniel, 19, 85
- James, 53
- John, 127, 128

Dean
- John, 152

Deniston
- Daniel, 9, 11, 18, 24, 60, 91, 94
- Daniel, Jr., 9

Dennison
- Daniel, 1

Denton
- _____, 24
- John, Capt., 3
- Jonas, 3, 24
- Robert, 21

Dickens
- Henry, 8

Dickenson
- Adam, 7, 23, 24, 32, 37
- John, 24, 57, 76, 90
- John, Captain, 90
- Joseph, 139

Dickey
- Michael, 26, 48, 131, 136

Dickinson
- _____, 148, 150, 152
- Adam, 7
- Captain, 116, 119, 122, 130
- John, 122
- John, Captain, 148
- Wm, 26

Dickton
- Joseph, 121, 138

Dill
- John, 6

Peter, 6
Diver
    Charles, 26
    Hugh, 26
Doage
    David, 99, 102, 104
Doak
    David, 81
Dobkins
    John, 8
Doggett
    Richard, 146
Dollis
    Charles, 14
Donaho
    Cornelius, 40
    Hugh, 137, 141
Donalin
    John, 6
Donerly
    Charles, 132
    John, 7
    William, 7
Donnerly
    Charles, 150, 152
    ffrancis, 13
Dooley
    Henry, 47, 136, 141
Dougherty
    Michael, 49
    William/Wm, 137, 153
Douglas
    Hugh, 129
Douglass
    Hugh, 129
    James, 129
Dove
    _____, 90
Downey
    Samuel, 21, 138
Downing
    James, 30
    John, 20
    Samuel, 40, 72

Downs
    _____, 24, 32
    Capt., 1
    Henry, 4, 9, 13, 23, 54, 67
    Henry, Jr., 11, 13, 14, 23, 29
Draper
    George, 6
    John, 129
    Widow, 53
    William, 43
Dryden
    David, 95, 106, 122
Drydon
    David, 28, 80
Duel
    Charles, 7
Duffield
    Robert, 129
Duglass
    George, 39
    Hugh, 126
    James, 126
    Jonathan, 34
Dunbarr
    John, 21
Duncan
    William, 113
Dunkle
    John, 77
Dunlap
    _____, 150
    Robert, 125, 128
Dunlop
    Robert, 29, 39, 40, 45, 60
Dunn
    Francis, 40
Dye
    Jacob, 8
Dyer
    James, 5
    Roger, 29
    William, 66, 67
Earley
    Jeremiah, 58

Mordicai, 20
Early
    Jeremiah, 47
    John, 71, 97
Edmiston
    David, 14
    James, 85
Edmondson
    _____, 1
    James, 13, 39, 50, 52
    John, 40
    Mathew, 1, 15, 22, 34
    William, 50
Edmondston
    Matthew, 5
Elliot
    John, 5
    William/Wm, 23, 34, 70, 125, 128
Elliott
    William, 125
Elswick
    John, 21
English
    _____, 96, 132
    Joseph, 109
    Mathew, 6
    Thomas, 6
    William, 6
Ephraim
    Buck, 7
Ervin
    Henry, 147
Erwin
    _____, 125
    Andrew, 26, 34, 48, 59, 61, 62, 65
    Benjamin, 26
    David, 141
    Edward, 22, 26, 124
    Edward, Jr, 121, 123, 124
    Francis, 26, 120
    Francis, Junr., 136
    John, 26
    Robert, 96
    Samuel, 139

Estell
    Wallace, 41, 44, 47, 50
Estham
    Francis, .6
Estill
    _____, 118, 123, 128
    John, 118, 123, 129, 130, 135, 141
    Wallace/Wallis, 28, 46, 128, 129, 147
Evan
    Uriah, 6
Evans
    _____, 72, 96, 138
    Daniel, 19, 28, 51
    Evan, 65, 67
    Mark, 2, 6, 8, 10
    Nathaniel/Nath, 65, 72, 82, 105, 122
    Peter, 107, 112, 146
Ewing
    James, 117, 147
Ezekiel
    George, 5
Fairfax
    Lord, 100, 101, 142
Farguson
    John, 5
    Samuel, 14, 28
Faught
    Andrew/Andw, 143
Feemster
    _____, 129
    Thomas, 94, 118, 129, 152
Ferguson
    Henry, 92
Fimster
    Thomas, 83
Fincher
    Samuel, 37
Findlay
    Jno, 131
Findley
    John, 121
Finla
    _____, 36

    John, 1, 15, 34, 36, 42, 76
    William, 55, 59, 68
    Wm, 39
Finlay
    William, 31, 59
Finley
    John, 74, 101, 123, 140, 149
    Robert, 140
    William, 22, 72, 140
Finly
    Robert, 32
Finney
    Michael, 30, 50, 52, 82
Fleming
    William, 113, 124
Forman
    John, 20
Foster
    Andrew, 44
Fought
    Andrew, 65, 134
    John, 33
Fowler
    John, 124, 128, 133
    Robert, 26, 41, 130, 140, 141
Foyle
    Robert, 34
Fraizer
    James, 154
Fram
    James, 14
Frame
    David, 129
    James, 32
    Thomas, 115
    William, 26
Frances
    John, 27
Francis
    John, 35, 57, 62, 66, 100
Francisco
    Ludwic/Ludwick, 6, 12, 44, 87, 133
    Stiffell, 8
Frazier
    _____, 71, 154
    James, 50, 52, 104
    John, 14, 109
    Patrick, 31, 35, 37, 49, 109
    Robert, 8, 95, 134, 137
    Samuel, 143
    William, 16, 97
Freelan
    James, 129
Frelen
    John, 125
Fuller
    Henry, 50, 52
Fulton
    _____, 26, 63
    Hugh, 19, 102
    James, 12, 21, 38, 45, 48, 50, 69
    John, 23, 73, 89, 150
    Thomas, 23, 60, 83, 93, 110, 111
    Widow, 47
    William, 122
F[illegible]rnice
    John, 33
Galespie
    James, 68, 130
    John, 140
Galespie
    Thomas, 130
Galespy
    James, 23, 36, 55, 63, 73
    Robert, 126
    William, 7, 122
Galispy
    William, 32
Gallespy
    William, 119
Galliad
    James, 51
Gamble
    James, 81, 108
    Joseph, 74, 83, 84, 87, 97
    Robert, 27
Gamwell
    James, 130, 145

Joseph, 106
Gardner
    Alexander, 5
    Francis, 5
    Thomas, 5, 93
Garrison
    Paul, 6
Garwin
    Edward, 93
Gathive
    _____, 139
Gay
    Capt, 5
    Henry, 57
    James, 83, 86, 90, 116, 132
    John, 23
    Robert/Robt, 1, 13, 34, 44, 60, 84
    Samuel, 1, 44
    Widow, 115, 121
    William/Wm, 23
Gent
    Abraham, 134
Gerrall
    William, 39
Gerrott
    Wm, 37
Gibson
    Alexander, 5, 121
    George, 40, 148
    Robert, 10, 56
    Samuel, 40, 116
Gilbert
    Felix, 66, 77, 78, 79, 83, 84, 87, 91, 96, 103, 104, 107, 109, 117, 123, 125, 138, 139, 150
Gilberts
    Felix, 75
Gilham
    Thomas, 37, 60
Gilkason
    Robert, 5
Gilkison
    Archibald, 140
Gill
    James, 2
Gillespy
    James, 140
Gillilan
    Nathan, 152
Gilliland
    Nathan, 38, 46, 93
Gillispy
    William, 153
Gilmer
    _____, 137
Gilmore
    James/Jas, 40, 102, 110, 148
    John, 86, 100, 149
    Peachey Ridgway (Ridgeway), 104, 106
Givens
    _____, 17, 97, 133
    James, 17, 104, 133, 134, 141
    Samuel/Saml, 4, 17, 19, 38, 48, 58, 65, 129
    William, 129, 147
Givins
    _____, 41
    James, 39
Goldman
    Henry, 51
    Jacob, 20, 51
    John, 20
Good
    Conrod, 111
Goodman
    Jacob, 88
Goodson
    Thomas, 130
Gordon
    Thomas, 9, 19, 146
Gorrell[Gorrett?]
    James, 40
Gorrett
    James, 40
    Wm, 45
Gragg
    Robert, 133

    William, 121
Graham
    _____, 90, 135, 136
    Archd, 51
    John, 5, 22, 130
    Robert, 20
    William/Wm, 49, 51, 63, 90, 136
Grattan
    John, 143
Gratton
    _____, 138
    John, 82, 111, 126
Gray
    Jacob, 55
    Robert, 79
Grayon
    Thomas, 129
Green
    Francis, 111
Greenlee
    James, 55, 96, 118, 145
    John, 118
Greer
    Andrew, 140, 151
Gregg
    Roberts, 134
Grider
    Benja, 26
Griffeths
    Mathusaleth, 6
Griffith
    Thomas, 3
Grigory
    Nap, 35
Grimes
    _____, 92
Grubbs
    Francis, 26
    Thomas, 7
Grymes
    _____, 86, 94, 95
    Archibald, 85
    Francis, 138
    John, 1, 98

    William, 91, 94, 98, 128
Gum
    Jacob, 35
    John, 123, 138
Gunnoe
    Alexander, 26
Guy
    John, 34
    Samuel, 34
    William/Wm, 34
Gwinns
    James, 128
Gwins
    John, 17, 39
Hair
    Matthew, 121
Halderman
    Jacob, 69
Hall
    _____, 76
    Andrew, 150
    Edward, 9, 16, 38
    Edwd, 10
    James/Jas., 22, 27, 28
    John, 121, 137
    Moses, 80, 83
    Robert, 118
    William, 40, 65, 67, 78, 121, 141,
        145
    William, jr., 59
Hambleton
    Thomas, 129
Hamilton
    Alexander, 125, 128
    Andrew, 1, 2, 29, 57, 60, 121, 148
    Archibald, 71, 88, 122, 137, 148
    Audley, 87, 91, 94
    Isaiah, 51
    James, 14, 78, 89, 91
    John, 148, 152
    Patrick, 126
    Robert, 149
    Samuel, 130
    William/Wm, 15, 20, 21, 26, 31, 76

Hanah
: Joseph, 95

Handley
: _____, 125
: John, 73, 89, 145

Handlon
: William, 5

Hands
: _____, 47

Hankins
: John, 26
: William, 7

Hanley
: John, 34

Hanna
: John/Jno, 137, 148

Hannah
: John, 40, 122
: Joseph, 101

Hans Burger
: Steven, 33

Harbeson
: William, 85

Harbison
: William, 100

Harden
: Henry, 41, 49

Hardin
: Benjamin, 3
: John, 50

Harding
: Henry, 7

Hare
: John, 34, 36, 45, 48, 80

Harges
: John, 52

Hargrove
: John, 30

Hargus
: John, 50

Harman
: Jacob, 6
: Valintine, 6

Harmon
: Adam, 6, 46
: Jacob, 7
: Jacob, Jr., 59
: Jacob, Sr., 8
: John, 8

Harper
: Hance, 28, 94
: Mathew, 28, 41, 46
: Michael, 28

Harplore
: Nicholas, 109

Harrald
: William, 31, 49

Harrel
: William, 7

Harris
: Henry, 39
: James, 20

Harrison
: Benjamin, 116, 123, 124, 126, 147, 152
: Daniel, 30, 31, 41, 77
: Jeremiah, 3, 46
: John, 13, 19, 23, 83, 85, 98, 100, 112, 140, 151
: John, Junr., 98
: Matthew, 152, 153
: Mr., 153
: Nehemiah, 152
: Reuben/Reubin/Ruben/Rubin, 33, 89, 112, 126, 152
: Thomas, 3, 83, 86, 131
: Zebulon, 33, 37, 87, 139

Harrisson
: Jeremiah, 10
: Thos, 10

Harrold
: Richard, 18

Hart
: _____, 85
: Aron, 51
: Charles, 6
: Miles, 51
: Mr., 83

Silas, 36, 57, 63, 66, 67, 74, 75, 79, 84, 86, 92, 108, 123, 124, 138, 149
Simon, 6
Hartsaw
    Frederick, 54
Harvie
    John, 92
Havener
    Nicholas, 77, 92
Havenor
    Nicholas, 77
Hawkins
    Benjamin, 119
Haws
    Peter, 66
Hay
    James, 7
Hayes
    Andrew, 19
    David, 20
    John, 18
Hays
    _____, 10, 43, 69, 70, 117
    Adrew/Andrew/Andr, 20, 25, 29, 31, 43, 60, 68, 69, 74, 82, 84, 149
    Charles, 68, 149
    Hugh, 108
    John, 7, 8, 20, 149
    John, decd, 58
    Patrick, 8, 9, 13, 43, 47, 57, 70, 71, 73
Hemphill
    Samuel, 152
Henderson
    Alexander/Alexr, 14, 39
    David, 14
    James, 144
    John, 4, 19, 27, 42, 46, 61, 67, 87, 104, 107, 114, 116, 121, 124, 130, 132, 140
    Jones, 138
    Joseph, 145
    Samuel/Saml, 14, 39, 83, 133
    William, 38, 63, 66, 77, 93
Henry
    James, 150
Herdman
    John, 89
    John, Jr, 152
Hering
    Frederick, 6
Herman
    Adam, 6
    George, 6
Heron
    Alexander, 129
Herren
    Alexr, 10
Herrin
    Alexander, 3
    William, 152
Herron
    Alexander, 77, 123, 133, 144
Hicklen
    Hugh, 41, 44
    John, 44, 118, 123, 129, 147
    Thomas/Thos, 44, 135
    Thomas, Jr., 135
Hill
    Andrew, 26
    John, 7
    Johnston, 77
    Thos, 40
Hind
    John, 39
    William, 73
Hinds
    John, 67, 81
    Samuel, 134
    William, 39, 77
Hines
    William, 58
Hite
    _____, 126
Hix
    Joseph, 129

Hodge
    William, 60
Hodges
    John, 148
    Samuel, 113, 115, 141
Hoffman
    Henry, 116
Hog
    Peter, 92, 107, 139
Hogshead
    David, 63, 66
    James, 123, 124
    John, 5, 123, 124, 146, 152, 153
    Michael, 82, 116
    William/Wm, 5, 35, 43
Holdman
    Daniel, 13, 19
    David, 1
    William, 50, 52, 85, 136
Holdston
    Henry, 53, 61
    Henry, Jr, 54
    Henry, Sr, 53
Homes
    John, 39
Hook
    Michael, 51
    Robert, 7, 71
Hooks
    Robert, 49
Hopkins
    _____, 152
    Archibald, 111
    John, 79, 89, 123, 146
Horse
    Peter, 17
Houston_____, 125
    John, 121
    Robert, 76
Hover
    Basson, 74
    Pasley, 67
How
    Joseph, 21

Howe
    Joseph, 129
Hues
    Thomas, 26
Hugart
    _____, 32
    James, 15
    Thomas, 113, 115
    William, 122
Hugh
    William, 7
Hughart
    Thomas, 148
Hughes
    _____, 153
    Aaron/Aron, 135, 152
    Francis, 34
    James, 99, 113
Hughs
    _____, 152
    Francis, 27, 35
Hull
    Richard, 53
Humble
    Uriah, 69
Hundley
    Alexander, 153
Hunter
    James, 44, 72
    John, 47
    William, 44, 72
Hurst
    William/Wm, 7, 26, 31, 33
Huston
    Archibald, 85, 134
    James, 40, 101
    John, 29, 43, 47, 98
    Robert, 42, 63, 66
    Samuel, 89
Hutcheson
    George, 86
    John, 78
    John, Jr., 50
    John, Sr, 50

William, 25
William (Georges Son), 86
Hutchings
   John, 52
   John, jr., 52
Hutchinson
   George, 126
   William, 144
Hutchison
   John, 4, 116
   John, Jr., 105
   William, 1
Ingles
   _____, 128, 129
   John, 40
   Thomas, 40
   Wm, 40
Ingless
   _____, 98
Inglis
   _____, 109, 123
   William, 105
Ingram
   Alexander, 51
Inman
   Lazarus, 140
Isaac
   Elijah, 40
   Elisha, 6
Jackson
   _____, 22, 37, 94, 148
   Samuel, 56
   Widow, 35
   William/Wm, 15, 22
Jameson
   John, 38, 40, 44
Jefferson
   Thomas, x
Jenings
   _____, 56, 62, 82, 84, 92, 104
Jennings
   _____, 1, 2, 22, 34, 37, 43, 100, 113, 115, 116, 121, 123, 124, 127, 133

Job
   Calep, 7, 26
   Isaac, 129
   Joshua, 7
John
   _____, 53, 61, 119
Johnson
   Ezekel, 125
   Wm, 14
Johnston
   James, 135
   Michael, 52
   Wm, 39
Jones
   _____, 87, 90, 134
   Calep, 7
   Calop, 15
   Gabriel, 18, 58, 104, 120
   John, 52, 121
   Parson, 75
Kanady
   Joseph, 110
Kaufman
   Michael, 16, 20
Keffman
   Henry, 136
Kelly
   Alexander, 81
   Michael, 154
Kenaday
   _____, 43, 70
   Joseph, 46, 47, 57
   Josephs, 49
Kenady
   _____, 78
   Captain, 68
   Joseph, 71
Kender
   Peter, 6
Kennady
   William/Willm, 113, 135
Kent
   Jacob, 130
Kerr

_____, 122
David, 25
James, 62, 148, 151
John, 91
Richard, 51
William, 134
Kerrell
  Jacob, 7
Kervine
  William, 2
Kerwin
  William, 2
Kidd
  Daniel, 145, 147
Kile
  Alexander, 128
Kill Patrick
  George, 4
Killpatrick
  Thomas, 4
Kilpatrick
  Robert, 74
  Thos, 44
King
  _____, 26, 76, 79, 126
  John, 26, 34, 48, 59, 64, 99
  Thomas, 46
  William, 1, 3, 4, 11
Kingkade
  _____, 77
  John, 60
Kinkead
  Samuel, 4
  David, 120
  William, 121
Kinny
  Mathew, 151
Kirkham
  Henry, 116
Kirkley
  Francis, 47
  Francis, jr, 71
Kirkpatrick
  John, 52
  Thomas, 40, 52
Kirtley
  Capt, 99
  Frances, 97
  Francis, 109, 117
Knox
  _____, 32
  James/Jas, 37, 57, 66
Kyle
  Alexander, 80
Lamb
  William, 8
Land
  Thomas, 7
Lane
  John, 6
Langdon
  Joseph, 24
Lapsley
  _____, 131
  Joseph, 5, 28, 29, 50, 65, 96, 124
Larton
  Israel, 6
Lasley
  James, 9, 88
Laverty
  Ralph, 7, 57, 90, 129
  William, 129
Lawrance
  William, 129
Lawrence
  John, 7
Leard
  James, 131
Leath
  Ephraim, 26
Ledford
  all the, 6
  John, 62, 64
  William, 62
Ledgerwood
  William, 19, 42, 46, 63
  Wm, 10, 15, 21, 40
Leech

Ephraim, 7
Leeper
    Andrew, 70, 83
    Gawin, 122, 138
    William, 46
Leopard
    William, 53
Lesley
    James, 25
Lessly
    James, 137
Lestley
    James, 25
Lewis
    _____, 22, 74, 101, 107, 108, 112, 113, 115, 120, 152
    Andrew, 2, 9, 107, 124, 126
    Captain, 130
    Charles, 87, 91, 94, 118, 150
    Charles, Captain, 148, 150
    Colo., 2, 98, 126
    George, 2, 27, 37, 84, 118, 123
    John, 46, 94, 118
    John, Colo., 15, 23
    Thomas, 58, 104, 117, 129
    William, 9, 91, 93, 95, 102, 105, 113, 116
Linam
    Andrew, 20
Linvell
    _____, 34, 147
Loakey
    Thos, 13
Lockard
    James, 15
    Samuel, 8
Lockart
    Andrew, 134
    Jacob, 4, 40, 44
    James, 7, 19, 21, 24, 25, 26, 27, 39, 41, 42, 44, 49, 60, 85, 87, 91, 93, 94, 99, 101, 102, 111
    Randal/Randall, 78, 82
    Samuel, 37, 63

    William/Wm, 24, 42
Lockey
    Thomas, 2
Lockhard
    James, 10
Lockhart
    James, 10
Lockridge
    Andrew, 113
    James, 76
    Robert, 60
Lofton
    James, 13
Logan
    David, 23, 30, 39
    John, 121, 153
    William, 74, 76
Long
    _____, 57, 82, 100, 101, 104, 110, 116, 127, 143
    Henry, 16, 27, 71, 97, 154
    Joseph, 5, 40, 65, 98
    Nicholas, 20
    Paul, 16
    Widow, 71, 116
    William/Wm, 14, 38, 92, 119
Looney
    _____, 5, 21, 82, 90
    Absolom, 117
    David, 85
    John, 117
    Robert, 64
    Robert, Jr., 61
    Samuel, 34
    Thomas, 6
Loony
    Adam, 40
Lourey
    William, 117
Love
    Abraham, 79
    Daniel, 23, 34, 44, 77, 85, 88, 123, 124
    Ephraim, 46, 89, 138

John, 47
Joseph, 38, 51
Philip/Phillip, 128, 129, 130, 132, 144
Samuel, 112
Lowrey
William, 141
Lowry
John, 53, 61
Jon., 54
Loy
Stephen, 126
Luney
_____, 11
Lung
Henry, 33
Nicholas, 27, 42
Paul, 27
Philips, 42
Luny
Paul, 12
Lusk
James, 44
Samuel, 5
William, 2, 68, 76, 80
Lyle
Daniel, 42, 76, 100, 106, 107, 109, 110, 125, 140
John/Jno, 21, 26, 29, 30, 31, 61, 109, 110, 140
John, Junior, 121
John, Sr., 125
Mathew, 28, 55
Matthew, 109, 110
Samuel, 106, 107, 108, 122
Widow, 121
Lynn
John, 4, 15, 19, 21
Lyon
Humberston, 6, 20
Steven, 20
Madison
_____, 94, 96, 105

John, 3, 36, 54, 58, 83, 97, 102, 104, 117, 133, 134
Magavock
James, 100
Magill
James, 125
Magoit
John, 27
Magort
Hans/Hance, 33, 71
John, 18
Magot
Hance, 42, 47, 150
Magott
Hance, 154
Mairs
James, 20
Malcome
John, 79, 83
Man
Barnat, 116
Manes
Hugh, 52
Mann
Barnet, 47
Bernerd, 121
William, 148
Marshall
John, 30, 64
Martain
Wm, 40
Martin
Joseph, 44, 93
Patrick, 4, 9, 38, 40, 44, 91, 147
William/Wm, 40, 44, 52, 88, 93, 129
Mason
John, 6, 28, 59
Mathews
_____, 74, 94, 95, 97, 101, 116, 121, 131
George, 97, 99, 102, 105, 116, 144
John, 5, 21, 30, 36, 50, 51, 83
John, Jr., 52, 118

Joshua, 50, 52
Richard, 51, 52, 74
Sampson, 51, 52, 86, 87, 91, 93, 94, 95, 101, 110, 126, 146, 148, 151
William, 55, 111, 122

Maury
Adam, 70

Maxwell
John, 3, 17, 30, 50, 52, 76, 108, 136

Maxwill
John, 22

May
Joseph, 71

Mays
James, 15, 23, 24

McAdoe
John, 51

Mcadoo
John, 137

Mcafee
_____, 139
George, 135, 139
James, 39, 53, 54, 93, 96
James, Jr., 139
James, Sr., 135

McAfee
_____, 135

Mcanair
Daniel, 2

Mcanaire
Daniel, 15

Mcananre
Daniel, 5

Mcanare
Daniel, 5, 22

Mcbride
Francis, 21
William, 21, 130

McCall
James, 53

McCammis
David, 26

McCampbell
James, 120

McClanachan
John, 118
Robert, 94

McClanahan
Robert, 50

McCleary
James, 75
John, 52, 57, 60

McClelhill
Joseph, 4, 22, 44

McClellan
Robert, 4

McClellon
Robert, 40

McClenachan
_____, 136
Alexander, 138, 145
Elijah, 48, 50, 54, 55, 86, 87, 145
John, 148
Rob, 67
Robert, 46, 47, 52, 58, 65, 78, 84, 86, 87, 92, 94, 101, 105, 109, 113, 145, 147
William, 136, 137

McClenahan
Robert, 3, 17, 22, 46

McClenhan
John, 44
Robert, 44

McClenon
Robt, 40

McClintock
William/Wm, 4, 40, 44

McClung
John, 145
William, 12, 21, 28

McClure
Alexander, 42, 55, 68, 73
Andrew, 120
Habert, 78
Halbert, 141
Harbert, 8

    Hugh, 150
    James, 121, 129
    John, 22, 38, 60, 138, 145, 151
    Moses, 61, 63, 65, 66, 95, 113
    Nathaniel, 76
    Samuel, 35, 50, 51, 78
    William, 134
McColley
    John, 52
McCord
    Andrew, 25
McCorkall
    Alexander, 50
    Patrick, 50
McCorkle
    Alexander, 52
    James, 3, 38, 40
    Patrick, 52
    Robert, 38
    Samuel, 46
McCormick
    David, 51
    Joshua, 51
McCown
    Francis, 16, 86
    James, 9, 16, 25, 93
    John, 43
McCowns
    James, 8
McCoy
    James, 18, 41
    John, 79
McCreary
    James, 44
    John, 24, 44, 115, 152
McCreery
    John, 138, 148, 150
McCrorey
    James, 113
McCrorie
    William, 80
McCroskey
    David, 74
    John, 68

    John, jr, 60
    Patrick, 44
McCuley
    John, 50
McCune
    Andrew, 130
    Francis, 5
    James, 5
    Samuel/Saml, 14, 130
McCurry
    William, 47
McCutcheon
    _____, 125, 128
    James, 44
    John, 43, 44
    Robert, 23, 34
    Samuel, 44, 88, 151
    William/Wm, 20, 43, 88, 110, 116,
        139
    William (Merchant), 128
McCutchin
    Robt, 14
McDaniel
    Bryan, 96, 100
    Widow, 100
McDonald
    Alexander, 93
    Bryan, 135
    Edward, 51, 57
    James, 51
    Joseph, 51
McDonall
    Bryan, 90
    Hugh, 32
McDowell
    James, 60, 95, 96, 140, 145
    Saml, Capt., 145
    Samuel, 98, 109, 110, 121, 135, 140,
        150, 153
Mcelroy
    Alexander, 128
McElwain
    Moses, 147
McFarland

Duncan, 44, 148
John, 20
Mcfarlin
Robert, 20
Mcfarling
Alexander, 129
Duncan, 129
Robert, 129
Mcfarron
John, 2, 53, 64, 96
Thomas, 118
Mcfeeters
Alexander, 40
John, 44, 52
William, 4, 9, 40, 44, 52
Wm, Jr., 44
McGee
William, 87
McGill
James, 62, 65, 121, 124, 141, 144
John, 26, 41
William, 2, 26, 80
McGinney
John, 34
McGomery
Robert, 90
McGown
John, 53, 56
Mckam
John, 86
McKay
John, 61
Mckeachy
James, 108
Mckearny
James, 146
Mckee
James, 109, 110
Samuel, 134
William, 141, 145
McKenney
John, 4
McKenny
Alexander, 44

John, 5, 44
McKoy
Alexander, 7
James, 7, 18, 26, 31, 90
Moses, 7
Zachariah, 26
Zachery, 7
McMahen
John, 131
McMahon
John, 97, 144
Robert, 26, 31, 109, 145
McMullin
Edward, 125
John, 125
McMurry
Alexander, 40
John, 40
William/Wm, 62, 125
McMurty
_____, 135, 139
Joseph, 135, 139
McNab
Baptist, 55, 66
William, 40
Mcnabb
Baptist, 61, 65
James, 141
William, 38, 42
McNeal
James, 7, 26
Neal, 51
McNeil
John, 105, 107
McNeill
Daniel, 138
McPharron
John, 12
McPheetters
John, 121
William, Jr, 121
McRoberts
Samuel, 135, 146
Means

Hugh, 50
Meek
    John, 23
    Thomas, 23
Memury
    William, 32
Me[_]sha[?]
    Abraham, 40
Miligan
    Charles, 11
Milkin
    Charles, 12
Miller
    Abraham, 42
    Adam, 1, 6, 12, 33
    Alexander/Alexr, 29, 60, 68, 69
    David, 51, 63
    Henry, 68
    Hugh, 129
    Jacob, 33, 104
    James, 5, 20, 21, 42, 46, 53
    John, 5, 20, 28, 34, 44, 100, 129, 147, 153
    John, Jr, 69
    Robert, 20
    William, 20, 21, 51
Millican
    _____, 63
    Charles, 49, 51, 53, 61
Millikin
    _____, 30
Mills
    Hugh, 51, 92
    James, 4, 5
    John, 2, 63, 85, 144
    William, 4
Mires
    Jacob, 51
Mitchell
    David, 10
    James, 21, 25, 63, 71, 72
    John, 4, 7, 23, 46, 72
    Thomas, 72

Mizer
    John, 16
Mocke
    John, 34
Moffet
    John, 5
Moffett
    George, 116, 124, 126, 133, 134, 140
    James, 138
Moffitt
    George, 149
Monsey
    Samuel, 26, 112, 147
Montgomerie
    James, 2, 4, 6, 16, 32, 61
    John, 71, 108
    Robert, 32, 64
    Samuel, 20
Montgomery
    _____, 119
    James, 12, 119, 135, 144
Montier
    James, 111
Moodey
    James, 19
Moody
    James, 25, 38, 40, 41, 72
    Robert, 14, 16, 73
Moon
    Edward, 51
Moore
    _____, 19, 21
    David, 30, 65, 69, 72, 96, 145
    Elizabeth, 101
    James, 40, 149
    James Jr, 136
    John, 7, 18, 19, 25, 50, 124, 150, 152
    Moses, 147
    Philip, 39
    Riley, 19, 27
    Robert, 50

Thomas, 8, 12, 19, 27, 28, 64, 107, 151, 152
William, 28
Moris
   David, 70
Morris
   Hans, 61
Morrison
   James, 40
Moser
   Adrew, 6
Muldrough
   Andrew, 7
Murray
   _____, 112
   Henry, 103, 115
Murty
   Joseph, 150
Nealey
   James, 98
Nealy
   James, 38
Neelley
   James, 101, 109, 113, 128, 129
Neilly
   James, 50, 51, 90, 91, 94
   John, 90, 92
   Robert, 90
Neist
   Thomas, 47
Nellson
   David, 124
Nelson
   David, 41, 115
Netherton
   Henry, 32
Newell
   James, 129
Nicholas
   _____, 125
   Jacob, 30, 42, 87, 90, 99, 103, 106, 123-125, 150
Niely
   Samuel, 6

Noal
   Nicholas, 7
Noble
   Erasmus, 129
   John, 52
   William, 52
Norris
   Robert, 20
Null
   Nicholas/Nichs, 42, 139
Nut
   William, 3
Nutt
   _____, 36, 65
   William, 19
O'Dell
   Samuel, 27, 32
Offrail
   Morris, 12
Offriel
   Maurice, 44
Offrield
   Morice/Moric, 3, 16
Ofrield
   Morice/Morrice, 1, 4
O'frield
   Maurice, 40
Ogle
   Benjamin, 40
Oleston
   John, 51
   Samuel, 51
Oliver
   Aron, 146
Orry
   James, 68
Osborn
   George, 39
   Jeremiah, 39
Overall
   William, 26
Oyle
   Benjamin, 6
Page

Alexander, 129
Painter
_____, 83, 116, 132, 141
Alexander, 27, 47, 89
Palmer
William, 4, 93
Parent
Josiah, 26
Thomas, 26
William/Wm, 26
Paris
George, 85
Parkey
Henry, 71, 85
Parsenger
Jacob, 139
Parsinger
Jacob, 87
Patrick
John, 93, 130, 140
Little, 33
Robert/Robt, 5, 16, 17, 22, 31, 32, 36, 38, 39, 59
Patterson
_____, 150
Edward, 51
Erwin, 20, 25, 51
George, 96
James, 27, 120
John, 131, 144
Robert, 9, 17, 56, 64, 73, 81
William, 72, 81, 134
Pattison
John, 76
Patton
_____, 25, 29
Colo, 10, 112
Jacob, 51, 53, 64
James/Jams, 10, 38, 45, 51, 52, 53, 56
John, 15, 17, 29, 35, 67
Mathew/Matthew, 15, 53, 67, 79, 126, 133
William, 106

Paul
Audley, 74, 108
John, 35, 56
Pauling
Henry, 150
Paxton
_____, 77, 96
John, 28, 45, 46, 49, 50, 52, 65, 76, 79, 105, 144, 149, 150
Samuel, 50, 51, 52
Thomas, 66, 85
Thomas, Sr, 35
William, 51, 52, 95, 105
Pearis
George, 40, 90
Peary
George, 40
James, 38, 40, 42
Thomas, 4, 40, 42
Peiry
George, 44
James, 44, 46
Thomas, 44
Pellam
William, 20, 53
Pence
Jacob, 8, 139
Valintine, 8, 75
Volentine, 42
Pepper
Samuel, 129
William, 40
Perry
John, 52
Persenger
Jacob, 133
Peteet
Jonathan John, 52
Peters
_____, 136, 137
Peterson
Jacob, 109
Phegan
Philip, 28

Philips
- James, 40, 42, 62
- John, 24, 33, 102
- Robert, 44
- Steven, 26

Phillips
- James, 4, 5, 143
- Jno, 135
- John, 139

Pickens
- _____, 17, 36, 56
- Andrew/Adrew, 4, 9, 16
- Gabriel, 27, 36, 79
- John, 1, 9, 11, 14, 17, 19, 31, 56

Pickins
- _____, 13
- Gabriel, 15, 18

Pickle
- Henry, 74, 92, 151

Pierce
- William/Wm, 1, 11, 12, 16

Piery
- Thomas, 40

Pilsher
- Richard, 14

Pilson
- Richard, 39

Poage
- _____, 96, 102, 122
- George, 71, 91, 107, 118, 119, 147
- John, 21, 31, 51, 56, 74, 78, 87, 91, 97, 99, 102, 105, 106, 108, 112, 117, 126, 130, 131, 133
- Robert/Robt, 18, 30, 36, 38, 41, 49, 55, 86, 87, 91, 93, 95, 99, 105
- Thomas, 94, 95, 97

Poge
- John, 9
- Robert, 9

Pointer
- Alexander, 56

Poin[?]
- Joseph, 50

Ponder
- Daniel, 87

Pooper
- Lambert, 22, 47

Porter
- William, 149

Potts
- John, 61, 119, 135, 150

Preston
- Colo, 78
- John, 4
- William/Wm, 45, 64, 79, 83, 95, 96, 100, 107, 115, 118, 135, 136, 137

Price
- Daniel, 100, 101, 154
- William, 28

Props
- Michael, 66, 77, 111, 126

Pullen
- Loftus, 28, 41, 44, 46, 113, 129
- Lofty, 43

Pullin
- Loftus, 54, 147

Pullings
- Loftus, 133

Rader
- Mathais, 89

Ralston
- William, 51, 134

Raltstone
- Robert, 5

Ramsay
- _____, 68, 76
- William, 76

Ramsey
- _____, 54, 107
- James, 140
- John/Jno., 4, 39, 55, 61, 71, 73, 94, 116, 120, 131, 140
- Josiah, 135
- Margaret, 124
- Robert, 10, 19
- Thomas, 64
- William, 34, 100

Rankins
> George, 65, 67

Ray
> George, 38
> John, 152

Reaburn
> Henry, 63, 69, 88
> James, 43, 55
> John, 105
> Joseph, 124

Reader
> Adam, 131

Reah
> William, 111

Reed
> Peter, 39
> Richard, 64
> Robert, 107, 146, 151, 153
> Thomas, 44, 151

Reid
> Thomas, 40

Renix
> _____, 50, 52, 110
> Robert, 5, 21, 51, 102
> William, 147

Rentfro
> Captain, 117
> Peter, 5
> Stephen/Steven, 12, 30, 51, 57, 90, 100

Richards
> John, 130
> Josias, 40, 44

Richardson
> Daniel, 29

Richeson
> Daniel, 3

Richey
> Alexander, 38, 40, 89
> John, 97, 109, 131

Rider
> Adam, 12
> Mathias, 132

Risk
> _____, 60, 117, 128
> John, 44, 52, 72, 116, 117, 139

Robb
> Wm, 14

Robertson
> James, 9, 115, 120
> Mathew, 76, 81
> Matthew, 148

Robeson
> Robert, 44

Robinson
> _____, 53
> Capt., 2
> David, 51, 113, 115, 120, 123, 125, 142
> Esther, 47
> George, 4, 6, 11, 86, 90
> Isaac, 131, 132
> James, 38, 49, 58, 60, 115, 125, 144
> John, 14, 19, 25, 33, 37, 40, 93, 96, 132, 134
> John, Senior, 54
> Joseph, 30, 51, 149
> Joseph, Jr., 90
> Margaret (Widow), 125
> William/Wm, 6, 38, 47, 94, 96, 105, 106, 107, 109, 113, 123, 125, 128

Rogers
> Jacob, 16, 18, 30

Rolston
> John, 8

Roseborough
> James, 49

Ross
> Hugh, 39

Rowland
> James, 90, 100
> Thomas, 146

Ruckman
> John, 40

Ruddle
> Cornelious, 146
> John, Sr., 3

Ruder
　　_____, 146
Rufner
　　Peter, 42
Rusk
　　_____, 75
Russell
　　Andrew/Andr, 4, 8, 13, 17, 86, 93, 102
　　Bryce, 105
　　William/Wm, 31, 33, 41
Rutherford
　　Joseph, Senr, 112
　　Thomas, 109, 111
Rutledge
　　Edward, 91
　　James, 22
Rutlidge
　　Thos, 14
Rutlidges
　　Geo, 14
Ryon
　　Joseph, 52
Salley
　　George, 52
　　John Peter, 52
Salling
　　George, 50
　　John Peter, 5, 30, 50
Sancion
　　Daniel, 51
Sareh
　　Mathias, 51
Sawyers
　　James, Junior, 148
Sayers
　　Alexander, 20, 53, 95
　　James, 112
　　James Jr., 134, 146
　　William, 20, 95
Scholl
　　Capt., 3
　　Peter, 37, 39
Scilar[Seilar?]
　　Plunkard, 61
Scot
　　_____, 24, 32
　　Andrew, 46, 82
　　George, 8, 23
　　James, 7, 21, 32
　　John, 32, 87, 90, 92
　　Major, 40, 46
　　Robert, 7, 16, 17, 18, 24, 40, 44, 95, 101
　　Samuel, 7
　　Thomas, 2, 46
　　William, 50, 52
Scott
　　Andrew, 126
　　Robert, 75
Searight
　　James, 134
Seewright
　　John, 138, 145
Seilar
　　Plunkard, 53
Seller
　　Henry, 42
　　John, 154
Sellore
　　Henry, 30
Seltser
　　Mathias, 3
Seltzer
　　Mathias/Mattias, 11, 12
Sevenson
　　James, 23
Sevier
　　Valentine/Volentine/Volintine, 21, 44, 85
Shankland
　　Edward, 49, 74
　　Robert, 42, 67, 95
Shanklin
　　_____, 99, 119
　　Edward, 85, 111, 124, 125, 129
　　John, 146
　　Robert, 99

Sharkey
    Patrick, 64
Sharp
    _____, 83
    Edward, 105
    Mathew, 8
Shaver
    Paul, 109
Shaw
    Abraham, 44
    John, 28
    Thomas, 52
Sheilds
    Thomas, 71, 86
Shields
    John, 25
Shipay
    _____, 90
Shipler
    Henry, 39
Shirkey
    Patrick, 96
Shirley
    Michael, 139, 150
    Patrick, 135
Shirly
    Richard, 26
Shoemaker
    George, 131
    Hamilton, 51
Simpson
    _____, 74
    James, 7, 32, 39, 50, 52, 62, 76, 100, 108, 110, 137, 153
Sinclar
    _____, 118
    Charly, 20
Sivers
    _____, 79
Sixby
    John, 5
Skaggs
    Henry, 129
    James, 6

Skidmore
    James, 121, 153
Skilleren
    George, 99
Skillern
    George, 98, 101, 116, 120, 121, 129, 151
    Skilleron
    George, 39
Slater
    John, 56
Sloan
    _____, 85
    Widow, 53, 56
Smiley
    Alexander, 52
    John, 50, 52
    Walter, 38, 135, 142
Smith
    _____, 100
    Abraham, 36, 66, 67, 79, 83, 110, 126, 129, 138
    Alexander, 139
    Daniel, 27, 77, 79, 82, 84, 89, 107, 109, 111, 112, 121
    Henry, 15, 18, 26, 30, 31, 36, 83, 86
    John, 8, 9, 15, 18, 34, 50, 52, 98, 128
    John, Capt, 15
    John, Major, 61
    Jonathan, 144, 151, 153
    Joseph, 52
    Levy, 129
    Philip, 6
    Robert, 8
    Tobias, 51
    William, 1, 18, 34, 46
    Wm, Captain, 15
    Zachariah, 105
Snodon
    William, 129
Soduskie
    Andrew, 69
Sollers

Soper
    John, 26
Soper
    Joseph, 125
Spear
    Henry, 12
    John, 40, 44
Spears
    George, 108, 131
    Henry, 3, 26
    Hugh, 4
    John, 4, 5
Speer
    Henry, 11
Sproul
    John, 50, 52
Sprowl
    Samuel, 42
Stales
    John, 47
Staley
    John, 27
Stalnaker
    Adam, 51
    George, 51
    Jacob, 51
    Samuel, 51
Staly
    John, 21
Starknecker
    Samuel, 6
Steel
    Andrew, 44, 70, 73, 140
    James, 150
    John, 140
    Robert, 108
    Samuel, 9, 47, 58, 70, 102, 140, 146, 149
    Widow, 142
Steele
    _____, 147
Steell
    Robert (Miller), 146
Stern
    Frederick, 51, 129

Steuart
    Thomas, 22, 29
Steven
    John, 140
Stevenson
    David, 14, 17, 36, 80
    James, 34
    John/Jno, 7, 15, 21, 22, 47, 49, 52, 63, 68, 70, 80, 85, 98, 109, 111, 126, 140, 141
    Robert, 134
    Thomas, 13, 34, 61, 81
    Thomas, Jr, 80
    William/Wm, 17, 66, 75, 77
Stewart
    _____, 112
    Alexander, 60, 68, 91, 92, 114
    Archabald Archibald/Archd, 36, 39, 55, 91
    Colonel, 126
    David, 42, 46, 52, 94, 109
    John, 73, 74, 128, 134
    Thomas, 9, 31, 32, 38, 47, 58, 75, 92
    Walter, 131, 142, 144
Stinson
    James, 100
    Thomas, 2, 6, 11
Stone
    Henry, 92, 151
Stonlick
    Samuel, 20
Storey
    Thomas, 134
Stover
    Daniel, 12, 27
Stride
    John, 20
Stroud
    John, 6, 20
Stuart
    _____, 14, 148
    Archibald, 14, 84
    Benjamin, 138, 150
    David, 4, 5, 8, 13, 17, 40

Francis, 144
James, 7
John, 71, 84
Thomas/Thos, 10, 13, 77
Walter, 144
Stump
    Michael, 3, 39
Suart
    David, 7
Summerfield
    Francis, 6
Summers
    John, 98, 100, 122, 148
Swatley
    Mark, 79, 111, 126
Tar
    Edward, 98
Tarr
    _____, 61
    Edward, 106
Tate
    _____, 81
    Cooper John, 29
    John, 31, 38, 72, 75, 77, 84, 99, 101, 102, 128, 147, 150
Taylor
    George, 76
    Isaac, 12, 21, 25, 33, 42, 50, 54, 61, 62, 108, 113, 140
    Isaac, Jr., 37
    William, 108
Teat
    Thomas, 44
Tedford
    James, 147
Tees
    _____, 101, 105
    Joseph, 17, 36
    Widow, 77
    William, 91, 92, 94, 95, 97, 101, 114, 140, 150
Telford
    James, 146
Terrald
    John, 7
Terry
    Jesper, 51
    William, 51
Thomas
    _____, 86, 87, 90, 108
    James, 21
    John, 6, 82, 86, 100, 108, 131, 152
    Rees, 34
    Widow, 111
Thompson
    _____, 98
    Adam, 38, 40
    Alexander/Alexr, 1, 4, 6, 13, 81, 86, 92, 93, 105, 136
    Hugh, 6, 14, 17
    James, 13, 28, 71, 150
    John, 14, 21, 55, 62, 73, 92, 93, 136, 137
    Mathew, 7, 8, 67, 95, 101
    Robert, 136
    Thomas, 37
    William/Wm, 3, 4, 6, 8, 17, 22, 23, 25, 54, 93, 95, 125
    William, Jr., 4, 8
Thomsom
    Alexander, 8
Thomson
    Alexander, 2
    Wm, 10
    Wm, Jr., 14
Thorn
    _____, 3, 11, 32
    Peter, 22, 47
Thornhill
    Samuel, 33
Timble
    James, 49
    John, 52, 62
Tincher
    _____, 147
    Samuel, 29
Tinker
    _____, 137, 142

Todd
    James, 40
    Low, 67
    William, 40
Tom
    _____, 15
Tosh
    Tasker, 6, 51
    Thomas, 6, 28, 51, 59, 138, 146
Trimble
    _____, 87
    David, 5, 15, 111, 132
    James, 1, 5, 50, 52, 77, 79, 81, 82, 85, 95, 100, 136
    John/Jno, 1, 3, 4, 5, 29, 36, 38, 40, 41, 44, 45, 79, 87, 110, 111, 121
    Robert, 116
    Walter, 5, 149
Trishell
    John, 4
Turk
    Robert, 9
    Thomas, 26, 73, 89, 91
Turpin
    Soloman/Solomon, 87, 92, 112
Tyler
    Francis, 58
Umpris
    John, 125
Underwood
    John, 56, 66
Urrey
    James, 33, 47
Vance
    George, 4, 14
    James, 40
    John, 20, 40, 44, 89, 125
    Mathew, 52
    Rachel, 39
Vansell
    Edmund, 129
Vause, 98, 105, 106, 107, 109, 113, 115, 123, 125, 126, 128, 129, 130, 132

Viare
    John, 8
Viney
    Andrew, 21
Vinyard
    Christopher, 121
Voss
    Ephraim, 6, 59
Vought
    Andrew, 63, 88
Wade
    Dawson, 129
Wadington
    William, 40
Waggoner
    Ludwick, 67, 108
Waite
    Joseph, 41
Wait
    James, 47, 89, 106
Waits
    James, 64
Walding
    Wm, 12
Walker
    _____, 78, 94
    Alexander, 4, 7, 63, 71, 83, 86, 117, 122, 137, 143, 149
    Alexander, Jr., 144
    Benjn, 10
    Charles, 37, 57, 60, 84
    James, 12, 29
    John, 43, 68
    Joseph, 49, 52, 76, 78, 150
    Samuel, 51, 52
Wall
    Conrod, 121
Wallace
    John, 93
    Peter, 21, 28, 50, 124, 141
    Samuel, 1, 4, 5, 11, 40, 52, 60, 103, 104, 141, 144
Wallis
    James, 9

Ward
    John, 39, 49
    William, 44, 96, 101, 106, 121, 130
Wardlaw
    John, 117
Waring
    Michael, 92, 146
Warrell
    George, 33
Warren
    Michael/Michl, 131, 152
Warring
    Michael, 90
Warwick
    _____, 64
Waters
    _____, 80
Watkins
    William, 135
Watterson
    Thomas, 131, 141
Waughul
    Joseph, 94
Weems
    Thomas, 26, 70
Weer
    Samuel, 146
Wees
    Jacob, 109
Westfall
    Jacob, 39
    John, 39
    Wm, 39
White
    Bryant, 5
    Isaac, 9, 38, 47, 131, 133, 140
    John, 137
    William, 35, 43
Whitley
    Paul, 81
    Soloman, 40
Whooley
    Christian, 125
    Peter, 125
    William, 125
Wiley
    Robert, 108
Wilkins
    Samuel/Saml, 1, 3, 10, 17
Willbey
    James, 20
Williams
    _____, 35
    James, 125
    John, 83
    Robert, 34
    William, 21
Williamson
    Charles, 26
Willson
    Charles, 136
    John, 76
    Thomas, 143
    Thomas, (Chestnut Hill), 143
    Thomas, CH, 143
Wilson
    Captain, 24
    Charles, 79, 116
    George, 41, 43, 54, 121
    Herculus, 28
    James, 24, 25, 52
    John, 14, 25, 38, 44, 47, 52, 60, 75, 85, 87, 94, 128, 129, 147, 148
    John, Jr., 44
    Mathew, 44
    Robert, 39
    Samuel/Saml, 42, 45, 46, 128
    Stephen, 44, 129
    Thomas, 6, 65, 66, 80, 121
    William, 44, 52, 57, 60, 129, 147
Wiltshire
    Nathaniel, 20
Wiltsil
    Martin, 69
Wolson
    James, 50
Wood
    _____, 20

John, 51
Woodley
    Jacob, 152, 153
Woodroof
    Nathaniel, 39
Woods
    _____, 8, 17, 21, 26, 39, 58, 77, 79, 84, 93
    John, 51
    Richard, 21, 30, 36, 55, 76, 81, 82, 116
    Samuel, 130
Woolman
    Jacob, 5
Worklaw
    William, 34
Wortlaw
    John, 70
Wortlow
    William, 25
Wright
    _____, 32
    Alexander, 31, 38, 42, 46, 47, 57, 58
    Peter, 32, 37, 125
    Thomas, 28, 125
    Widow, 131
    Wm, 14, 38
Young
    _____, 38, 91, 118, 145
    Hugh, 4, 40, 44
    Jame/James, 4, 8, 40, 60, 99
    John, 34, 44, 66, 69, 124, 125, 140
    Patrick, 40, 75, 89
    Robert, 38, 40, 42, 44, 46, 67, 71, 126
    Samuel/Saml, 44, 78
    Widow, 117
Zinn
    Garret, 53

Rivers, Runs, Springs, Creeks, and Other Water Features

Back Creek, 82, 94, 148
Big Spring, 140
Blacks Draft, 78
Blacks run, 35
Branch below James Moore Junior's, 136
Branch near Feemster's, 129
Briery Branch, 110
Broad Spring, 76
Brockes Creek, 34
Bryery Branch, 74
Buchanan's Mill Creek, 92
Buffalo/Buffaloe/Buffallow/Buffelo/
Buffelow Creek, 74, 79, 100, 105, 110, 124, 144
    Bent/Fork of, 49, 85
Bull Pasture River, 94, 118, 123, 128, 129
Bullett's Springs, 147
Caldwell's Creek, 119
Calf Pasture/Calfpasture, 1, 2, 15, 23, 34, 41, 46, 57, 60, 82, 92, 152
    Head of, 29
Charles Campbell's run, 136
Patrick Campbell's run, 55
Cape Caphon, 27
Carr's Creek, 96
Catabo/Catapo/Catawbo Creek, 6, 12, 30, 39, 40, 54, 90, 93, 95, 96, 118, 135, 139, 144
Chamberlaine's run, 63
Christian's/Christian Creek, 25, 44, 45, 51, 78, 79, 81, 93, 102, 104, 105, 106, 116, 126, 146
Christy's Creek, 46, 91
Collett's run, 8
Cook's Creek, 86, 129
Cow Pasture River, 2, 7, 15, 22, 28, 32, 57, 94, 118, 123, 128-130, 137, 141, 148
    Great Lick in, 2
Craig's Creek, 53, 54, 61, 118, 119, 135, 139, 150
Cub run, 75
Dry branch/Drybranch, 92, 142
Dry River, 77, 79, 129
    Forks of, 15, 17, 18
    Little Fork of, 67

Dry run, 36
Duck Ponds, 108, 133, 134
Dunlaps Creek, 150
Evan's Run, 72, 96
Falling Springs, 94
John Finla's great Spring, 76
Finla's Spring, 36
Flint run, 41
Forks of the [South?] River, 97
Goody's Run, 31
Great Spring, 74
Gry Branch, 93
Guy Branch, 93
Holdston's River, 51, 53
Jackson's/Jackson River, 15, 22, 37, 94, 148
James/Jame River, 8, 12, 61, 76, 85, 105, 106, 110, 118, 119, 121, 124, 129, 138, 144, 153
   Falls of, 8
   Forks of, 30, 36, 100
   Main Branch of, 51
   North Branch of, 21, 42, 80, 100, 105, 106, 110, 124, 144
   North Fork of, 5, 50, 51
   South Fork of, 5
Jenings's Branch, 56
John's/John Creek, 53, 61, 119
   Mouth of, 119
Jumping run, 8
Creek near Daniel Kidd's, 145
Lapsley's Run, 131
Lewis Creek, 74
Linvell's Creek, 34, 147
Little Warm springs, 150
Long Meadow Run, 17, 116
Lost River, 47
Luney's Creek, 11
Run above Madison's Plantation, 94
River, Forks of near John Madison's, 36
Main River, 97
Marsh between this Court House and the tinkling Spring, 52
Massisippi, 14

Head of Meadow Creek, 126
Middle River, 17, 22-24, 32, 34-36, 62, 72, 79, 97, 99, 121, 124, 133, 134
Mole Hill Draft, 147
Mossey Creek, 72, 111
Naked Creek, 17, 36, 39, 99, 126, 138
New River, 5, 6, 40, 46, 53, 59, 95, 98, 128, 129, 132, 144
North Mill Creek, 109
North River, 1, 2, 21, 23, 29, 34-36, 39, 44, 52, 57, 67-69, 76, 77, 79, 8-83, 84, 105, 107, 109, 124, 127, 131, 133, 135, 150
Nutts Mill Creek, 36, 65
Pass run, 11
Patterson's Creek, 150
Peak Creek, 109, 113, 123, 129, 132
Peter's Creek, 136, 137
Pine Run, 70
Piney Run, 22
Poage Run, 102
Potomack/Potomak/Potowmack River, 126
   South Branch/Fork of, 15, 67, 74, 92, 126
Waters of Purgatory, 38
Ramsay's/Ramsey's, 54, 68
Reed Creek, 5, 14, 38, 53
the River, 5, 6, 7, 16, 26
River, Forks of, 36
Roan Oak/Roane Oak, 7, 14, 51, 53, 54, 64, 132
   Brances of, 6
   Forks of, 20
   North Branch/Fork of, 6, 132
   South Branch/Fork of, 5, 6, 20
Rockfish River, 58
Shanando River, 33, 41, 154
Shanklins Run, 99
South branch, 29, 30, 39, 46, 72
South fork, 39
South River, 2, 3, 8, 10, 16, 17, 31, 54, 55, 61, 95, 97, 104, 134, 135, 137, 140
   Forks of, 97
   Mouth of, 104, 134, 137

River by Henry Spears's Plantation, 26
Stewarts Run, 112
Stoney Creek, 3
Stoney Run, 42, 99
Stuart, Benjamin branch, 138
Stuarts Creek, 148
Swift/Swit Run, 1, 6, 9, 23, 24, 30, 31, 32, 34, 35, 36, 41, 44, 46, 47, 58, 71, 77, 97, 99, 100, 101, 117, 120, 123, 124, 126, 127, 129, 152, 153
    South Branch, 31
Tavern Spring, 61, 64
Tinker Creek, 137, 142
Tinkling/Tinckling Spring, 3, 4, 8, 10, 13, 14, 25, 35, 52, 75, 76, 78, 81, 86, 94, 108, 112
Tom's Creek, 15
Turn of the Waters by Charles Walker's, 57
Warm Springs, 94, 130, 138, 148, 152
Run above William Ward's House, 106
Warm springs (Little), 150
Waters in Jenning's Gap, 115, 121
Waters of the long Glade, 62
Welshmans Run, 136, 141
Western Waters, 132
Williams Creek, 35
Wood's River, 20

Roads

[Note: Roads are cross-indexed to all locations and persons mentioned. Spellings and descriptions have been standardized to aid in identifying roads and to simplify the preparation of this index. This was a necessity as many road descriptions changed slightly in the orders as different landmarks were cited. The reader should also keep in mind that various roads went under similar general designations and should bear this in mind when determining the identity of each road.]

road over the Blue Ridge at Woods's old pass to the line of Albemarle (to meet proposed road from Albemarle Court House), 21

road from the New Rockfish Gap to the line of Albemarle and thence to the road that leads over the Secretary's ford, 92

road from George Mathews's mill to Francis Alexanders thence to the new road that leads to Rockfish Gap, 99

road from Mathews's mill to Tees's Gap through Francis Alexander's plantation, 101

road from Francis Alexander's to William Tees's crossing the Long Meadow, 101

road from Black James Armstrong's to William Long's mill and thence to James Alexander's, 14

road from Benjamin Allen's mill to the North River, 1

road from James Givens's mill by Hugh Allen's house to the Stone Meeting house, 134

road from Davidson's ford to Edward Rutledge's and thence to John Allison's ford and by John

Kerr's to the Stone Meeting House, 89, 91

road from James Thompson's by John Allison's ferry on the North River to John Paxton's, 150

road from the North River to John Anderson's, 2

road from John Anderson's to the Court House, 2, 31

road from Robert Poage's to the river near John Anderson's house, 18

road from John Anderson's meadow to Mathews's mill, 131, 144

road from the Court House/Staunton to William Anderson's, 45, 111

road from Mossey Creek to William Anderson's, 111

road from the Dry Branch Gap of the North Mountain to Archers mill, 92, 142

road from John Archer's to John Ramsey's, 71

road from John Archer's mill to Robert Fowler's, 130, 140

road from the Dry Gap to Mr. John Archer's mill, 149, 151

view for potential road over Armer's or Rockfish gaps, 47-48

road from Black James Armstrong's to William Long's mill and thence to James Alexander's, 14

road from Thomas Armstong's to the Calfpasture waters, 152

road from Andrew Hays's mill on Back Creek to Timber Ridge Meeting House, 82

road from John Poage's by William M^cbride's shop to the main road between Bailey and Brown's, 130

road from James Baird's to the Lick by Robert Scotts, 75

road from Joseph May's to James Ball's, 71

road from the Tinkling Spring Meeting House to James Ball's, 75 road from Carr's (Kerr's) shop via Baskins's ford thence up a ridge between Daniel Deniston's and John Poage's, and thence into the road from Robert Poage's to the Court House, 87, 91, 122

road from the top of the Ridge to John Terrald's and James Beard's, 7

road from James Beard's/James Beard's ford to Chamberlaine's Run thence to the Stone Meeting House, 63, 122, 127

road from James Beard's through Robert Shankland's land to the North River, 67

road from John Stevenson's to James Beard's, 85

road from Thomas Connelly's house to James Beard's ford, 137

road from William Beard's to the Stone Meeting House, 97

road from John Stevenson's to William Beard's, 109

road from Lord Fairfax's line to William Beard's, 142

road from Bedford Gap to the old road near John Neilly's, 90

road from the Stone House to Bedford line, 91, 92

road from Crosby's field to Bedford line, 107

bridle way from Buchanan's ferry to the top of the Blue Ridge joining Bedford line, 117

road from the Great Lick to Bedford line to the road leading to Captain Renfroe's, 117

road from the Welshman's Run to the Bedford line, 136, 141

road from Thomas Tosh's to the road cleared by Richard Doggett to the Bedford line, 146

road from James River across the mountain to the Bedford line, 153

road from James Carter's mill to the Court House (via the first ford above Bell's land), 5

road near David Bell's plantation, 63

road from the foot of the mountain at Woods's Gap to James Bell's on the South River, 17 road from the forks between the Widow Steel's and James Bell's, 142

road round John Bennet's plantation, 133

road from William Bethell's road to Peter Rufner's mill, 42

(petition of the inhabitants of the Cowpasture) road from Patrick Davis's to the road that leads from Col. John Lewis's to Beverley's Big Meadows, 23

road from Patrick Davis's to the road that leads to Beverley's Big Meadow, 24

road from Benjamin Borden's to Beverley Manor line, 13

roads from the North River to Beverley Manor line, 35

road from Alexander Miller's to Beverly Manor line, 68

road from the Wilderness Bridge to Beverley Manor line, 70, 117

road from Beverley Manor line to the Indian Road, 70

road from Evan's Run to Beverley Manor line, 72

road from Beverley Manor line to the forks of the road near Hugh Fultons, 102

road from Charles Campbell's Long Meadow Branch by Joseph Kanady's to Beverley Manor line, 110

road from John Harrison's at the Big Spring to the county line, 140

road from Bingaman's ferry to the waters of Roan Oak near Tobias Bright's and from the Widow Draper's to Jacob Brown's, 53

road from Bingaman's Ferry to Robinson's land above John Bingaman, Jr's, 53

road from the end of Bingaman's Road on Robinson's land to James Miller's on Reed Creek, 53

road from the Tinkling Spring to Black's Draft, 78

road from the Tinkling Spring to Black's Run and thence to Middle River, 35

road from the Duck Ponds to Alexander Blair's, 108

(petition of the inhabitants of the west side of the Blue Ledge) road over the Blue Ridge, 14

road from the top of the Blue Ridge at the head of Swift Run to Capt. Downs's place (formerly Alexander Thomson's), 1 (petition of the inhabitants of the west side of the Blue Ledge) road over the Blue Ridge, 14

road from the Inhabitants of Roan Oak to the top of the Blue Ridge/Brunswick County line (later Lunenburg County), 2

road from the Ridge that divides the waters of New River from the waters of the south branch of Roan Oak, and thence over the Blue Ridge, 6

road over the Blue Ridge at Woods's old pass to the line of Albemarle (to meet proposed road from Albemarle Court House), 21

road from Israel Christian's to meet the road (cleared by Thomas Steuart) over the Blue Ridge, 22

road (cleared by Thomas Steuart/Stewart) over the Blue Ridge, 22, 29, 31, 38

road over Thorn's Gap in the Blue Ridge, 33

road from Shanando River to the top of the Blue Ridge, 33

road from the road that leads from Chester's Ford to Frederick County line to the top of the Blue Ridge (to meet a Road cleared by Culpeper County), 41

bridle way from Buchanan's ferry to the top of the Blue Ridge joining Bedford line, 117

road from the North Mountain Meeting House to Borden's, 20

(petition of the inhabitants of the lower Cowpasture) road from the lower Cowpasture to Burden's [Borden's] tract, 32

road from Borden's to the North Branch of James River, 42

road from James Cowan's to Borden's line, 72

road from William Ward's house to Borden's patent line, 101

road from the road above William Ward's house to Borden's patent line, 106

road from Benjamin Borden's to James Fulton's, 12

road from Gilbert Campbell's ford to Benjamin Borden's, 13

road from Benjamin Borden's to Beverley Manor line, 13

road from Benjamin Borden's house to Providence Meeting House, 35 road from Isaac Taylor's to the Widow Borden's, 42

road from John Bowyer's to William Lusk's, 76

road from the North River to John Bowyer's, 107

road from David Cloyd Jr.'s to John Bowyer, Gent.'s plantation on James River, 119

road from John Bowyer's plantation on James River by Seder [Cedar?] Bridge to Mathews's Road, 121

road from Graham's clearing by the Great Lick to Alexander Boyd's, 90

road from Samuel Braford's meadow to the Indian Road, 41

road from Samuel McDowell's by James Cowden's store house to Samuel Brafford's/Brawford's, 150, 153

road from Grimes's land by Breckenridge's house thence into the main road, 92

road from Major Breckenridge's to the Great Lick, 149

road from John Thomas's mill to Thomas Brian's/Bryan's, 100, 108

road from Abraham Smith's to the foot of the mountain at Briery Branch Gap, 110

road from the Ridge above Tobias Bright's that divides the waters of New River from the branches of Roan Oak to the lower ford of Catabo Creek, 6, 39

road from Bingaman's ferry to the waters of Roan Oak near Tobias Bright's and from the Widow Draper's to Jacob Brown's, 53

road from the Broad Spring in the forks of James River to the ferry, 76

(petition of inhabitants of Linvell's Creek) road from Brock's Creek to Francis Hughes and thence to the main road that leads to Fredericksburg, 34

road from the North Mountain Gap called Brock's Gap near Thomas Neist's to the mouth of the Lost River leading to North Shenandore, 47

road from Brock's Gap to Hampshire County Line, 74

road from the Court House to Brock's Gap, 79

Brock's Gap road, 84

road from Edward Shanklin's to Widow Thomas's old place near Brock's Gap, 111 road from Paxton's ford at the North River to the foot of the Poplar Hill through Brown's land, 77

road from Samuel Young's to Brown's, 78

road from John Poage's by William M^cbride's shop to the main road between Bailey and Brown's, 130

new road from the town [Staunton] by Young's mill and thence to the Glebe (replacing the old road by Brown's bridge), 145

road from Bingaman's ferry to the waters of Roan Oak near Tobias Bright's and from the Widow Draper's to Jacob Brown's, 53

road from Jacob Brown's on Roan Oak to Isaac Taylor's, 54

road from the second branch between Mr. Brown's and John Houston's to the Great Road by the Widow Lyle's, 121

road from the Court House/Staunton via Maj. Browns/Brown's Bridge/ Browns Meeting House and to the Glebe (and parts thereof), 41, 44, 109, 112, 117, 138, 145

road from Patrick Martin's to Brown's Meeting House, 147

road from Charles Campbell's house to Alexander Brownlee's and thence to James Fulton's, 50

road from the Inhabitants of Roan Oak to the top of the Blue Ridge/Brunswick County line (later Lunenburg County), 2

road from Calep Job's to James McKoy's. crossing the river at the Brush Bottom ford and along the river by Henry Spear's Plantation, 26

road from John Thomas's Mill to Thomas Bryan's/Brian's, 100, 108

road from Charles Millican's to William Bryan's, 49

road from the end of William Carravan's road on his plantation to William Bryan's on Roan Oak, 51

road from Basson Hover's on the South Fork of the South Branch of the Potomac by the Bryery Branch to Silas Hart's, 74

bridle way from Buchanan's ferry to the top of the Blue Ridge joining Bedford line, 117 road from James Young's Mill to Alexander Richey's smiths shop and thence to Buchanan's mill, 38, 40

road from the Gry [Dry? Guy?] branch to Buchanan's mill, 93

road from Buchanan's ford on James River to the main road already established over Cedar bridge, 153

road from Colonel Buchanan's on the north side of James River to the Pedlar ford, 119, 124

road from Walter Stewart's to the best ford on James River between the ferry and Col. Buchanan's and thence to the main road leading to John Mills's, 144

road from the Court House and via John Buchanan's mill to the Indian Road that leads by Fulton's, 26

road from Grymes's clearing to the head of the run above Madison's plantation, thence to New River on the lands of John Buchanan Gent. and thence to Fort Lewis and Fort Chiswell, 94-95

road from Renix's to James River at John Buchanan's house, 110

road from Vause's over the New River on the Land of John Buchanan and thence by Ingles's ferry to the Lead Mines (and portions thereof), 98, 128

road from William Buchanan's to the Court House, 4

road from Staunton to Buchanan's Mill Creek on the road leading to William Long's mill, 92

road from the Bent of Buffeloe to Michael Dougherty's, 49

road from the ford of the north branch of James River to James Stinson's on Buffelow, 100

road from the north branch of James River to Buffelow (via John Paxton's), 105, 110

road from Buffelo to James Gilmore's, 110

road from Thomas Paxton's by Hart's bottom to the fork of Buffelow, 85

road from the North River ford to Buffaloe Creek/Buffaloe Creek ford, 79, 81, 105

road by John Paxton's house to Buffaloe Creek, 79

road from Buffelow Creek to Edward Sharps, 105

road from the north branch of James River round the Poplar Hills to Buffalo Creek, 124, 144

road from William Elliot's to McCutcheon's mill thence through Buffaloe Gap, 125, 128

road through Buffalo Gap to Staunton/the road leading to Staunton, 148, 149, 151, 154

road from John Hodge's to the Buffalo Gap road, 148

road from Pedler ford to Bullett's Springs, 147

road from Estill's mill in the Bullpasture to George Lewis's in the Cowpasture, 118, 123

road from Hicklen's in the Bullpasture to Thomas Feemster's in the Cowpasture, 129

road from William Wilsons Mill into the new road at the foot of the Bullpasture and thence into the branch near Feemster's, 129

road from Nutt's Mill Creek near James Cadwell's to the Court House, 36, 65

road from William Long's to Caldwell's Creek, 119

road from Andrew Hamiltons in the Calfpasture through Jennings'sGap, 1

road from the great lick in the Cowpasture by Col. Lewis's land to Andrew Hamilton's in the Calfpasture, 2

(petition of the inhabitants of the Calfpasture) road from William Gay's to Robert McCutchceon's and thence to Robert Campbells, 23

(petition of the inhabitants of the Cowpasture) road from Wallace Estill's mill to the road on the head of the Calfpasture, 28-29

(petition of inhabitants of the Calfpasture) road from William Guy's to Robert McCutcheon's mill and thence to Robert Campbell's, 34

road the Calfpasture to Swift Run Pass, 41

road from Wallace Estell's/Estill's to the Calfpasture Road, 41, 46

(petition of the inhabitants of the Cowpasture and Calfpasture) road from Andrew Hamilton's to the turn of the (Calfpasture) waters by Charles Walker's, 57, 60

road from Jennings's Gap to the turn of the Calfpasture waters, 82, 92

road from Thomas Armstong's to the Calfpasture waters, 152

road from Gilbert Campbell's ford to Benjamin Borden's, 13

road from Campbell's schoolhouse to Renix's Road, 52

road from the North River to Campbell's schoolhouse, 52

road from William Long's mill to Charles Campbell's, 38

road from Charles Campbell's to the cross roads above James Fulton's, 38, 63

road from Charles Campbell's house to Alexander Brownlee's and thence to James Fulton's, 50

road from Charles Campbell's Long Meadow Branch by Joseph Kanady's to Beverley Manor line, 110

road from Charles Campbell's Run to John Davis's mill, 136

road from George Campbell's to William McClenachan's mill, 137

road from James Campbell's to the Catapo Road, 64

road from James Campbell's to the head of Roan Oak waters, 64

road from the North Mountain Meeting House to John Campbell/John Campbell's field, 19, 42

road from John Campbell/John Campbell's field to the Court House, 19, 27, 42

road from James Cowan's meadow to Patrick Campbell's run, 55

road round Patrick Campbell's plantation, 69

(petition of the inhabitants of the Calfpasture) road from William Gay's to Robert McCutchceon's and thence to Robert Campbells, 23

(petition of inhabitants of the Calfpasture) road from William Guy's to Robert McCutcheon's mill and thence to Robert Campbell's, 34

road from Cape Caphon to meet the road near Thomas Moore's, 27

road from Carr's (Kerr's) shop via Baskins's ford thence up a ridge between Daniel Deniston's and John Poage's, and thence into the road from Robert Poage's to the Court House, 87, 91, 122

Carr's Creek roads, 96

road from the Widow Sloan's plantation to the end of Caravan's new road, 56 road from the end of William Carravan's road on his plantation to William Bryan's on Roan Oak, 51

road from Charles Millican's to William Carravan's, 51

road from lower end of Cowpasture to Carter's mill, 7

road from James Carter's mill to the Court House (via the first ford above Bell's land), 5

road from Carvin's to Millican's, 63

road from Charles Millican's to the end of Carwin's Road and thence to the Widow Sloan's, 53

road from the Ridge above Tobias Bright's that divides the waters of New River from the branches of Roan Oak to the lower ford of Catabo Creek, 6, 39

road from Charles Milkin's to the first fording on Catabo Creek, 12

road from Millikin's to the first ford on Catapo, 30

road from Frederick Hartsaw's mill on Craig's Creek to the Catapo, 54

road from James Campbell's to the Catapo Road, 64

road from the Catapo Road to Warwick Gap, 64

road from the Stone House to James Mcafee's or James McCown's on Catapo, 93

road from Looney's ferry to the first ford of Catawbo, 90

road from Graham's clearing to Catawbo, 90

road from the ford of Catabo to John M^{c}farron's, 96

road from Grymes's clearing to Catapo, 95

road from Catawbo to Pedler ford on James River, 118

road from Fort William to the head of Catawbo, 135

road from James Montgomery's at Catawbo to the side of Craig's Creek Mountain, 135

road from James Montgomery's lower line to the old county line leading from Catawbo to the New River, 144

road from Buchanan's ford on James River to the main road already established over <u>Cedar bridge</u>, 153

road from James Beard/James Beard's ford to <u>Chamberlaine's Run</u> thence to the Stone Meeting House, 63, 122, 127

road from the <u>Cherry Tree Bottom ford</u> to Millikin's, 30

road from the road that leads from <u>Chester's Ford</u> to Frederick County line to the top of the Blue Ridge (to meet a Road cleared by Culpeper County), 41

road from the Tinkling Spring to Stuart and <u>Christian's</u> road, 13, 14

road from between Captain Wilson's and John McCreary's via James Lockart's field, James Wilson's field and Capt. <u>Christian's</u> to the road that leads from Patton's mill to the Tinkling Spring, 24-25

road from Long Meadow bridge to the South River at Israel <u>Christian's</u>, 16

road from the South River at Israel <u>Christian's</u> to Woods's Gap, 16

road from the Piney Run to Israel <u>Christian's</u>, 22

road from Israel <u>Christian's</u> to meet the road (cleared by Thomas Steuart/Stewart) over the Blue Ridge, 22

road from Israel <u>Christian's</u> to the mountain, 31, 32

main road through the Israel <u>Christian's</u> lot in the town of Staunton, 54, 77, 83

road round Israel <u>Christian's</u> meadow fence, 94, 96

road from the Court House to William <u>Christian's</u>, 84

road from William <u>Christian's</u> to the saw mill, 84

road from James McCown's to Patton's mill place on <u>Christians Creek</u>, 25

road from the Court House/Staunton to <u>Christian's Creek</u>, 44, 45, 51, 78, 79, 102, 104, 105, 106, 116, 146

road from <u>Christian's Creek</u> to the Tinkling Spring, 81

road from <u>Christian's Creek</u> to Rockfish Gap, 93

road from Christian's Creek to Tees's, 105

road down Christian's Creek as far as George Hutchinson's deceased by Col. Lewis's, 126

road from this Court House to Christy's Creek, 46, 91

road from the Court House to where the Church is to be built and thence to the Timber Grove, 10

road round the plantation of Margaret Clark (near the road from Risk's mill to Providence), 128, 150

road from the Court House to the Clerks Office, 3

road from William Clighorn's to the waters of Purgatory, 38

road from David Cloyd's to John M^cfarron's, 64

road from David Cloyd's plantation to the Roan Oak Road, 64

road from David Cloyd Jr.'s to John Bowyer, Gent.'s plantation on James River, 119

road from Michael Cloyd's house to the branch below James Moore Jr.'s, 136

road from Coburn's mill to the county line, 22

(petition of the inhabitants of the South branch) road from Patton's mill to Coburn's mill, 29

road from the South River above Joseph Hanah's crossing Coles ford to Mathew Thompson's, 95

(petition of the southwest inhabitants of the county) road from Ezekiel Colhoun's to Wood's River from thence to the top of the ridge dividing Wood's River and the south fork of Roan Oak, 20

road from the fork of the new road near Jumping Run or Abraham Collett's and thence to the Court House, 8, 9

road from the Stone Meeting House to Thomas Conerley's, 97

road from Thomas Connelly's house to James Beard's ford, 137

road from John Seewright's mill to Thomas Connerly's, 145

road from Mr. Hart's to the Meeting House on Cook's Creek, 83, 86 road from Abraham Smith's to the road that leads to Swift Run Gap (via John Douglass's, crossing Dry River above James McClure's field, crossing Cook's Creek between William Snodon's and Alexander Heron's meadow fence and by Edward Shanklin's to the main road that leads to Swift Run Gap), 129

road from the county line to Stoney Creek, 3

road from Calep Jones's mill to the county line, 7, 15

road from the county line to John Staly's mill, 21

road from Coburn's mill to the county line, 22

road from Michael Props's to the county line, 77

road from John Gratton's to the county line on the south side of the North Mountain, 82

road from the Great Lick to the county line, 101

road from North Mill Creek from the upper tract to the county line below Jacob Peterson's, 109

road from Tinker Creek to the county line, 137

road from John Harrison's at the Big Spring to the county line, 140

road from the county line to the fork of the road by John Harrison's, 151

road from Hughs's lane by Mr. Matthew Harrison's mills to the county line, 152, 153

road from William King's to the Court House and thence to Samuel Gay's, 1

road from John Anderson's to the Court House, 2, 31

road from Jennings's Gap to Daniel M^canair's and thence via John Finla's to the Court House, 2, 15, 133

road from the Court House to the Tinkling Spring, 3, 4, 8, 13

road from the Court House to the Clerks Office, 3

road from the top of the North Mountain to William King's and thence to the Court House (and portions thereof), 3, 4, 11, 40

road from William Buchanan's to the Court House, 4

road from James Carter's mill to the Court House (via the first ford above Bell's land), 5

road from the Court House to the Timber Broge, 7

road from the Court House to the top of the [Blue] Ridge near Rockfish Gap, 8

road from the fork of the new road near Jumping Run or Abraham Collett's and thence to the Court House, 8, 9

road from John Pickens's mill to the Court House, 9

road from the Court House to the Indian Road near Robert Craven's, 10

road from the Court House to where the Church is to be built and thence to the Timber Grove, 10

road from the Timber Grove to the North Mountain Meeting House to the Court House, 15

(petition of inhabitants of south branch of Potomac) road from John Patton's to the forks of Dry River and via Capt. John Smith's to the Court House, 15

road from John Mizer's to the Stone Meeting House by the Court House road, 16

road from the Court House/Staunton to Middle River (including via the head of the Race paths), 17, 34, 62, 79, 121

road from the forks of Dry River to the Court House, 18

road from the Court House/Staunton to Robert Poage's, 18, 49, 99, 105

road from the Court House to Moore's mill, 18, 21

road from the North Mountain Meeting House to the Court House, 19, 21, 93

road from John Campbell's/John Campbell's field to the Court House, 19, 27, 42

road from the Court House and via John Buchanan's mill to the Indian Road that leads by Fulton's, 26

road from Nutt's Mill Creek near James Cadwell's to the Court House, 36, 65

road from the North River near Silas Hart's Gent. to the Court House, 36

road from the Court House/Staunton via Browns Meeting House/Major Brown's/Brown's Bridge and to the Glebe (and portions thereof), 41, 44, 109, 112, 117, 138, 145

road from the Court House to James Moody's, 41

road from the Court House to Givins's mill, 41

road from Kenaday's mill to the Court House, 43

road from the Court House/Staunton to Christian's Creek, 44, 45, 51, 78, 79, 104, 105, 106, 116, 146

road from the Court House to William Anderson's, 45, 111

road from this Court House to Christy's Creek, 46, 91

several roads from the Court House to Silas Hart's, 57, 63, 66, 67

road from Thomas Moore's to the Court House, 63

road from the Court House to Brock's Gap, 79

road from the Court House to William Christian's, 84

road from Abraham Smith's to the Court House, 83

road from the Court House to Robert McClenachan's, 86

old road from the Court House to Robert McClenachan's, 87

road from the Court House to Trimble's ford, 87

road from Carr's (Kerr's) shop via Baskins's ford thence up a ridge between Daniel Deniston's and John Poage's, and thence into the road from Robert Poage's to the Court House, 87, 91, 122

road from the Court House to Edward Tar's, 98

road from Benjamin Stuart's branch to the Court House road, 138

road from John Coutt's crossing Shanando River by Henry Long's into the new road leading to Massanutten, 154 road from James Cowan's to the Indian Road, 39, 49

road from James Cowan's meadow to Patrick Campbell's run, 55

road from James Cowan's line to David Moore's, 69, 70

road from James Cowan's to Borden's line, 72

road from Samuel McDowell's by James Cowden's store house to Samuel Brafford's, 150, 153

road from the great lick in the Cowpasture by Col. Lewis's land to Andrew Hamilton's in the Calfpasture, 2

road from lower end of Cowpasture to Carter's mill, 7

road from Jackson's River to Co. John Lewis's land in the Cowpasture, 15

road from Daniel McAnare's through Jennings's Gap to the Cowpasture, 22

road from the Cowpasture to Lewis's great bottom, 22

(petition of the inhabitants of the Cowpasture) road from Patrick Davis's to the road that leads from Col. John Lewis's to Beverley's Big Meadows, 23

(petition of the inhabitants of the Cowpasture) road from Wallace Estill's mill to the road on the head of the Calfpasture, 28-29

road from Wright's mill to the Cowpasture near Hugart's or Knox's, 32

(petition of the inhabitants of the lower Cowpasture) road from the lower Cowpasture to Burdens [Borden's] tract, 32

(petition of the inhabitants of the Cowpasture and Calfpasture) road from Andrew Hamilton's to the turn of the (Calfpasture) waters by Charles Walker's, 57, 60

road from Estill's mill in the Bullpasture to George Lewis's in the Cowpasture, 118, 123

road from the turn of the waters of the Cowpasture River to Robert Hall's, 118

road from Hicklen's in the Bullpasture to Thomas Feemster's in the Cowpasture, 129

road from the Cowpasture to Gilmer's Gap, 137

road from James Givens's to the head of the Cowpasture River, 141

road from Craig's mills to the mouth of the South River to the Great Road Leading to Staunton, 134, 137 road from the Tinkling Spring to Mr Craig's, 86

road from James Craig's mill up the South River to John Patrick's, 140

road from Frederick Hartsaw's mill on Craig's Creek up the said creek and across the mountain to James M^{c}afee's, 54

road from Frederick Hartsaw's mill on Craig's Creek to the Catapo, 54

road from the mouth of Craig's Creek to Fort Young, 118

road from James Montgomerie's to the foot of the mountain towards Craig's Creek, 119

road from Joseph Murtys house down Craig's Creek and Pattersons Creek into the main road from John Crawfords to the Stone House, 150

road from James Montgomery's at Catawbo to the side of Craig's Creek Mountain, 135

road from the North River to Craven's, 23

road from Robert Craven's to Samuel Wilkins's, 3

road from Robert Craven's to the Indian Road, 3, 11

road from the Court House to the Indian Road near Robert Craven's, 10

road from Naked Creek to Robert Craven's, 17

road from Robert Craven's to the marked road that leads to Swift Run Pass, 44

road from the North River to Robert Craven's and thence by Volentine Sevier's, 44

road from Robert Craven's to the fork of the road below John Harrison's, 83

road from Robert Craven's to the ford at the North River at John Fowler's, 133

road from Ramsey's cabin to John Crawford's, 107

road from Joseph Murty's house down Craig's Creek and Patterson's Creek into the main road from John Crawford's to the Stone House, 150

road from Crocket's to King's Gap, 26

road from Crosby's field to Bedford line, 107

road from Cub Run to Robert Scott's, 75

road from the road that leads from Chester's Ford to Frederick County line to the top of the Blue Ridge (to meet a Road cleared by Culpeper County), 41

road from Hays's Gap to Captain Culton's, 117

new market road from Edward Erwin's to Swift Run road from Edward Erwin's leading by William Curry's, Edward Erwin, Jr.'s, the old road to John Fowler's still house, passing through Edward Shanklin's lane to David Nelson's, thence to the South Branch Road at Houston's meadow and thence to the forks below Jacob Nicholas's, 124-125

road from Samuel Davidson's to Woods's Gap, 79

road from Samuel Davidson's ford to Edward Rutledge's and thence to John Allison's ford and by John Kerr's to the Stone Meeting House, 89, 91

road from Davis's Mill to John Ramsey's on South River, 61

road from Davis's cabin to the Warm Springs, 152

road from David Davis's mill to the top of the mountain above William King's, 1

road from James Davis's to the landing road, 30

road from Samuel Stalnaker's on Holdston's River to James Davis's, 51

road from John Davis's mill to Woods's new cleared Gap, 26

road from the Stone Meeting house to John Davis's mill, 41

road from Thomas Watterson's field to John Davis's mill, 131

road from Charles Campbell's Run to John Davis's mill, 136

(petition of the inhabitants of the Cowpasture) road from Patrick Davis's to the road that leads from Col. John Lewis's to Beverley's Big Meadows, 23

road from Patrick Davis's to the road that leads to Beverley's Big Meadow, 24

road from Samuel Davis's to the mountain at Woods's Gap, 77

road from William Davis's to Timber Ridge Meeting House, 106

road from Volintine Sevier's old place to Daniel Davison's, 85

road from Daniel Davison's house to John Stevenson's, 85

road from Alexander Sayer's mill to James Davison's on Holdston's River, 53 road from John Davison's to the Stone Meeting House, 127

road from John Robinson's mill by the Den to the county road leading to Warwick, 134

road from Carr's shop via Baskins's ford thence up a ridge between Daniel Deniston's and John Poage's, and thence into the road from Robert Poage's to the Court House, 87, 91, 122

road from the Pedler ford on James River and up the river eight miles to Capt. Dickenson's, 119

road from within eight miles of the Pedler ford to Captain Dickenson's, 122

road from Captain Charles Lewis's to where Dickinson's road joins the road leading from Staunton to Warm Springs, 148

road from the forks of Lewis and Dickinson's road to the Warm Springs, 152

road from Peter Wright's to Adam Dickenson's, 37

road from Dove's to Captain John Dickenson's, 90

road from the Panther/Painter Gap to Captain John Dickenson's, 90, 116

road from the Warm Springs to the forks of the road leading to Captain John Dickinson's, 148

road from Joseph Dickenson's to the Stone Meeting house, 139

road from Thomas Tosh's to the road cleared by Richard Doggett to the Bedford line, 146

road from John Wilson's by Dooley's, Barnet Mann's, and John Love's, and thence to James Wait's, 47

road from the Bent of Buffeloe to Michael Dougherty's, 49

road from Abraham Smith's to the road that leads to Swift Run Gap (via John Douglass's, crossing Dry River above James McClure's field, crossing Cook's Creek between William Snodon's and Alexander Heron's meadow fence and by Edward Shanklin's to the main road that leads to Swift Run Gap), 129

road from Dove's to Captain John Dickenson's, 90

road from the top of the Blue Ridge at the head of Swift Run to Capt. Downs's place (formerly Alexander Thomson's), 1 road from Downs's to the Stone Meeting House, 24, 32

road from Henry Downs's through William Thompson's former plantation to the Stone Meeting House, 54

road from Henry Downs, Jr.'s to the Meeting House, 11

road from the Lower Meeting House to Henry Downs, Jr.'s, 13, 14

road from Henry Downs, Jr.'s to the Stone Meeting House, 23, 29

road from Bingaman's ferry to the waters of Roan Oak near Tobias Bright's and from the Widow Draper's to Jacob Brown's, 53

road from the Gry [Dry? Guy?] branch to Buchanan's mill, 93

road from the Dry Branch/Dry Branch Gap of the North Mountain to Archers mill, 92, 142

road from the Dry Gap to Mr. John Archer's mill, 149, 151

(petition of inhabitants of south branch of Potomac) road from John Patton's to the forks of Dry River and via Capt. John Smith's to the Court House, 15

road from John Patton's/John Patton's old place to the forks/little fork of Dry River, 17, 67

road from the forks of Dry River to the Court House, 18

road from Abraham Smith's to the road that leads to Swift Run Gap (via John Douglass's, crossing Dry River above James McClure's field, crossing Cook's Creek between William Snodon's and Alexander Heron's meadow fence and by Edward Shanklin's to the main road that leads to Swift Run Gap), 129

road from the little fork of the Dry Run to the North River, 36

road from the Dry River Gap to the road that leads over Swift Run Gap, 77

road cut from the old road through the Dry River Gap of the mountain (road from Dry River Gap (via Siver's mill and Charles Wilson's) to the county line), 79

road from the Duck Ponds to Alexander Blair's, 108

road from the Duck Ponds to the Middle River, 133, 134

road from the North River to Robert Dunlop's, 29

road from the Little Warm Springs to the fork of the road on Dunlap's Creek, 150 road from Reed Creek to Eagle Bottom and thence to the top of the ridge that divides the waters of New River and those of the south fork of Roan Oak, 5

road from Jeremiah Earley's to the top of the Ridge at Swift Run, 58

road from James Edmondson's mill to the Fork Meeting House, 50

road from William Elliot's to McCutcheon's mill thence through Buffaloe Gap, 125, 128

road from English's to Madison's plantation, 96

road from Vause's by Ingles's/English's ferry to Peak Creek on the North side of the New River, 109, 113, 123, 129, 132

road from Bernerd Mann's to Edward Erwin Jr.'s, 121

new road from Edward Erwin's to the Market Road that leads to Swift Run Gap, 123, 129

old road from Jennings's Gap to Swift Run (including old market road from Edward Erwin's to the fork below Jacob Nicholas's), 124

new market road from Edward Erwin's to Swift Run (road from Edward Erwin's leading by William Curry's, Edward Erwin, Jr.'s, the old road to John Fowler's still house, passing through Edward Shanklin's lane to David Nelson's, thence to the South Branch Road at Houston's meadow and thence to the forks below Jacob Nicholas's, 124-125

road from Jennings's Gap to Edward Erwin Jr.'s (via William Fleming's), 123, 124

road from Estill's mill in the Bullpasture to George Lewis's in the Cowpasture, 118, 123

road from Wallace Estell's/Estill's to the Calfpasture road, 41, 46

road from William Wilson's mill to Wallace Estell's mill, 44

(petition of the inhabitants of the Cowpasture) road from Wallace Estill's mill to the road on the head of the Calfpasture, 28-29

road from Samuel Wilson's house to Wallace Estill's, 128

road from Wallace Estill's to Tincher's, 147

road from Evan's Run to Beverley Manor line, 72

road from Evans's Run to David Moore's, 96

road from the Stone house to Evans's mill, 138

road from Lord Fairfax's line to the road that leads over Swift Run Pass, 100, 101

road from Lord Fairfax's line to William Beard's, 142

road from William Wilson's Mill into the new road at the foot of the Bullpasture and thence into the branch near Feemster's, 129

road from Hicklen's in the Bullpasture to Thomas Feemster's in the Cowpasture, 129

road from Jennings's Gap to Daniel M^canair's and thence via John Finla's to the Court House, 2, 15, 133

road from Finla's Spring to the Meeting House, 36

road from the Tinkling Spring/Tinkling Spring Meeting House to John Finley's/Finla's Great Spring, 74

road from Jennings's Gap to Edward Erwin Jr.'s (via William Fleming's), 123, 124

road from James Edmondson's mill to the Fork Meeting House, 50

road from Grymes's clearing to the head of the run above Madison's plantation, thence to New River on the lands of John Buchanan Gent. and thence to Fort Lewis and Fort Chiswell, 94-95

road from Vause's to Fort Chiswell, 109

road from Fort Defiance to Handley's mill, 125

road from Grymes's clearing to the head of the run above Madison's plantation, thence to New River on the lands of John Buchanan Gent. and thence to Fort Lewis and Fort Chiswell, 94-95

road from Fort Lewis to the Great Lick, 101

road from the Stone House to Fort Lewis, 105, 107, 108, 112

road from Fort Lewis to Vause's, 113, 115

road round the hill where Fort Lewis stands, 115, 120

road from Fort Lewis to Peter's Creek, 136

road from Fort William to the Market Road, 100

road from Fort William to the head of Catawbo, 135

road from the mouth of Craig's Creek to Fort Young, 118

new market road from Edward Erwin's to Swift Run (road from Edward Erwin's leading by William Curry's, Edward Erwin, Jr.'s, the old road to John Fowler's still house, passing through Edward Shanklin's lane to David Nelson's, thence to the South Branch Road at Houston's meadow and thence to the forks below Jacob Nicholas's, 124-125

road from John Fowler's fording to the Stone Meeting House, 128

road from Robert Craven's to the ford at the North River at John Fowler's, 133

road from John Archer's mill to Robert Fowler's, 130, 140

road from Patrick Frazier's to the Stone Meeting House, 109

road from William Frazier's to Hance Magort's and thence to the top of the [Blue] Ridge at Swift Run Pass, 71, 97, 154

road from the forks of the South River to William Frazier's, 97

the Indian Road from Frederick County line to Tom's Creek, 15

road from James McCoy's to Frederick County line, 18

road from the road that leads from Chester's Ford to Frederick County line to the top of the Blue Ridge (to meet a Road cleared by Culpeper County), 41

road from Rockfish Gap to the road that leads to the falls of James River and Fredericksburg, 8

(petition of inhabitants of Linvell's Creek) road from Brock's Creek to Francis Hughes and thence to the main road that leads to Fredericksburg, 34

road from the Court House and via John Buchanan's mill to the Indian Road that leads by Fulton's, 26

road from the forks at the Widow Fulton's to Joseph Kenaday's mill, 47

road from Beverley Manor line to the forks of the road near Hugh Fultons, 102

road from Benjamin Borden's to James Fulton's, 12

roads from Charles Campbell's to the cross roads above James Fulton's, 38, 63

road from Charles Campbell's house to Alexander Brownlee's and thence to James Fulton's, 50

50road from the Widow Gay's to Samuel Hodge's, 115

road from the Widow Gay's to the dividing of the waters in Jennings's Gap, 121

road from Painter Gap to James Gay's, 132

road from Charles Walker's to Robert Gay's, 84

road from William King's to the Court House and thence to Samuel Gay's, 1

(petition of the inhabitants of the Calfpasture) road from William Gay's to Robert McCutchceon's and thence to Robert Campbell's, 23

road from George Gibson's at the House Mountain to John Hanna's mill, 143

road from the North River where James Gill dwelled to the South River, 2

road from Nathan Gillilan's to Staunton, 152

road from the Cowpasture to Gilmer's Gap, 137

road from Buffelo to James Gilmore's, 110

road from James Gilmore's house to Renix's old place, 110

road from Pickens's mill to the Indian Road near Givens's old place, 17

road from the Court House to Givins's mill, 41

road from Givens's mill to the forks of the [South?] River, 97

road from John Madison's to Givens's mill, 133

road from James Givins's mill to the road over Woods's new Gap at the foot of the mountain, 39

road from James Givens's mill by Hugh Allen's house to the Stone Meeting house, 134

road from James Givens's to the head of the Cowpasture River, 141

road from the Glebe to John Risk's mill, 52

road from the Court House/Staunton, via Major Brown's/Brown's Meeting House/Brown's Bridge, to the Glebe (and portions thereof), 41, 44, 109, 112, 117

road from the Glebe to the town of Staunton, 177, 138

new road from the town [Staunton] by Young's mill and thence to the Glebe (replacing the old road by Brown's bridge), 145

road from Michael Prop's to Conrod Good's, 111

road from Thomas Gordon's to Aron Oliver's, 146

road from Graham's clearing to Catawbo, 90

road from Graham's clearing by the Great Lick to Alexander Boyd's, 90

road from Graham's clearing to James Johnston's, 135

road from the Great Lick to Graham's clearing, 136

road from John Gratton's to the county line on the south side of the North Mountain, 82

road from John Grattan's to the Stone Meeting House, 143

road from Gratton's Store to Naked Creek, 138

road from the great lick in the Cowpasture by Col. Lewis's land to Andrew Hamilton's in the Calfpasture, 2

road from Grymes's land to the Great Licks, 86

road from Graham's clearing by the Great Lick to Alexander Boyd's, 90

road from Fort Lewis to the Great Lick, 101

road from the Great Lick to the county line, 101

the Warwick Road near the Great Lick, 115

road from the Great Lick to Bedford line to the road leading to Captain Rentfroe's, 117

road from the Great Lick to Graham's clearing, 136

road from Major Breckenridge's to the Great Lick, 149

road from Joseph Long's mill to James Young's mill thence to the Great Road on James Morrison's plantation, 40

road from Joseph Long's mill to the Great Road near Thompson's, 98

road from the second branch between Mr. Brown's and John Houston's to the Great Road by the Widow Lyle's, 121 road from Craig's mill to the mouth of the South River and from the mills to the Great Road leading to Staunton, 134, 137

road from Grimes's land by Breckenridge's house thence into the main road, 92

road from the Gry [Dry? Guy?] branch to Buchanan's mill, 93

road from Grymes's land to the Great Licks, 86

road from Grymes's clearing to the head of the run above Madison's plantation, thence to New River on the lands of John Buchanan Gent. and thence to Fort Lewis and Fort Chiswell, 94-95

road from Grymes's clearing to Catapo, 95

road from Col. Lewis's and from Staunton to John Grymes's, 98

road (on the south side of James River) from the ferry and ford to Sloan's land above William Harbeson's and thence to Archibald Grymes's land and the gap of the mountain, 85-86

(petition of inhabitants of the Calfpasture) road from William Guy's to Robert McCutcheon's mill and thence to Robert Campbell's, 34

road from the Gry [Dry? Guy?] branch to Buchanan's mill, 93

road from Jacob Halderman's to Hampshire County line, 69

road between Hall's mill and the main county road round Joseph Walker's fence, 76

road from the cross road below Patrick Hays's (meeting with the road by Edward Hall's at the foot of the mountain), 9

road from Edward Hall's to William Long's mill, 38

road from George Lewis's to Robert Hall's, 118

road from the turn of the waters of the Cowpasture River to Robert Hall's, 118

road from William Hall's to the Mountain Road, 65

road from William Hall's mill to William McKee's, 141, 145

road from Andrew Hamilton's in the Calfpasture through Jennings's Gap, 1

road from the great lick in the Cowpasture by Col. Lewis's land to Andrew Hamilton's in the Calfpasture, 2 (petition of the inhabitants of the Cowpasture and Calfpasture) road from Andrew Hamilton's to the turn of the (Calfpasture) waters by Charles Walker's, 57, 60

road from King's mill or Naked Creek to Patrick Hamilton's and thence by John Poage's mill to the Staunton Road, 126

road from the Stone Meeting House to King's mill (through William Hamilton's fenced ground), 76, 79

road from Jacob Halderman's to Hampshire County line, 69

road from Brock's Gap to Hampshire County line, 74

road from a ford near Esther Robinson's to a marked tree near Hand's meadow, 47

road from Fort Defiance to Handley's mill, 125

road from the South River above Joseph Hanah's crossing Coles ford to Mathew Thompson's, 95

road from George Gibson's at the House Mountain to John Hanna's mill, 148

road from Joseph Hannah's to Mathew Thompson's, 101

road (on the south side of James River) from the ferry and ford to Sloan's land above William Harbeson's and thence to Archibald Grymes's land and the gap of the mountain, 85-86

road from the Widow McDaniel's to William Harbison's, 100

road from Adam Harmon's to the river and north branch of Roan Oak, 6

wagon road from Michael Prop's to Daniel Harrison's, 77

road from John Harrison's to the Meeting House road, 19

road from Robert Craven's to the fork of the road below John Harrison's, 83

road from George Scot's on Middle River to John Harrisons, 23

road from Smith's bridge to the forks of the road near John Harrison's, 100

road from the forks of the road below John Harrison's to Reubin Harrison's meadow and thence to Daniel Smith's bridge, 112

road from John Stevenson's to the top of the Ridge by John Harrison Jr.'s. deceased, 98 road from John Harrison's at the Big Spring to the county line, 140

road from the county line to the fork of the road by John Harrison's, 151

road from Hughs's lane by Mr. Matthew Harrison's mills to the county line, 152, 153

road from Mr. Matthew Harrison's mills to the road leading to Swift Run Gap, 152, 153

main road round Rubin Harrison's Plantation, 33

road from Daniel Smith's to Rubin Harrison's meadow, 89

road from Thomas's mill to Thomas Harrison's, 86

road from Adam Reader's Mines to Issac Robinson's and thence to the Widow Wright's and from thence to Thomas Harrison's, 131

road from Mr. Hart's to the Meeting House on Cook's Creek, 83, 86

road from Thomas Paxton's by Hart's bottom to the fork of Buffelow, 85

road from the North River near Silas Hart's Gent. to the Court House, 36

several roads from the Court House to Silas Hart's, 57, 63. 66, 67

road from Basson Hover's on the South Fork of the South Branch of the Potomac by the Bryery Branch to Silas Hart's, 74

road from Henry Stone's to Silas Hart's, 92

road from Frederick Hartsaw's mill on Craig's Creek up the said creek and across the mountain to James M^{c}afee's, 54

road from Frederick Hartsaw's mill on Craig's Creek to the Catapo, 54

road from the cross road below Hays on the north side of the South River to the ridge, 10

road from Hays's fulling mill to Timber Ridge Meeting House, 29, 69

road from Hays's mill to Providence Meeting House, 43

road from Hays's mill to Alexander Miller's, 69

road from Hays's to Kenaday's mill, 70

road from Adrew Hays's mill to Captain Kenady's, 68

road from Andrew Hays's to Robert Kilpatrick's, 74

road from Andrew Hays's mill on Back Creek to Timber Ridge Meeting House, 82

the old road from Alexander Walkers by James Moore's to Andrew Hays's, 149

the new road from Alexander Walkers by Charles Hay's to Andrew Hays's, 149

road from John Hays's Mill to Providence Meeting House and thence to the county road, 20

road from the cross road below Patrick Hays's (meeting with the road by Edward Hall's at the foot of the mountain), 9

road round Patrick Hays's plantation, 13

road that goes by Kenaday's to Patrick Hays's, 43

road from Hays's Gap to Captain Culton's, 117

road round James Henderson's plantation, 144

road from Abraham Smith's to the road that leads to Swift Run Gap (via John Douglass's, crossing Dry River above James McClure's field, crossing Cook's Creek between William Snodon's and Alexander Heron's meadow fence and by Edward Shanklin's to the main road that leads to Swift Run Gap), 129

road from Hicklen's in the Bullpasture to Thomas Feemster's in the Cowpasture, 129

road from William Wilson's mill to the new road near John Hicklen's, 147

road from Hite's Mines to the road that leads to Swift Run Gap, 126

road from John Hodge's to the Buffalo Gap road, 148

road from Samuel Hodge's to Jennings's Gap, 113

road from the Widow Gay's to Samuel Hodge's, 115

road from Painter Gap to Samuel Hodge's, 141

road from McClenachan's mill to William Holdman's, 136

road from Henry Holdston's to the Tavern Spring beyond James Montgomery's, 61

road from Samuel Stalnaker's on Holdston's River to James Davis', 51

road from Alexander Sayer's mill to James Davison's on Holdston's River, 53 road from Hopkins's mill to the road leading to Swift Run Gap Road, 152

road from George Gibson's at the House Mountain to John Hanna's mill, 148

new market road from Edward Erwin's to Swift Run (road from Edward Erwin's leading by William Curry's, Edward Erwin, Jr.'s, the old road to John Fowler's still house, passing through Edward Shanklin's lane to David Nelson's, thence to the South Branch Road at Houston's meadow and thence to the forks below Jacob Nicholas's, 124-125

road from the second branch between Mr. Brown's and John Houston's to the Great Road by the Widow Lyle's, 121

road from Basson Hover's on the South Fork of the South Branch of the Potomac by the Bryery Branch to Silas Hart's, 74

road down Christian's Creek as far as George Hutchinson's deceased by Col Lewis's, 126

road from Staunton by John Hutchinson's to the old road leading from Mathews's mill to John Ramsey's, 116

road from Hughs's lane by Mr. Matthew Harrison's mills to the county line, 152, 153

(petition of inhabitants of Linvell's Creek) road from Brock's Creek to Francis Hughes and thence to the main road that leads to Fredericksburg, 34

road from Craven's to the Indian Road, 3, 11

road from the Court House to the Indian Road near Robert Craven's, 10

Indian Road, 11, 22, 23

the Indian Road from Frederick County line to Tom's Creek, 15

road from Pickens's mill to the Indian Road near Givens's old place, 17

road from the Court House and via John Buchanan's mill to the Indian Road that leads by Fulton's, 26

road from James Cowan's to the Indian Road, 39, 49

road from Samuel Braford's meadow to the Indian Road, 41

Indian Road from the north fork to the main branch of James River, 51

road from the Indian Road to David Moore's mill, 65

road from Beverley Manor line to the Indian Road, 70

road from Vause's over the New River on the Land of John Buchanan and thence by Ingles's ferry to the Lead Mines (and portions thereof), 98, 128

road from Vause's on Roanoke by Ingles's ferry to Peak Creek on the North side of the New River, 109, 113, 123, 129, 132

road from the Widow Jackson's to Williams Creek, 35

road from Samuel Jackson's[?] to the second ford on Jennings's Branch, 56

road from Jackson's River to Co. John Lewis's land in the Cowpasture, 15

road from the north fork of James River to Looney's ford on the south fork of James River, 5

road from Rockfish Gap to the road that leads to the falls of James River and Fredericksburg, 8

road by the waters of James River, 12

road from Looney's ferry to the north branch of James River, 21

road from David Moore's mill to Robert Poage's mill place in the forks of James River, 30

roads in the forks of James River, 36, 100

road from Borden's to the North Branch of James River, 42

road from the North fork of James River near John Mathews's to Renix's Road, 50

Indian Road from the north fork to the main branch of James River, 51

road from James River to the forks below Charles Millican's, 61

road from the Broad Spring in the forks of James River to the ferry, 76

road from the North Branch of James River to William Lusk's, 80

road (on the south side of James River) from the ferry and ford to Sloan's land above William Harbeson's and thence to Archibald Grymes's land and the gap of the mountain, 85-86

road from the ford of the north branch of James River to James Stinson's on Buffelow, 100 road from the north branch of James River to Buffelow (via John Paxton's and Abraham Brown's), 105, 110

road from the north branch of James River to Edward Tarr's old shop, 106

road from Renix's to James River at John Buchanan's house, 110

road from Catawbo to Pedler ford on James River, 118

road from the Pedler ford on James River and up the river eight miles to Capt. Dickenson's, 119

road from Colonel Buchanan's on the north side of James River to the Pedlar ford, 119

road from David Cloyd Jr.'s to John Bowyer, Gent.'s plantation on James River, 119

road from John Bowyer's plantation on James River by Seder [Cedar?] Bridge to Mathews's Road, 121

road from the north branch of James River round the Poplar Hills to Buffalo Creek, 124, 144

road from Col. Buchanan's to the Pedlar ford on James River, 124

road from William Lawrence's to the ferry on James River, 129

road from the ferry on James River to the Warm Springs opposite John McClure's, 138

road from Walter Stewart's to the best ford on James River between the ferry and Col. Buchanan's and thence to the main road leading to John Mills's, 144

road from Buchanan's ford on James River to the main road already established over Cedar bridge, 153

road from James River across the mountain to the Bedford line, 153

road from Samuel Jackson's[?] to the second ford on Jennings's Branch, 56

road from Andrew Hamiltons in the Calfpasture through Jennings's Gap, 1

road from Jennings's Gap to Daniel M^{c}anair's and thence via John Finla's to the Court House/Staunton (and portions thereof), 2, 15, 133

road from Daniel M^{c}anare's through Jennings's Gap to the Cowpasture, 22

road from Jennings's [Gap] to Swift Run Gap (via the Long Glade and the North River (Swift Run) to the main road to Swift Run Gap) (and portions thereof), 34-35, 43, 57, 62, 100, 104, 127

road from Jennings's Gap to Charles Walker's, 37

road from Jennings's Gap to the turn of the waters near the head of the Calfpasture, 82, 92 road from Archibald Stuart's to the top of the mountain near Rockfish Gap (from Woods Gap to Jennings's Gap and between the North and South mountains to the North River), 84

road from Samuel Hodge's to Jennings's Gap, 113

road from the turns of the waters in Jenning's Gap, 115

road from Jennings's Gap to Barnat Man's, 116

road from the Widow Gay's to the dividing of the waters in Jennings's Gap, 121

old road from Jennings's Gap to Swift Run Gap, 123

road from Jennings's Gap to Edward Erwin Jr.'s (via William Fleming's), 123, 124

old road from Jennings's Gap to Swift Run (including old market road from Edward Erwin's to the fork below Jacob Nicholas's), 124

road from Calep Job's to James McKoy's. crossing the river at the Brush Bottom ford and along the river by Henry Spear's Plantation, 26

road from the mouth of John's Creek through the mountains to the Wagon Road, 53

road from the mouth of John's Creek over the mountains to John M^{c}farron's, 53

road from the mouth of John's Creek to the top of the gap near Montgomery's, 119

road from Graham's clearing to James Johnston's, 135

road from James Johnston's to Josiah Ramsey's cabin, 135

road from Jones's ford to John Scot's thence to Thomas's mill (and portions thereof), 87, 90

road from John Madison's house to Jones's ford, 134

road from Parson Jones's to Rusk's mill, 75

road from Calep Jones's mill to the county line, 7, 15

road from the fork of the new road near Jumping Run or Collett's and thence to the Court House, 8, 9

road from Charles Campbell's Long Meadow Branch by Joseph Kanady's to Beverley Manor line, 110

road from Tate's mill to Alexander Kelly's, 81

road that goes by Kenaday's to Patrick Hays's, 43

road from Kenaday's mill to the Court House, 43

road from Adrew Hays's mill to Captain Kenady's, 68

road from Hays's to Kenaday's mill, 70

road from Kenady's to Walker's, 78

road from the forks at the Widow Fulton's to Joseph Kenaday's mill, 47

road from James Roseborough's to Joseph Kenaday's, 49

road from Joseph Kenady's to the Landing Road, 71

road from Carr's (Kerr's) shop via Baskins's ford thence up a ridge between Daniel Deniston's and John Poage's, and thence into the road from Robert Poage's to the Court House, 87, 91, 122

road from Kerr's shop to the main road near Poage's, 122

road from the Stone Meeting House to James Kerr's, 151

road from the Stone Meeting House to James Kerr's, 148, 151

road from Samuel Davidson's ford to Edward Rutledge's and thence to John Allison's ford and by John Kerr's to the Stone Meeting House, 89, 91

road from Andrew Hays's to Robert Kilpatrick's, 74

road from the Stone Meeting House to King's mill (through William Hamilton's fenced ground), 76, 79

road from King's mill or Naked Creek to Patrick Hamilton's and thence by John Poage's mill to the Staunton Road, 126

road from John King's mill on Naked Creek to John King's mill on the Middle River, 99

road from William King's to the Court House and thence to Samuel Gay's, 1

road from David Davis's mill to the top of the mountain above William King's, 1

road from the top of the North Mountain to William King's and thence to the Court House (and portions thereof), 3, 4, 11, 90

road from Crocket's to King's Gap, 26

road from the Widow Tee's to the top of the Ridge at Kingkade's Gap, 77

bridle way from Widow Long's to Henry Kirkham's, 116

road from Capt. Kirtley's to Swift Run Pass, 99

road from James Davis's to the Landing Road, 30

road from Joseph Kenady's to the Landing Road, 71

road from Pedler ford to Lapley's Run, 131

road from William Lawrence's to the ferry on James River, 129

road from Vause's over the New River on the Land of John Buchanan and thence by Ingles's ferry to the Lead Mines (and portions thereof), 98, 128

road from John Stevenson's to Andrew Leeper's, 70

road from Andrew Leeper's to the mountain opposite to John Madison's, 83

road from James Lessly's to the fork of the road leading to Staunton, 137

road from the great lick in the Cowpasture by Col. Lewis's land to Andrew Hamilton's in the Calfpasture, 2

road from the Cowpasture to Lewis's great bottom, 22

road from Col. Lewis's and from Staunton to John Grymes's, 98

road down Christian's Creek as far as George Hutchinson's deceased by Col. Lewis's, 126

road from the forks of Lewis and Dickinson's road to the Warm Springs, 152

road from Walker's place to Charles Lewis's thence to the Warm Spring, 94 road from Captain Charles Lewis's to where Dickinson's road joins the road leading from Staunton to Warm Springs, 148

road from George Lewis's house to Charles Walker's, 84

road from George Lewis's to Robert Halls, 118

road from Estill's mill in the Bullpasture to George Lewis's in the Cowpasture, 118, 123

road from Jackson's River to Co. John Lewis's land in the Cowpasture, 15

(petition of the inhabitants of the Cowpasture) road from Patrick Davis's to the road that leads from Col. John Lewis's to Beverley's Big Meadows, 23

(petition of inhabitants of Linvell's Creek) road from Brock's Creek to Francis Hughes's and thence to the main road that leads to Fredericksburg, 34

road from Linvell's Creek to Mole Hill Draft, 147

road from the Little Warm Springs to the fork of the road on Dunlap's Creek, 150

road from between Captain Wilson's and John McCreary's via James Lockart's field, James Wilson's field and Capt. Christian's to the road that leads from Patton's mill to the Tinkling Spring, 24-25

road through Randall Lockart's plantation, 78

road from the Widow Long's to James Thompson's, 71

road from Long's saw mill to Andrew Scot's, 82

road from Joseph Long's mill to James Young's mill thence to the Great Road on James Morrison's plantation, 40

bridle way from Widow Long's to Henry Kirkham's, 116

road from John Coutt's crossing Shanando River by Henry Long's into the new road leading to Massanutten, 154

road from Joseph Long's mill to the Great Road near Thompson's, 98

road from Black James Armstrong's to William Long's mill and thence to James Alexander's, 14

road from Edward Halls to William Long's mill, 38

road from William Long's mill to Charles Campbell's, 38

road from Staunton to Buchanan's Mill Creek on the road leading to William Long's mill, 92

road from William Long's to Caldwell's Creek, 119

road from Jennings's [Gap] to Swift Run Gap (via the Long Glade and the North River (Swift Run) to the main road to Swift Run Gap), 34-35, 43, 57, 62, 100, 104, 127

road from Francis Alexander's to William Tees's crossing the Long Meadow, 101

road from the Long Meadow bridge to Rockfish Gap Road, 143

road from Long Meadow bridge to the South River at Israel Christian's, 16

road from the north fork of James River to Looney's ford on the south fork of James River, 5

road from Looney's ferry to the north branch of James River, 21

road from the Tavern Spring in the Gap to Robert Looney's mill, 64

lower road from the North River to Looney's, 82

road from Looney's ferry to the first ford of Catawbo, 90

road from the North Mountain Gap called Brocks Gap near Thomas Neist's to the mouth of the Lost River leading to North Shenandore, 47

road from Alexander Thomsom's to the top of the [Blue] Ridge leading to Louisa County, 8

road from Ephraim Love's to the main road that leads from the south branch over Swift Run Pass, 46

road from Ephraim Love's to James Wait's, 89

road from John Wilson's by Dooley's, Barnet Mann's, and John Love's, and thence to James Wait's, 47

road from the road that on the mountain near Alexander Thompson's to the Lower Meeting House, 4

road from John Pickens's mill to the Lower Meeting House, 9, 14

road from the Lower Meeting House to Henry Downs, Jr.'s, 13, 14 road from Middle River to the Lower Meeting House, 17

road from the Lower Meeting House to Naked Creek, 17

road from the Inhabitants of Roan Oak to the top of the Blue Ridge/Brunswick County line (later Lunenburg County), 2

road from Roan Oak to the top of the [Blue] Ridge adjoining Lunenburg County [formerly Brunswick] (to meet potential road from Lunenburg Court House), 4, 16, 20

road from Charles Miligan's to Luney's Creek and thence to George Robinson's, 11

road round William Lusk's plantation, 2

road from the North River to William Lusk's, 68

road from John Bowyer's to William Lusk's, 76

road from the North Branch of James River to William Lusk's, 80

road from the second branch between Mr. Brown's and John Houston's to the Great Road by the Widow Lyle's, 121

road from Samuel McDowell's by Matthew Lyle's to James M^ckee's, 109, 110

road from Samuel Lyle's house through William Taylor's land to the county road, 108

road from Grymes's clearing to the head of the run above Madison's plantation, thence to New River on the lands of John Buchanan Gent. and thence to Fort Lewis and Fort Chiswell, 94-95

road from English's to Madison's plantation, 96

road from Robert Poage's to Pickens's mill, thence to the forks of the river near John Madison's and thence to Swift Run Gap, 36

road from Andrew Leeper's to the mountain opposite to John Madison's, 83

road from John Madison's to Givens's mill, 133

road from John Madison's house to Jones's ford, 134

road from William Frazier's to Hance Magort's and thence to the top of the [Blue] Ridge at Swift Run Pass (and portions thereof), 71, 97, 154

road from Stoney Run to Hance Magot's, 42

road from the smith shop near Jacob Rogers's to John Magort's, 18 road from John Wilson's by Dooley's, Barnet Mann's, and John Love's, and thence to James Wait's, 47

road from Jennings's Gap to Barnat Man's, 116

road from Bernerd Mann's to Edward Erwin Jr.'s, 121

road from Fort William to the Market Road, 100

new road from Edward Erwin's to the Market Road that leads to Swift Run Gap, 123, 124

road from Patrick Martin's to Brown's Meeting House, 147

the Masanuting Road, 43

road from John Coutt's crossing Shanando River by Henry Long's into the new road leading to Massanutten, 154

road from Mathews's plantation to the new road that leads to Rockfish Gap, 94, 95, 97

road from Mathews's mill to Tees's Gap through Francis Alexander's plantation, 101

road from Staunton by John Hutchinson's to the old road leading from Mathews's mill to John Ramsey's, 116

road from John Bowyer's plantation on James River by Seder [Cedar?] Bridge to Mathews's Road, 121

road from George Mathews's mill to Francis Alexanders thence to the new road that leads to Rockfish Gap, 99

road that leads to Rockfish Gap from George Mathews's house, 116

road from John Anderson's meadow to George Mathew's/Mathews's mill, 131, 144

road from the North fork of James River near John Mathews's to Renix's Road, 50

road from John Mathews Jr.'s deceased to the top of Sinclar's Gap, 118

road through Sampson Mathews's plantation, 93, 95

road from the Pine Run to Adam Maury's, 70

road from Joseph May's to James Ball's, 71

road from Frederick Hartsaw's mill on Craig's Creek up the said creek and across the mountain to James M^cafee's, 54 road from the Stone House to James Mcafee's or James McCown's on Catapo, 93

road from Bryan McDaniel's to James M^cafee's, 96

road from Joseph McMurty's mill through McAfee's Gap to the Wagon Road, 135, 139

road from Daniel M^canare's through Jennings's Gap to the Cowpasture, 22

road from Jennings's Gap to Daniel M^canair's and thence via John Finla's to the Court House/Staunton (and portions thereof), 2, 15, 133

road from John Poage's by William M^cbride's shop to the main road between Bailey and Brown's, 130

road from Robert McClanachan's house to the road that leads to the Tinkling Spring, 94

road from McClenachan's mill to William Holdman's, 136

road from the Court House to Robert McClenachan's, 86

old road from the Court House to Robert McClenachan's, 87

road from George Campbell's to William McClenachan's mill, 137

road from Abraham Smith's to the road that leads to Swift Run Gap (via John Douglass's, crossing Dry River above James McClure's field, crossing Cook's Creek between William Snodon's and Alexander Heron's meadow fence and by Edward Shanklin's to the main road that leads to Swift Run Gap), 129

road from the ferry on James River to the Warm Springs opposite John McClure's, 138

road from Patton's mill (formerly belonging to Andrew McCord) to the Tinkling Spring, 25

road from James McCown's to Patton's mill place on Christian's Creek, 25

road from the Stone House to James Mcafee's or James McCown's on Catapo, 93

road from James McCoy's to Frederick County line, 18

road from between Captain Wilson's and John McCreary's via James Lockart's field, James Wilson's field and Capt. Christian's to the road that leads from Patton's mill to the Tinkling Spring, 24-25

road from John McCreery's to James Moffett's, 138

road from William Elliot's to McCutcheon's mill thence through Buffaloe Gap, 125, 128 (petition of the inhabitants of the Calfpasture) road from William Gay's to Robert McCutchceon's and thence to Robert Campbell's, 23

(petition of inhabitants of the Calfpasture) road from William Guy's to Robert McCutcheon's mill and thence to Robert Campbell's, 34

road from the Widow McDaniel's to William Harbison's, 100

road from Bryan McDaniel's to James M^cafee's, 96

road through James McDowell's plantation, 95

road round James McDowell's plantation, 95

road from Samuel McDowell's by Matthew Lyle's to James M^ckee's, 109, 110

road from David Moore's to Capt. Samuel McDowell's, 145

road from Samuel McDowell's by James Cowden's store house to Samuel Brafford's/Brawford's, 150, 153

road from the mouth of John's Creek over the mountains to John M^cfarron's, 53

road from David Cloyd's to John M^cfarron's, 64

road from the ford of Catabo to John M^cfarron's, 96

road from Samuel McDowell's by Matthew Lyle's to James M^ckee's, 109, 110

road from William Hall's mill to William McKee's, 141, 145

road from Calep Job's to James McKoy's. crossing the river at the Brush Bottom ford and along the river by Henry Spear's Plantation, 26

road from Joseph McMurty's mill through McAfee's Gap to the Wagon Road, 135, 139

road from the head of Meadow Creek to the causeway at Vause's, 126

road from William Thompson's to the Meeting House, 6

road from Henry Downs, Jr.'s to the Meeting House, 11

road from John Harrison's to the Meeting House road, 19

road from Finla's Spring to the Meeting House, 36

road from Mr. Hart's to the Meeting House on Cook's Creek, 83, 86 road from the Court House/Staunton to Middle River, 17, 34, 62, 79, 121

road from Middle River to the Lower Meeting House, 17

road from George Scot's on Middle River to John Harrison's, 23

road from Scot's to the Middle River, 24, 32

road from the Tinkling Spring to Black's Run and thence to Middle River, 35

road from the South Branch to Staunton between Mossey Creek and Middle River, 72

road from this Court House to the Middle river (via the head of the Race paths), 17, 34, 62, 79, 121

road from John King's mill on Naked Creek to John King's mill on the Middle River, 99

road from the Duck Ponds to the Middle River, 133, 134

road from Charles Miligan's to Luney's Creek and thence to George Robinscn's, 11

road from Charles Milkin's to the first fording on Catabo Creek, 12

road from Alexander Miller's to Beverly Manor line, 68

road from the North River to Alexander Miller's, 69

road from Hays's mill to Alexander Miller's, 69

road from the end of Bingaman's Road on Robinson's land to James Miller's on Reed Creek, 53

road from Stephen Rentfroe's to John Miller's, 100

road from Carvin's to Millican's, 63

road from Charles Millican's to William Bryan's, 49

road from Charles Millican's to William Carravan's, 51

road from Charles Millican's to the end of Carwin's Road and thence to the Widow Sloan's, 53

road from James River to the forks below Charles Millican's, 61

road from the Cherry Tree Bottom ford to Millikin's, 30

road from Millikin's to the first ford on Catapo, 30

road from Walter Stewart's to the best ford on James River between the ferry and Col. Buchanan's and thence to the main road leading to John Mills's, 144

road from the fork of Roan Oak to the top of the ridge that divides the waters of Roan Oak and Mississippi, 14

road from John Mizer's to the Stone Meeting House by the Court House road, 16

road from John McCreery's to James Moffett's, 138

road from Linvell's Creek to Mole Hill Draft, 147

road from James Montgomerie's to the foot of the mountain towards Craig's Creek, 119

road from John Montgomerie's to Robert Steel's, 108

road from Henry Holdston's to the Tavern Spring beyond James Montgomery's, 61

road from James Montgomery's at Catawbo to the side of Craig's Creek Mountain, 135

road from James Montgomery's lower line to the old county line Leading from Catawbo to the New River, 144

road from the mouth of John's Creek to the top of the gap near Montgomery's, 119

road from the Court House to James Moody's, 41

road from the Court House to Moore's mill, 18, 21

road from David Moore's mill to Robert Poage's mill place in the forks of James River, 30

road from the Indian Road to David Moore's mill, 65

road from James Cowan's line to David Moore's/More's, 69, 70

road from Evans's Run to David Moore's, 96

road from the Rocks below the town [Staunton] to Elizabeth Moore's, 101

road from Michael Cloyd's house to the branch below James Moore Jr.'s, 136

the old road from Alexander Walkers by James Moore's to Andrew Hays's, 149

road from the North Mountain Meeting House to John Moore's, 19 road from William Walding's to meet the road near Thomas Moore's, 12

road from Cape Caphon to meet the road near Thomas Moore's, 27

road from Thomas Moore's to the Court House, 63

road from David Moore's to Capt. Samuel McDowell's, 145

road from Joseph Long's mill to James Young's mill thence to the Great Road on James Morrison's plantation, 40

road from the South Branch to Staunton between Mossey Creek and Middle River, 72

road from Mossey Creek to William Anderson's, 111

road from William Hall's to the Mountain Road, 65

road from Stewart's Run to Murray's place, 112

road from Joseph Murty's house down Craig's Creek and Patterson's Creek into the main road from John Crawford's to the Stone House, 150

road from the Lower Meeting House to Naked Creek, 17

road from Naked Creek to Robert Craven's, 17

road from the North River to Naked Creek near David Stevenson's and thence to the Stone Meeting House, 36, 138

road from the North River to Naked Creek, 39

road from John King's mill on Naked Creek to John King's mill on the Middle River, 99

road from King's mill on Naked Creek to Patrick Hamilton's and thence by John Poage's mill to the Staunton Road, 126

road from Gratton's Store to Naked Creek, 138

road from Bedford Gap to the old road near John Neilly's, 90

road from the North Mountain Gap called Brocks Gap near Thomas Neist's to the mouth of the Lost River leading to North Shenandore, 47 new market road from Edward Erwin's to Swift Run (road from Edward Erwin's leading by William Curry's, Edward Erwin, Jr.' s, the old road to John Fowler's still house, passing through Edward Shanklin's lane to David Nelson's, thence to the South Branch Road at Houston's meadow and thence to the forks below Jacob Nicholas's, 124-125

road from Thorn's Gap to Henry Netherton's, 32

road from the New Meeting House to Robert Scot's, 18

road from Timber Ridge to New Providence, 26

road from Reed Creek to Eagle Bottom and thence to the top of the ridge that divides the waters of New River and those of the south fork of Roan Oak, 5

road from the Ridge above Tobias Bright's that divides the waters of New River from the branches of Roan Oak to the lower ford of Catabo Creek, 6, 39

road from the Ridge that divides the waters of New River from the waters of the south branch of Roan Oak, and thence over the Blue Ridge, 6

the road on New River, 46

road from the New River near Garret Zinn's to the waters of Roan Oak, 53

road from Ephraim Voss's/Vause's to the New River, 59

road from Grymes's clearing to the head of the run above Madison's plantation, thence to New River on the lands of John Buchanan Gent. and thence to Fort Lewis and Fort Chiswell, 94-95

road from Vause's over the New River on the Land of John Buchanan and thence by Ingles's ferry to the Lead Mines (and portions thereof), 98, 128

road from Vause's on Roanoake by English's/Ingles's/Inglis's ferry to Peak Creek on the north side of New River, 109, 113, 123, 129, 132

road from James Montgomery's lower line to the old county line Leading from Catawbo to the New River, 144

old road from Jennings's Gap to Swift Run (including old market road from Edward Erwin's to the fork below Jacob Nicholas's), 124 new market road from Edward Erwin's to Swift Run (road from Edward Erwin's leading by William Curry's, Edward Erwin, Jr.'s, the old road to John Fowler's still house, passing through Edward Shanklin's lane to David Nelson's, thence to the South Branch Road at Houston's meadow and thence to the forks below Jacob Nicholas's, 124-125

road from North Mill Creek from the upper tract to the county line below Jacob Peterson's, 109

road from the top of the North Mountain to William King's and thence to the Court House (and portions thereof), 3, 4, 11, 90

road from John Gratton's to the county line on the south side of the North Mountain, 82

road from Archibald Stuart's to the top of the mountain near Rockfish Gap (from Woods's Gap to Jennings's Gap and between the North and South mountains to the North River), 84

road from the Dry Branch Gap of the North Mountain to Archers mill, 92, 142

road from the North Mountain Gap called Brocks Gap near Thomas Neist's to the mouth of the Lost River leading to North Shenandore, 47

road from the Timber Grove to the North Mountain Meeting House to the Court House, 15

road from the North Mountain Meeting House to the Court House/Staunton, 19, 21, 93

road from the North Mountain Meeting House to John Cambell's/John Campbell's field, 19, 42

road from the North Mountain Meeting House to John Moore's, 19

road from the North Mountain Meeting House to Borden's, 20

road from John Tate's/John Tate's Mill to the North Mountain Meeting House, 72, 75, 99, 101

road from Benjamin Allen's mill to the North River, 1

road from the North River to John Anderson's, 2

road from the North River where James Gill dwelled to the South River, 2

road from the North River to meet the county road, 21

road from the North River to Craven's, 23

road from the North River to Robert Dunlop's, 29

road from Jennings's [Gap] to Swift Run Gap (via the Long Glade and the North River (swift Run) to the main road to Swift Run Gap), 34-35, 43, 57, 62, 100, 104, 127

roads from the North River to Beverley Manor line, 35

road from the North River to Naked Creek near David Stevenson's and thence to the Stone Meeting House, 36, 138

road from the little fork of the Dry Run to the North River, 36

road from the North River near Silas Hart's Gent. to the Court House, 36

road from the North River to Naked Creek, 39

road from the North River to Robert Craven's and thence by Volentine Sevier's, 44

road from the North River to Campbell's schoolhouse, 52

road from James Beard's through Robert Shankland's land to the North River, 67

road from the North River to William Lusk's, 68

road from the North River to Alexander Miller's, 69

road from the North River to James Simpson's place, 76

road from George Taylor's field to William Ramsay's mill and thence to the wagon ford of the North River, 76

road from Paxton's ford at the North River to the foot of the Poplar Hill through Brown's land, 77

road from the North River ford to Buffaloe Creek/Buffaloe Creek ford, 79, 81, 105

road from Paul Whitley's to the main road between the North River and the Poplar Hills, 81

lower road from the North River to Looney's, 82

road from the North River to the Road near Sharp's, 83

road from Archibald Stuart's to the top of the mountain near Rockfish Gap (from Woods's Gap to Jennings's Gap and between the North and South mountains to the North River), 84

road from the North River to John Bowyer's, 107

roads below the North River, 109

road from John Richey's old place on the North River to the Stone Meeting House, 131

road from Robert Craven's to the ford at the North River at John Fowler's, 133

road from the North River to the South River, 135

road from James Thompson's by John Allison's ferry on the North River to John Paxton's, 150

road from the North Mountain Gap called Brocks Gap near Thomas Neist's to the mouth of the Lost River leading to North Shenandore, 47

road from Nutt's Mill Creek near James Cadwell's to the Court House, 36, 65

road from the South River to the foot of the old Gap, 55

road from Thomas Gordon's to Aron Oliver's, 146

road cleared to the top of the mountain at Swift Run Pass (to meet proposed road from Orange County), 58

road from Alexander Walker's to the Painter Gap, 83, 86

road from the Painter/Panther Gap to Captain John Dickinson's, 90, 116

road from Painter Gap to James Gay's, 132

road from Painter Gap to Samuel Hodge's, 141

road between John Willson's Gap and the Panther Gap, 76

road from the Panther/Painter Gap to Captain John Dickenson's, 90, 116

road from Pass Run over Thorn's Gap, 11

road from John Patrick's to Rockfish Gap, 130

road from James Craig's mill up the South River to John Patrick's, 140 road from Joseph Murty's house down Craig's Creek and Patterson's Creek into the main road from John Crawford's to the Stone House, 150

road from the Tinkling Spring Meeting House to Col. Patton's bridge, 10

road from between Captain Wilson's and John McCreary's via James Lockart's field, James Wilson's field and Capt. Christian's to the road that leads from Patton's mill to the Tinkling Spring, 24-25

road from James McCown's to Patton's mill place on Christian's Creek, 25

road from Patton's mill (formerly belonging to Andrew McCord) to the Tinkling Spring, 25

(petition of the inhabitants of the South branch) road from Patton's mill to Coburn's mill, 29

road from Col. Patton's mill place to the Tinkling Spring Meeting House, 112

the old road by John Paxton's to James Patton's house, 45

(petition of inhabitants of south branch of Potomac) road from John Patton's to the forks of Dry River and via Capt. John Smith's to the Court House, 15

road from John Patton's to the forks of Dry River, 17, 67

road from John Poage's to Audley Paul's, 108

road from Paxton's ford at the North River to the foot of the Poplar Hill through Brown's land, 77

the main roads from Poage's to Paxton's, 96

road by John Paxton's, 28

the old road by John Paxton's to James Patton's house, 45

road by John Paxton's house to Buffaloe Creek, 79

road from the north branch of James River to Buffelow (via John Paxton's), 105, 110

road from James Thompson's by John Allison's ferry on the North River to John Paxton's, 150

road from Thomas Paxton's by Hart's bottom to the fork of Buffelow, 85 road from Vause's on Roanoke by Inglis's/Ingles's/English's ferry to Peak Creek on the north side of the New River, 109, 113, 123, 129, 132

road from Catawbo to Pedler ford on James River, 118

road from the Pedler ford on James River and up the river eight miles to Capt. Dickenson's, 119

road from Colonel Buchanan's on the north side of James River to the Pedlar ford, 119

road from within eight miles of the Pedler ford to Captain Dickinson's, 122

road from Col. Buchanan's to the Pedlar ford on James River, 124

road from Pedler ford to Lapley's Run, 131

road from Pedler ford to Bullett's Springs, 147

Pennsylvania road, 84

road from Fort Lewis to Peter's Creek, 136

road from Peter's Creek to Tinker Creek, 137

road from North Mill Creek from the upper tract to the county line below Jacob Peterson's, 109

road from Pickins's to the Tinkling Spring, 13

road from Pickens's mill to the Indian Road near Givens's old place, 17

road from Robert Poage's to Pickens's mill, thence to the forks of the river near John Madison's and thence to Swift Run Gap, 36

road from Pickens's grist mill to the Stone Meeting House, 56

road from John Pickens's mill to the Lower Meeting House, 9, 14

road from John Pickens's mill to the Court House, 9

road from the Pine Run to Adam Maury's, 70

road from the Piney Run to Israel Christian's, 22

the main roads from Poage's to Paxton's, 96

road from Carr's (Kerr's) shop via Baskins's ford thence up a ridge between Daniel Deniston's and John Poage's, and thence into the road from Robert Poage's to the Court House, 87, 91, 122

lane near John Poage's house (altering road by cutting down the hill and bridging a hollow), 102, 106

road from John Poage's to Audley Paul's, 108

road from King's mill or Naked Creek to Patrick Hamilton's and thence by John Poage's mill to the Staunton Road, 126

road from John Poage's by William M^{c}bride's shop to the main road between Bailey and Brown's, 130

road from the Court House/Staunton to Robert Poage's, 18, 49, 99, 105

road from Robert Poage's to the river near John Anderson's house, 18

road from David Moore's mill to Robert Poage's mill place in the forks of James River, 30

road from Robert Poage's to Pickens's mill, thence to the forks of the river near John Madison's and thence to Swift Run Gap, 36

road from the Stone Meeting House to Robert Poage's, 41

road from Poage Run to Robert Renix's plantation, 102

road from Paxton's ford at the North River to the foot of the Poplar Hill through Brown's land, 77

road from Paul Whitley's to the main road between the North River and the Poplar Hills, 81

road from the north branch of James River round the Poplar Hills to Buffalo Creek, 124, 144

(petition of inhabitants of south branch of Potomac) road from John Patton's to the forks of Dry River and via Capt. John Smith's to the Court House, 15

(petition of the inhabitants of the South Branch) road from the south fork of Potomac to the main road near Abraham Smith's, 67

road from Basson Hover's on the South Fork of the South Branch of the Potomac by the Bryery Branch to Silas Hart's, 74 road from Michael Prop's to the head of the south fork of Potomac, 126

road from Michael Prop's to the county line, 77

wagon road from Michael Prop's to Daniel Harrison's, 77

road from Michael Prop's to Conrod Good's, 111

road from Michael Prop's to the head of the south fork of Potomac, 126

road round the plantation of Margaret Clark (near the road from Risk's Mill to Providence), 128

road from John Hays's Mill to Providence Meeting House and thence to the county road, 20

road from Benjamin Borden's house to Providence Meeting House, 35

road from Hays's mill to Providence Meeting House, 43

road from Providence Meeting House to Timber Ridge, 60, 98

road from John Risk's to Providence Meeting House, 116, 117

road from William Clighorn's to the waters of Purgatory, 38

road from the Court House/Staunton to Middle River (including via the head of the Race paths), 17, 34, 62, 79, 121

road from the South River at Ramsey's over the mountain, 54

road from Ramsay's to the foot of the South Mountain, 68

road from Ramsey's cabin to John Crawford's, 107

road from Davis's Mill to John Ramsey's on South River, 61

road from John Archer's to John Ramsey's, 71

road from Staunton by John Hutchinson's to the old road leading from Mathews's mill to John Ramsey's, 116

road from James Johnston's to Josiah Ramsey's cabin, 135

road from George Taylor's field to William Ramsay's mill and thence to the wagon ford of the North River, 76

road from Bryce Russell's house to the main road near John Reaburn's, 105 road from Adam Reader's Mines to Issac Robinson's and thence to the Widow Wright's and from thence to Thomas Harrison's, 131

(petition by the inhabitants of the South branch) road from the Wagon Road up the south fork to Peter Reed's mill, 39

road from Reed Creek to Eagle Bottom and thence to the top of the ridge that divides the waters of New River and those of the south fork of Roan Oak, 5

road from Reed Creek to Warwick, 38

road from the end of Bingaman's Road on Robinson's land to James Miller's on Reed Creek, 53

road from the North fork of James River near John Mathews's to Renix's Road, 50

road from Campbell's schoolhouse to Renix's Road, 52

road from James Gilmore's house to Renix's old place, 110

road from Renix's to James River at John Buchanan's house, 110

road from Poage Run to Robert Renix's plantation, 102

road from the Great Lick to Bedford line to the road leading to Captain Rentfroe's, 117

road from Stephen Rentfroe's to John Miller's, 100

road from Young's Mill to Alexander Richey's smiths shop and thence to Buchanan's mill, 38, 40

road from John Richey's old place on the North River to the Stone Meeting House, 131

road from the top of the [Blue?] Ridge to Alexander Thomson's, 2

road from Roan Oak to the top of the [Blue?] Ridge to the Lunenburg County (to meet proposed road to Lunenburg Court House), 4, 16, 20

road from the Ridge above Tobias Bright's that divides the waters of New River from the branches of Roan Oak to the lower ford of Catabo Creek, 6, 39

road from the Ridge that divides the waters of New River from the waters of the south branch of Roan Oak, and thence over the Blue Ridge, 6

road from the top of the Ridge to John Terrald's and James Beard's, 7 road from the Court House to the top of the [Blue] Ridge near Rockfish Gap, 8

road from Alexander Thomsom's to the top of the [Blue] Ridge leading to Louisa County, 8

road through the county to the top of the [Blue] Ridge near Swift Run Gap, 9

road over the ridge, 14

road from Jeremiah Earley's to the top of the Ridge at Swift Run, 58

road from Frazier's to Hance Magort's and thence to the top of the Ridge at Swift Run Pass (and portions thereof), 71, 97, 154

road from the Widow Tee's to the top of the Ridge at Kingkade's Gap, 77

road from John Stevenson's to the top of the Ridge by John Harrison Jr.'s. deceased, 98

road from Risk's mill to Samuel Wallace's, 60

road round the plantation of Margaret Clark (near the road from Risk's mill to Providence), 128

road from John Risk's mill to Thomas Teat's shop, 44

road from the Glebe to John Risk's mill, 52

road from John Risk's/Risk's Mill to Providence Meeting House, 116, 117

road from Roan Oak to the top of the Blue Ridge/Brunswick County line (later Lunenburg County), 2

road from Roan Oak to the top of the [Blue] Ridge to the Lunenburg County (to meet proposed road from Lunenburg Court House), 4, 16, 20

road from Reed Creek to Eagle Bottom and thence to the top of the ridge that divides the waters of New River and those of the south fork of Roan Oak, 5

road from Adam Harmon's to the river and north branch of Roan Oak, 6

road from the Ridge above Tobias Bright's that divides the waters of New River from the branches of Roan Oak to the lower ford of Catabo Creek, 6, 39

road from the Ridge that divides the waters of New River from the waters of the south branch of Roan Oak, and thence over the Blue Ridge, 6

(petition of the inhabitants of Roan Oak) road by the waters of Roan Oak, 7 road from the fork of Roan Oak to the top of the ridge that divides the waters of Roan Oak and Mississippi-, 14

(petition of the southwest inhabitants of the county) road from Ezekiel Colhoun's to Wood's River from thence to the top of the ridge dividing Wood's River and the south fork of Roan Oak, 20

road from the end of William Carravan's road on his plantation to William Bryan's on Roan Oak, 51

road from the New River near Garret Zinn's to the waters of Roan Oak, 53

road from Bingaman's ferry to the waters of Roan Oak near Tobias Bright's and from the Widow Draper's to Jacob Brown's, 53

road from Jacob Brown's on Roan Oak to Isaac Taylor's, 54

road from David Cloyd's plantation to the Roan Oak Road, 64

road from James Campbell's to the head of Roan Oak waters, 64

road from Vause's on Roanoake by Inglis's/Ingles's/English's ferry to Peak Creek on the north side of New River, 109, 113, 123, 129, 132

road from the head of the north fork of Roanoake to Capt. John Robinson's mill, 132

road from Bingaman's Ferry to Robinson's land above John Bingaman, Jr's, 53

road from the end of Bingaman's Road on Robinsons land to James Miller's on Reed Creek, 53

road from a ford near Esther Robinson's to a marked tree near Hand's meadow, 47

road from Charles Miligan's to Luney's Creek and thence to George Robinson's, 11

road from Adam Reader's Mines to Issac Robinson's and thence to the Widow Wright's and from thence to Thomas Harrison's, 131

road from the head of the north fork of Roanoake to Capt. John Robinson's mill, 132

road from John Robinson's mill by the Den to the county road leading to Warwick, 134

road from Woods's Gap to the head of Rockfish, 58

road from the Court House to the top of the [Blue] Ridge near Rockfish Gap, 8 road from Rockfish Gap to the road that leads to the falls of James River and Fredericksburg, 8

view for potential road over Armer's or Rockfish gaps, 47-48

road from Archibald Stuart's to the top of the mountain near Rockfish Gap (from Woods's Gap to Jennings's Gap and between the North and South mountains to the North River), 84

road from Rockfish Gap passing by Alexander Stewart's to the old road near Archibald Stewart's, 91, 91-92

road from the New Rockfish Gap to the line of Albemarle and thence to the road that leads over the Secretary's ford, 92

road from Christian's Creek to Rockfish Gap, 93

road from Mathews's plantation to the new road that leads to Rockfish Gap, 94, 95, 97

road from George Mathews's mill to Francis Alexanders thence to the new road that leads to Rockfish Gap, 99

road over Rockfish Gap, 106, 107, 120

road from the Tinkling Spring to Rockfish Gap, 108

road that leads to Rockfish Gap from George Mathews's house, 116

road from John Patrick's to Rockfish Gap, 130

road from the Long Meadow bridge to Rockfish Gap Road, 143

road from Robert Scot's to the smith shop near Jacob Rogers's, 18

road from the smith shop near Jacob Rogers's to John Magort's, 18

road from James Roseborough's to Joseph Kenaday's, 49

road from the old road from Ruder's Mines to Michael Waring's, 146

road from William Bethell's road to Peter Rufner's mill, 42

road from Parson Jones's to Rusk's mill, 75

road from Bryce Russell's house to the main road near John Reaburn's, 105 road from Samuel Davidson's ford to Edward Rutledge's and thence to John Allison's ford and by John Kerr's to the Stone Meeting House, 89, 91

road from John Stevenson's to Thomas Rutherford's, 109, 111

road from Alexander Sayer's mill to James Davison's on Holdston's River, 53

road from Scot's to the Middle River, 24, 32

road from Long's saw mill to Andrew Scot's, 82

road from George Scot's on Middle River to John Harrison's, 23

road from Jones's ford to John Scot's thence to Thomas's mill (and portions thereof), 87, 90

road from Michael Waring's to John Scot's, 92

road from the New Meeting House to Robert Scot's, 18

road from Robert Scot's to the smith shop near Jacob Rogers's, 18

road from James Baird's to the Lick by Robert Scott's, 75

road from Cub Run to Robert Scott's, 75

road from the New Rockfish Gap to the line of Albemarle and thence to the road that leads over the Secretary's ford, 92

road from John Bowyer's plantation on James River by Seder [Cedar?] bridge to Mathews's Road, 121

road from John Seewright's mill to Thomas Connerly's, 145

road from the North River to Robert Craven's and thence by Volentine Sevier's, 44

road from Volintine Sevier's old place to Daniel Davison's, 85

road from Shanando River to the top of the Blue Ridge, 33

road from John Coutt's crossing Shanando River by Henry Long's into the new road leading to Massanutten, 154

road from Robert Shankland's to Stoney Run, 42

road from James Beard's through Robert Shankland's land to the North River, 67

road from the Stone Meeting House to Shanklin's place, 119

road from Edward Shanklin's to Widow Thomas's old place near Brock's Gap, 111

new market road from Edward Erwin's to Swift Run (road from Edward Erwin's leading by William Curry's, Edward Erwin, Jr.'s, the old road to John Fowler's still house, passing through Edward Shanklin's lane to David Nelson's, thence to the South Branch Road at Houston's meadow and thence to the forks below Jacob Nicholas's, 124-125

road from Abraham Smith's to the road that leads to Swift Run Gap (via John Douglass's, crossing Dry River above James McClure's field, crossing Cook's Creek between William Snodon's and Alexander Heron's meadow fence and by Edward Shanklin's to the main road that leads to Swift Run Gap), 129

road from Shanklin's Run to Stoney Run, 99

road from the North River to the Road near Sharp's, 83

road from Buffelow Creek to Edward Sharp's, 105

road from Shipay's to Thomas's mill, 90

road from the North River to James Simpson's place, 76

road from John Mathews Jr.'s deceased to the top of Sinclar's Gap, 118

road cut from the old road through the Dry River Gap of the mountain (road from Dry River Gap (via Siver's mill and Charles Wilson's) to the county line), 79

road (on the south side of James River) from the ferry and ford to Sloan's land above William Harbeson's and thence to Archibald Grymes's land and the gap of the mountain, 85-86

road from Charles Millican's to the end of Carwin's Road and thence to the Widow Sloan's, 53

road from the Widow Sloan's plantation to the end of Caravan's new road, 56

road from Smith's bridge to the forks of the road near John Harrison's, 100

(petition of the inhabitants of the South Branch) road from the south fork of Potomac to the main road near Abraham Smith's, 67

road from Abraham Smith's to the Court House, 83

road from Abraham Smith's to the foot of the mountain at Briery Branch Gap, 110 road from Abraham Smith's to the road that leads to Swift Run Gap (via John Douglass's, crossing Dry River above James McClure's field, crossing Cook's Creek between William Snodon's and Alexander Heron's meadow fence and by Edward Shanklin's to the main road that leads to Swift Run Gap), 129

road from Daniel Smith's to Rubin Harrison's meadow, 89

road from the forks of the road below John Harrison's to Reubin Harrison's meadow and thence to Daniel Smith's bridge, 112

(petition of inhabitants of south branch of Potomac) road from John Patton's to the forks of Dry River and via Capt. John Smith's to the Court House, 15

road from Abraham Smith's to the road that leads to Swift Run Gap (via John Douglass's, crossing Dry River above James McClure's field, crossing Cook's Creek between William Snodon's and Alexander Heron's meadow fence and by Edward Shanklin's to the main road that leads to Swift Run Gap), 129

(petition of the inhabitants of the South branch) road from Patton's mill to Coburn's mill, 29

road from the South branch to Swift Run Pass/Swift Run Gap, 30, 31, 46

(petition of the inhabitants of the South Branch) road from the south fork of Potomac to the main road near Abraham Smith's, 67

road from the South Branch to Staunton between Mossey Creek and Middle River, 72

new market road from Edward Erwin's to Swift Run (road from Edward Erwin's leading by William Curry's, Edward Erwin, Jr.'s, the old road to John Fowler's still house, passing through Edward Shanklin's lane to David Nelson's, thence to the South Branch Road at Houston's meadow and thence to the forks below Jacob Nicholas's, 124-125

(petition by the inhabitants of the South branch) road from the Wagon Road up the south fork to Peter Reed's mill, 39

road from Ramsay's to the foot of the South Mountain, 68

road from Archibald Stuart's to the top of the mountain near Rockfish Gap (from Woods's Gap to Jennings's Gap and between the North and South mountains to the North River), 84

road from the North River where James Gill dwelled to the South River, 2

road over Thorn's Gap (to begin at the South River), 3

road from the cross road below Hays's on the north side of the South River to the ridge, 10

road from Long Meadow bridge to the South River at Israel Christian's, 16

road from the South River at Israel Christians to Woods's Gap, 16

road from the foot of the mountain at Woods's Gap to James Bell's on the South River, 17

road from the South River at Ramsey's over the mountain, 54

road from the South River to the foot of the old Gap, 55

road from Davis's Mill to John Ramsey's on South River, 61

road from the South River above Joseph Hanah's crossing Coles ford to Mathew Thompson's, 95

road from Givens's mill to the forks of the [South?] River, 97

road from the forks of the South River to William Frazier's, 97

road from the mouth of the South River to James Frazier's, 104

road from Craig's mill to the mouth of the South River and from the mills to the Great Road leading to Staunton, 134, 137

road from the North River to the South River, 135

road from James Craig's mill up the South River to John Patrick's, 140

road from Calep Job's to James McKoy's., 26

road from Samuel Stalnaker's on Holdston's River to James Davis's, 51

road from the county line to John Staly's mill, 21

road from Jennings's Gap to Daniel Mcanair's and then via John Finla's to the Court use/Staunton (and portions thereof), 2, 15, 133

road from the Court House/town [Staunton] to Robert Poage's, 18, 49, 99, 105

road from Court House/Staunton to the North Mountain Meeting House, 19, 21, 93 road from Court House/Staunton, via Major Brown's/Brown's Meeting House/Brown's Bridge, and to the Glebe, 41, 44, 109, 112, 117, 138, 145

road from the Court House/Staunton to Christian's Creek, 44, 45, 51, 78, 79, 102, 104, 105, 106, 116, 146

road from William Anderson's to the town of Staunton, 45, 111

main road through the Israel Christian's lot in the town of Staunton, 54, 77, 83

road from the South Branch to Staunton between Mossey Creek and Middle River, 72

the several roads leading to the town of Staunton, 91, 96, 110

road from Staunton to Buchanan's Mill Creek on the road leading to William Long's mill, 92

road from Col. Lewis's and from Staunton to John Grymes's, 98

road from the Rocks below the town [Staunton] to Elizabeth Moore's, 101

road from Staunton by John Hutchinson's to the old road leading from Mathews's mill to John Ramsey's, 116

road from the Glebe to the town of Staunton, 117

streets of Staunton, 127, 148, 151

road from Craig's mill to the mouth of the South River and from the mills to the Great Road leading to Staunton, 134, 137

road from James Lessly's to the fork of the road leading to Staunton, 137

new road from the town [Staunton] by Young's mill and thence to the Glebe (replacing the old road by Brown's bridge), 145

road from Captain Charles Lewis's to where Dickinson's road joins the road leading from Staunton to Warm Springs, 148 road through Buffalo Gap to the road leading to Staunton, 148, 149, 151, 154

road from Nathan Gillilan's to Staunton, 152

road from King's mill or Naked Creek to Patrick Hamilton's and thence by John Poage's mill to the Staunton Road, 126

road from the forks between the Widow Steel's and James Bell's, 142

road from Steel's mill to James Telford's, 146

road from James Tedford's to Steele's mill, 147

road from John Montgomerie's to Robert Steel's, 108

road from Israel Christian's to meet the road (cleared by Thomas Steuart/Stewart) over the Blue Ridge, 22

road (cleared by Thomas Steuart/Stewart) over the Blue Ridge, 22, 29, 31, 38

road from the North River to Naked Creek near David Stevenson's and thence to the Stone Meeting House, 36, 38

road from John Stevenson's to Andrew Leeper's, 70

road from Daniel Davison's house to John Stevenson's, 85

road from John Stevenson's to James Beard's, 85

road from John Stevenson's to the top of the Ridge by John Harrison Jr.' s. deceased, 98

road from John Stevenson's to Thomas Rutherford's, 109, 111

road from John Stevenson's to William Beard's, 109

road from Rockfish Gap passing by Alexander Stewart's to the old road near Archibald Stewart's, 91, 91-92

road (cleared by Thomas Stewart) over the Blue Ridge, 22, 29, 31, 38

road from Walter Stewart's to the best ford on James River between the ferry and Col. Buchanan's and thence to the main road leading to John Mills's, 144

road from Stewart's Run to Murray's place, 112

road from the ford of the north branch of James River to James Stinson's on Buffelow, 100

road from Henry Stone's to Silas Hart's, 92

road from the Stone House to Bedford line, 91, 92

road from the Stone House to James Mcafee's or James McCown's on Catapo, 93

road from the Stone House to Fort Lewis, 105, 107, 108, 112

road from the Stone House to Evans's mill, 138

road from the Stone House to Tinker Creek, 142

road from Joseph Murty's house down Craig's Creek and Patterson's Creek into the main road from John Crawford's to the Stone House, 150

road from John Mizer's to the Stone Meeting House by the Court House road, 16

road from Henry Downs, Jr.'s to the Stone Meeting House, 23, 29

road from Downs's to the Stone Meeting House, 24, 32

road from the North River to Naked Creek near David Stevenson's and thence to the Stone Meeting House, 36, 138

road from the Stone Meeting House to Robert Poage's, 41

road from the Stone Meeting house to John Davis's mill, 41

road from Henry Downs's through William Thompson's former plantation to the Stone Meeting House, 54

road from Pickens's grist mill to the Stone Meeting House, 56

road from James Beard's/James Beard's ford to Chamberlaine's Run thence to the Stone Meeting House, 63, 122, 127

road from the Stone Meeting House to King's mill (through William Hamilton's fenced ground), 76, 79

road from Waters's field to the Stone Meeting House, 80

road from Davidson's ford to Edward Rutledge's and thence to John Allison's ford and by John Kerr's to the Stone Meeting House, 91 road from William Beard's to the Stone Meeting House, 97

road from the Stone Meeting House to Thomas Conerley's, 97

road from Patrick Frazier's to the Stone Meeting House, 109

road from the Stone Meeting House to Shanklin's place, 119

road from John Davison's to the Stone Meeting House, 127

road from John Fowler's fording to the Stone Meeting House, 128

road from John Richey's old place on the North River to the Stone Meeting House, 131

road from James Givens's mill by Hugh Allen's house to the Stone Meeting House, 134

road from Joseph Dickenson's to the Stone Meeting House, 139

road from Thomas Waterson's to the Stone Meeting House, 141

road from John Grattan's to the Stone Meeting House, 143

road from the Stone Meeting House to James Kerr's, 148, 151

road from the county line to Stoney Creek, 3

road from Stoney Creek to the new road, 3

road from Robert Shankland's to Stoney Run, 42

road from Stoney Run to Hance Magot's, 42

road from Shanklin's Run to Stoney Run, 99

road from the Tinkling Spring to Stuart and Christian's road, 13, 14

road from Archibald Stuart's to the top of the mountain near Rockfish Gap (from Woods's Gap to Jennings's Gap and between the North and South mountains to the North River), 84

road from Benjamin Stuart's branch to the Courthouse road, 138

road from the top of the Blue Ridge at the head of Swift Run to Capt. Downs's place (formerly Alexander Thomson's), 1

road from Alexander Thompson's to Swift Run Gap, 6

road through the county to the top of the [Blue] Ridge near Swift Run Gap, 9

road over Swift Run Gap/Swift Run Pass, 23, 24, 32, 47, 77, 117, 120, 123

road from the South branch road to Swift Run Gap, 30, 31, 46

road from Jennings's [Gap] to Swift Run Gap (via the Long Glade and the North River (Swift Run) to the main road to Swift Run Gap), 34-35, 43, 57, 62, 100, 104, 127

road from Robert Poage's to Pickens's mill, thence to the forks of the river near John Madison's and thence to Swift Run Gap, 36

road the Calfpasture to Swift Run Pass, 41

road from Robert Craven's to the marked road that leads to Swift Run Pass, 44

road from Ephraim Love's to the main road that leads from the south branch Over Swift Run Pass, 46

road from Jeremiah Earley's to the top of the Ridge at Swift Run, 58

road cleared to the top of the mountain at Swift Run Pass (to meet proposed road from Orange County), 58

road from Frazier's to Hance Magort's and thence to the top of the Ridge at Swift Run Pass, 71, 97, 157

road from the Dry River Gap to the road that leads over Swift Run Gap, 77

road from Capt. Kirtley's to Swift Run Pass, 99

road from Lord Fairfax's line to the road that leads over Swift Run Pass, 100, 101

new road from Edward Erwin's to the Market Road that leads to Swift Run Gap, 123, 124

old road from Jennings's Gap to Swift Run Gap, 123

old road from Jennings's Gap to Swift Run (including old market road from Edward Erwin's to the fork below Jacob Nicholas's), 124 new market road from Edward Erwin's to Swift Run road from Edward Erwin's leading by William Curry's, Edward Erwin, Jr.'s, the old road to John Fowler's still house, passing through Edward Shanklin's lane to David Nelson's, thence to the South Branch Road at Houston's meadow and thence to the forks below Jacob Nicholas's, 124-125

road from Hite's Mines to the road that leads to Swift Run Gap, 126

road from Abraham Smith's to the road that leads to Swift Run Gap (via John Douglass's, crossing Dry River above James McClure's field, crossing Cook's Creek between William Snodon's and Alexander Heron's meadow fence and by Edward Shanklin's to the main road that leads to Swift Run Gap), 129

road from Mr. Matthew Harrison's mills to the road leading to Swift Run Gap, 152, 153

road from Hopkins's mill to the road leading to Swift Run Gap Road, 152

road from the Court House to Edward Tar's, 98

road from Isaac Taylor's to Tarr's shop, 61, 62

road from the north branch of James River to Edward Tarr's old shop, 106

road from Tate's mill to Alexander Kelly's, 81

road from John Tate's/John Tate's Mill to the North Mountain Meeting House, 72, 75, 99, 101

road from Henry Holdston's to the Tavern Spring beyond James Montgomery's, 61

road from the Tavern Spring in the Gap to Robert Looney's mill, 64

road from George Taylor's field to William Ramsay's mill and thence to the wagon ford of the North River, 76

road from Isaac Taylor's to the Widow Borden's, 42

road from Jacob Brown's on Roan Oak to Isaac Taylor's, 54

road from Isaac Taylor's to Tarr's shop, 61, 62

old and new roads from Timber Ridge Meeting House [to] Isaac Taylor's, 140

road from Samuel Lyle's house through William Taylor's land to the county road, 108

road from John Risk's mill to Thomas Teat's shop, 44

road from the Widow Tee's to the top of the Ridge at Kingkade's Gap, 77 road from Christian's Creek to Tees's, 105

road from Francis Alexander's to William Tees's crossing the Long Meadow, 101

road from Mathews's mill to Tees's Gap through Francis Alexander's plantation, 101

road from James Tedford's to Steele's mill, 147

road from Steel's mill to James Telford's, 146

road from the top of the Ridge to John Terrald's and James Beard's, 7

road from Thomas's mill to Thomas Harrison's, 86

road from Jones's ford to John Scot's thence to Thomas's mill, 87, 90

road from Shipay's to Thomas's mill, 90

road from Edward Shanklin's to Widow Thomas's old place near Brock's Gap, 111

road from John Thomas's mill to Thomas Brians, 100, 108

road from Joseph Long's mill to the Great Road near Thompson's, 98

road from the road that on the mountain near Alexander Thompson's to the Lower Meeting House, 4

road from Alexander Thompson's to Swift Run Gap, 6

road from Joseph Hannah's to Mathew Thompson's, 101

road from the Widow Long's to James Thompson's, 71

road from James Thompson's by John Allison's ferry on the North River to John Paxton's, 150

road from the South River above Joseph Hanah's crossing Coles ford to Mathew Thompson's, 95

road from William Thompson's to the Meeting House, 6

road from Henry Downs's through William Thompson's former plantation to the Stone Meeting House, 54

road from the top of the Blue Ridge at the head of Swift Run to Capt. Downs's place (formerly Alexander Thomson's), 1

road from the top of the [Blue?] Ridge to Alexander Thomson's, 2 road from Alexander Thomsom's to the top of the [Blue] Ridge leading to Louisa County, 8

road over Thorn's Gap (to begin at the South River), 3

road from Pass Run over Thorn's Gap, 11

road from Thorn's Gap to Henry Netherton's, 32

road over Thorn's Gap in the Blue Ridge, 33

road from the Court House to the Timber Broge, 7

road from the Courthouse to where the Church is to be built and thence to the Timber Grove, 10

road from the Timber Grove to the North Mountain Meeting House to the Court House, 15

road from Timber Ridge to New Providence, 26

road from Providence Meeting House to Timber Ridge, 60, 98

road from Hays's fulling mill to Timber Ridge Meeting House, 29

road from Hays's mill to Timber Ridge Meeting House, 69

road from Andrew Hays's mill on Back Creek to Timber Ridge Meeting House, 82

road from William Davis's to Timber Ridge Meeting House, 106

old and new roads from Timber Ridge Meeting House [to] Isaac Taylor's, 140

road from Wallace Estill's to Tincher's, 147

road from Peter's Creek to Tinker Creek, 137

road from Tinker Creek to the county line, 137

road from the Stone House to Tinker Creek, 142

road from the Court House to the Tinkling Spring, 3, 4, 8, 13

road from the Tinkling Spring, 10

road from the Tinkling Spring to Stuart and Christian's road, 13, 14

road from Pickins's to the Tinkling Spring, 13

road from between Captain Wilson's and John McCreary's via James Lockart's field, James Wilson's field and Capt. Christian's to the road that leads from Patton's mill to the Tinkling Spring, 24-25

road from Patton's mill (formerly belonging to Andrew McCord) to the Tinkling Spring, 25

road from the Tinkling Spring to Black's Run and thence to Middle River, 35

road from the Tinkling Spring/Tinkling Spring Meeting House to John Finley's/Finla's Great Spring, 74, 76

road from the Tinkling Spring to Black's Draft, 78

road from Christian's Creek to the Tinkling Spring, 81

road from the Tinkling Spring to Mr Craig's, 86

road from Robert McClanachan's house to the road that leads to the Tinkling Spring, 94

road from the Tinkling Spring to Rockfish Gap, 108

road from the Tinkling Spring Meeting House to Col. Patton's bridge, 10

road from the Tinkling Spring Meeting House to James Ball's, 75

road from the Tinkling Spring/Tinkling Spring Meeting House to John Finley's/Finla's Great Spring, 74, 76

road from Col. Patton's mill place to the Tinkling Spring Meeting House, 112

the Indian Road from Frederick County line to Tom's Creek, 15

road from Thomas Tosh's to the road cleared by Richard Doggett to the Bedford line, 146

road from the Court House to Trimble's ford, 87

road through Rachel Vance's land, 39

road from Vause's to Fort Chiswell, 109

road from Fort Lewis to Vause's, 113, 115

road at Vause's, 125

road from the head of Meadow Creek to the causeway at Vause's, 126 road from Vause's over the New River on the Land of John Buchanan and thence by Ingles's ferry to the Lead Mines (and portions thereof), 98, 128

road from Vause's on Roanoke by Ingles's/Inglis's/English's ferry to Peak Creek on the North side of the New River, 109, 113, 123, 129, 132

road from Vause's to Samuel Wood's, 130

road from Vause's on Roanoake by English's ferry to Peak Creek on the north side of New River, 132

road from Ephraim Voss's/Vause's to the New River, 59

(petition by the inhabitants of the South branch) road from the Wagon Road up the south fork to Peter Reed's mill, 39

road from the mouth of John's Creek through the mountains to the Wagon Road, 53

road from Joseph McMurty's mill through McAfee's Gap to the Wagon Road, 135, 139

road from John Wilson's by Dooley's, Barnet Mann's, and John Love's, and thence to James Wait's, 47

road from Ephraim Love's to James Wait's, 89

road from William Walding's to meet the road near Thomas Moore's, 12

road from Kenady's to Walker's, 78

road from Walker's place to Charles Lewis's thence to the Warm Spring, 94

road from Alexander Walker's to the Painter Gap, 83, 86

the old road from Alexander Walker's by James Moore's to Andrew Hays's, 149

the new road from Alexander Walker's by Charles Hay's to Andrew Hays's, 149

(petition of the inhabitants of the Cowpasture and Calfpasture) road from Andrew road from Jennings's Gap to Charles Walker's, 37

Hamilton's to the turn of the (Calfpasture) waters by Charles Walker's, 57, 60

road from George Lewis's house to Charles Walker's, 84

road from Charles Walker's to Robert Gay's, 84

road through Joseph Walker's plantation, 52, 78

road between Hall's mill and the main county road round Joseph Walker's fence, 76

road from Risk's mill to Samuel Wallace's, 60

road from Samuel Wallace's to James Young's, 60

road from William Ward's house to Borden's patent line, 101

road from the road above William Ward's house to Borden's patent line, 106

road from Walker's place to Charles Lewis's thence to the Warm Spring, 94

road from the ferry on James River to the Warm Springs opposite John McClure's, 138

road from Captain Charles Lewis's to where Dickinson's road joins the road leading from Staunton to Warm Springs, 148

road from the Warm Springs to the forks of the road leading to Captain John Dickinson's, 148

road from the Little Warm Springs to the fork of the road on Dunlap's Creek, 150

road from the forks of Lewis's and Dickinson's road to the Warm Springs, 152

road from Davis's cabin to the Warm Springs, 152

road from Michael Waring's to John Scot's, 92

road from the old road from Ruder's Mines to Michael Waring's, 146

road from Reed Creek to Warwick, 38

road from John Robinson's mill by the Den to the county road leading to Warwick, 134

road from the Catapo Road to Warwick Gap, 64

the Warwick Road near the Great Lick, 115

road from Waters's field to the Stone Meeting House, 80

road from Thomas Waterson's to the Stone Meeting House, 141

road from Thomas Watterson's field to John Davis's mill, 131

road from Welshman's Run to the Bedford line, 136, 141

road from Paul Whitley's to the main road between the North River and the Poplar Hills, 81

road from the Wilderness Bridge to Beverley Manor line, 70, 117

road from Robert Craven's to Samuel Wilkins's, 3

road from the Widow Jackson's to Williams's Creek, 35

road from between Captain Wilson's and John McCreary's via James Lockart's field, James Wilson's field and Capt. Christian's to the road that leads from Patton's mill to the Tinkling Spring, 24-25

road cut from the old road through the Dry River Gap of the mountain (road from Dry River Gap (via Siver's mill and Charles Wilson's) to the county line), 79

road from between Captain Wilson's and John McCreary's via James Lockart's field, James Wilson's field and Capt. Christian's to the road that leads from Patton's mill to the Tinkling Spring, 24-25

road from John Wilson's by Dooley's, Barnet Mann's, and John Love's, and thence to James Wait's, 47

road between John Willson's Gap and the Panther Gap, 76

road from Samuel Wilson's house to Wallace Estill's, 128

road from William Wilson's mill to Wallace Estell's mill, 44

road from William Wilsons Mill into the new road at the foot of the Bullpasture and thence into the branch near Feemster's, 129

road from William Wilson's mill to the new road near John Hicklen's, 147

road from Vause's to Samuel Wood's, 130

(petition of the southwest inhabitants of the county) road from Ezekiel Colhoun's to Wood's River from thence to the top of the ridge dividing Wood's River and the south fork of Roan Oak, 20

road from James Young's mill to Woods's Gap, 8

road from the South River at Israel Christians to Woods's Gap, 16

road from Woods's Gap to the head of Rockfish, 58

road from the foot of the mountain at Woods's Gap to James Bell's on the South River, 17

road from Samuel Davis's to the mountain at Woods's Gap, 77

road from Samuel Davidson's to Woods's Gap, 79

road from Archibald Stuart's to the top of the mountain near Rockfish Gap (from Woods's Gap to Jennings's Gap and between the North and South mountains to the North River), 84

road over Woods's Gap, 93

road from John Davis's mill to Woods's new cleared Gap, 26

road from James Givins's mill to the road over Woods's new Gap at the foot of the mountain, 39

road over the Blue Ridge at Woods's old pass to the line of Albemarle (to meet proposed road from Albemarle Court House), 21

road from Wrights Mill to the Cow Pasture near Hugarts or Knox's, 32

road from Adam Reader's Mines to Issac Robinson's and thence to the Widow Wright's and from thence to Thomas Harrison's, 131

road from Peter Wright's to Adam Dickenson's, 37

road from Young's mill to Alexander Richey's smiths shop and thence to Buchanan's mill, 38, 40

new road from the town [Staunton] by Young's mill and thence to the Glebe (replacing the old road by Brown's bridge), 145

road from James Young's mill to Woods's Gap, 8

road from Joseph Long's mill to James Young's mill thence to the Great Road on James Morrison's plantation, 40

road from Samuel Wallace's to James Young's, 60

road from Samuel Young's to Brown's, 78

road from the New River near Garret Zinn's to the waters of Roan Oak, 53